D1394970

Mountain Lover

MOUNTAIN LOVER

DENNIS GRAY

The Crowood Press

First published in 1990 by
The Crowood Press
Gipsy Lane
Swindon
Wiltshire SN2 6DQ

British Library Cataloguing in Publication Data

Gray, Dennis
Mountain lover.
1. Mountaineering – Biographies
I. Title
796.522092

ISBN 1 85223 272 2

Acknowledgements
I would like to thank the following for help with
photographic material: Takao Kurosawa, Michael Scott,
Samuel Rosen, Jiri Novak, Jaromir Wolf, Mr and Mrs Uttley,
Mrs R. Leech, Terry Tullis, Ian Howell, Bob Pettigrew, *The
Glasgow Herald*, Paul Fatti, Mrs Audrey Whillans and John
Cleare.

Photoset and printed in Great Britain by
Redwood Press Limited, Melksham, Wiltshire

Contents

The Mountain Lover

For many days of rain, of seasonal monsoon rain, rain that dribbled,
　　dribbled everywhere
We sat, sitting in the waiting room at Raxaul station, sitting on the
　　frontier to Nepal, we waited, waited, waited
Patiently for trains, for equipment, food, for sunshine, friendship and
　　for laughter.
This waiting had become all powerful, all pervasive, cutting out our
　　small talk; imposing its silent reign; boring into us.
The tin roof of the waiting room had been tuned with perfect pitch
　　for rain to drum, drum, drum upon.
It beat soft, then loud, distant, then near, kettle, then snare; but
　　drum, drum, drum; drum it beat incessantly.
For the umpteenth time that day, a day exactly like the preceding
　　five, I raised myself off the wooden bench
To wander again outside.
I struggled along the rainswept platform, climbed over luggage,
　　avoided crouching human figures, and gained the open street
And found it all the same, all as it was before; rickshaws standing by
　　the kerb, the wet, scant-clad coolies;
'Baksheesh Sahib!'
Across the wet and muddy road the bazaar had gathered a lively
　　group of Indians round its portals in apparent but not certain
　　argument;
I set forth, intent on finding out what animated those turbanned
　　figures, clutching as a talisman the paperback
I had tried to read all morning.
For some reason, I can not yet explain, I stooped as I crossed the
　　road and, in mid-stride, looked up into the sky,
Away, and to the horizon –
Yes! There! A break in the clouds! The first for days! But what was
　　that among the swirling mists? ... It could not be,
For the Himalaya was some tens of miles away. Clouds,
It must surely be the clouds formed to such distinction by the
　　movements of pressure?
I had never seen anything so impressive for it was gigantic, a
　　mountain the like of which one only dreams of,
So perfect in its form.
Suddenly at my sleeve, I felt a tug. 'Oh God!' I thought, 'yet another
　　Haridjan, Baksheesh, Baksheesh, Baksheesh' – 'Clear off and leave
　　me in peace!'
I swung round, abruptly, forcibly.
There confronting me, was a rickshaw wallah, dressed only in a
　　faded dhoti, his thin frame racked with cold and hunger.
First I saw his eyes; black, shining, beautiful; beautiful, shining,
　　shining; humble yet proud; submissive yet defiant –

'It is Makalu Sahib!'

'Makalu', he repeated, rolled around the tongue with the usual Hindi
  inflexion, but said with awe, wonderment, indefinable

Longing.

I looked, disbelieving, first at him, then to that vision floating in the
  clouds.

I looked, and back at him and felt so full of pity for him and myself.

I choked, then gazed northwards just once more as the clouds re-
  asserted their supremacy, and the rain began to slither once again.

Makalu slowly disappeared before my eyes.

I moved away, back whence I had come but the coolie remained,

Immobile, transfixed;

With eyes turned to that distant horizon; a brown, wet, fellow
  human being.

I choked out an affirmative, 'Makalu – Yes' then stomped back
  angrily across the road, to slink back into the depths of the station
  waiting room

Where I continued waiting.

Dennis Gray

Dedication

For Stephen, Robin and Helen,
my children and best friends

Introduction

And seek thee great things for thyself? Seek them not!
Jeremiah

Everything was starting to spin around; the claustrophobia resulting from more than thirty people crammed into the small meeting room adjacent to the British Mountaineering Council's office was beginning to make me feel ill. The Management Committee of the Council was in session with delegates present from all over Britain, and an ill-tempered debate about climbing competitions had dominated the agenda for the past hour. One voice, incessant above all others, droned on and on beyond reasoned argument, obsessive and like an overwound gramophone. How had I managed to get myself into such a position that my precious life's hours were being wasted listening to this sort of thing?

I tried to concentrate on the debate in progress, but it was pointless. Events internationally had overtaken us; climbing competitions were here to stay and it seemed obvious to me that the BMC's role was to control and support them in a manner which did minimum damage to the traditional fabric of the sport. However, for some, the subject was highly contentious and the debate raged on, dominated by the same single speaker. I was not the only person there fed up with it all.

The room, now cluttered with bodies and office equipment, is an unprepossessing functional box of red brick, partitioning, glass and steel. On the wall is a giant painting of Eagle Crag at Buttermere by the late Bill Peascod, alongside photographs of Peter Boardman and Alex MacIntyre. In the corner is a bookcase made by a colleague as a memorial to two friends killed whilst ice climbing on Lochnagar.

My eyes were drawn to the photos of Alex and Peter. They had both done stints as the BMC's National Officer – over three years each – and had both moved on, keen to do their own thing. What times we had enjoyed together here! But now they were both dead; both killed in 1982, Peter on Everest and Alex on Annapurna. How I wished they were here to help focus the debate, and stop all this aimless time-wasting. Once again, 'How did I get here?' It had all started so long ago that I found it difficult to remember the sequence of events.

Had it not started when a small boy of eleven, wandering one day, by a series of coincidences, into the Hangingstones Quarry on Ilkley Moor, had beheld a vision in the form of a human spider? The sight of tall, lanky, white-haired Arthur Dolphin solo climbing up and down the rock faces with extraordinary agility and speed had inspired me to want to take up the sport. Arthur, as fine a mentor as any boy could ever have enjoyed, was the first of many friends to die in the mountains.

An outcrop climbing apprenticeship in Yorkshire and Derbyshire had led on to trips to the bigger cliffs and mountains of the Lake District, North Wales and finally Scotland. All this had happened against a background of social revolution, a widening of educational and work opportunities which had allowed an opening-up of travel and the development of mountain tourism. Visits followed to the Alps, and many other centres in Europe, the USA, the Andes, Africa, the Middle and Far East and the Himalaya. For over forty years I have followed the mountain path, and it has brought me many rich experiences. There have been many friendships and adventures too, providing me with a treasure-filled store of memories, as well as extreme pain and sorrow.

At the end of 1971 I attended a climbing club dinner; the other speaker that evening was the BMC President, Tony Moulam. He took me aside at one point, and asked me if I knew that the BMC was setting up a professional organisation and was about to appoint its first-ever National Officer. I had heard about these developments, from Bob Pettigrew. 'Are you interested?' asked Tony.

'Me? *Me*? You must be kidding!'

'We think you're the person for the job. What you wrote in *Rope Boy* is what most climbers think – we all need a little organisation but a lot of freedom.'

'I'm sorry, Tony, I just can't think of taking on such a job now,' I said, and thought no more of it.

Bob Pettigrew then began to bombard me with phone calls and cryptic letters, and eventually, under the pressure, I gave way and half-heartedly applied for the job. To my surprise I was appointed in January 1972, and now there I was, at the end of 1988, still with the Council. Seventeen years on, I was now the General Secretary with a staff of ten, and a member of so many committees that if challenged I could not have named them all!

The years at the BMC had been eventful. I had travelled widely and learned much about the media, government, sports administration and politics. My family had grown, and we had founded a small retail sports business. But it had all begun to go badly wrong, because of my commitment to climbing and my work in mountaineering, and now I had to admit that my life was a mess. I was recently divorced, and back living in Leeds 6, within a few hundred yards of where I had grown up! It was time for a fresh start and a new beginning. I was aware that I was getting old, and I didn't want to outstay my welcome at the BMC.

I dragged myself back to the debate. The same speaker was still holding forth and I felt a deep sense of frustration at his lack of sensitivity. I had travelled in Third World countries and seen their plight, and I knew that we were all now faced with Armageddon. In our own mountain world, the problems of conservation and access were crucial, and climbing competitions on artificial structures were irrelevant to the global scenario.

That Management meeting in September 1988 acted as a catalyst – I didn't want to spend one more minute of what time I had left in such a frustrating and wasteful way. I hesitated but a moment – I could always write, lecture, instruct and lead people in the mountains – it would be an adventure! So a few weeks later I gave notice. It had been a truly worthwhile personal experience, but it was time to move on.

I look forward now to the new decade; to an active retirement, climbing, travelling and exploring. And this is also a good time to look back, to try to take stock and to remember the fun, the adventures and the friendships. Perhaps this will help me fix a future course. Perhaps I will find the answer to Mathew Arnold's question, as some kind of justification for it all: 'Is it so small a thing, to have enjoyed the sun?'

The Old Rockers

Time, the subtle thief of youth.
John Milton

Before the last war, climbing in Britain was, despite the existence of small groups of activists from the working classes, such as the Creagh Dhu Club from Glasgow and the Sheffield Climbing Club, very much a sport for the well-to-do. The war, and the social revolution which was set in train with the end of hostilities, inevitably penetrated the closeted world of mountaineering, and changed it dramatically.

I grew up in the Woodhouse district of Leeds 6, and my background and my way of life at this time were markedly different from my contemporaries. My father was a theatrical entertainer by profession, and, although he had been born a Yorkshire Dalesman, he was now a 'townie'. My mother was from an Irish family; she was also musical and a city dweller. Their marriage was a fiery, tempestuous affair, but a love match as they had much in common. Our large broken-down stone house was often the venue for rehearsing acts, and musicians, singers and comedians were regular guests. The accent at these meetings was on popular music and entertainment (my father's great love was Variety and Music Hall), but as my sister and I grew older it was impressed upon us that serious theatre, the opera, the ballet and classical music were great and noble, and we were made to sit and listen in silence whenever such works were broadcast on the radio. My sister's interest led her eventually to becoming a professional singer for several years, but, while I loved the theatre and still do, I was more fascinated by literature and the printed word; and by sport.

My participation in mountaineering began by accident. At eleven I joined the Woodhouse troop of the Boy Scouts, and a chance visit to the Cow and Calf Rocks at Ilkley on an organised scouting trip that went wrong gave me the opportunity to see someone climb for the first time in my life. Today, with television coverage, even though it is still minimal, most people know about how climbers carry on their sport. At that time we knew nothing about it at all. In any case, we were mad keen on cricket – so much so that in winter we would clear the snow off our earth pitch on Woodhouse Moor so we could carry on playing! However, at the Cow and Calf Rocks I witnessed an inspirational vision – Arthur Dolphin rock climbing, solo, on a steep wall – and I was hooked. I wanted to be like him immediately and so I started travelling the 16 miles from Leeds to Ilkley on Samuel Ledgard's double-decker blue buses every Sunday morning. I would walk the mile or so from the town up to the rocks and loiter in the Hangingstones Quarry, adjacent to the Cow and Calf, hoping to talk to the climbers who came there every weekend. I longed for someone to take me climbing.

In retrospect I was a fanatic – a small boy of eleven years of age, driven by some sort of need to get out of the inner city and on to the rock. My father was acutely worried by all this talk of climbing and several times he forbade me to go, but my mother secretly encouraged me, and she could always be relied upon for the bus fares! Eventually, through my persistence, I began to get to know some of the regular climbers at Ilkley. They were a very radical bunch, an extreme reflection of

Ilkley Quarry, where I first saw climbing being done in 1947. It is now referred to as 'an old boot of a place'. (Photo: Dennis Gray)

society in general at that time. Everyone who had lived through the war years, and in particular those who had been in the services and had seen action, was hell-bent on changing the status quo. My first teenage years were spent in the company of the most unorthodox, non-conformist climbing group I have ever known. We met each other during the closing years of the 1940s, mainly at Ilkley but also at the other West Yorkshire outcrops such as Almscliff and, over a period of time, we gelled into a tight-knit group, becoming known within the climbing scene as the 'Bradford Lads'. We never were a club, nor did we wish to be for we were too anarchistic. We were anti-organisation, anti-rule and thought nothing of flouting authority.

The Yorkshire gritstone outcrops are mostly beautifully situated, despite their close proximity to the Leeds and Bradford conurbation. Brimham Rocks, Almscliff Crag and Shipley Glen are all beauty spots, and attract many tourists each summer weekend. However, I think all would agree that Ilkley's Cow and Calf, set on the edge of the moor and the most famous outcrop, does not benefit from the most attractive of locations. In fact, I have heard the Hangingstones Quarry referred to as an 'old boot of a place'! It was there that I learned to climb, under the watchful eyes of older members of the Lads like Alfie Beanland and later Arthur Dolphin himself. We climbed on hemp ropes, used shoulder belays, dressed in ex-War Department equipment, and used direct belay methods. We wore nailed boots, but for the harder climbs changed to rubber gym shoes. There were few if any karabiners or snap-links available, and those that were had not been tested and were unreliable.

The late 1940s were years of austerity for the whole of Europe, and in Britain things were so bad at times that you might have been forgiven for thinking we had been on the losing side. Not only was food rationed, but petrol, sweets and even clothes and furniture were only available with the necessary coupons. In the harsh winters of those years, there was little or no fuel. The kids I grew up with in the slums of Leeds were often in a desperate plight; their clothes were in rags, they were nearly always hungry and many of them suffered from rickets caused by vitamin deficiency, and were infested with bugs and lice. I was more lucky, since my father usually earned as much each night as their parents did in a week. There was a thriving black market where he could spend his money, for this was the age of the 'spiv', a gentleman who never worked himself, but who could always get you anything you desired . . . at a price.

At weekends, we climbers all mucked in together. What we had we shared, and deep friendships were formed which endure to this day. Some weekends I would have nothing to contribute, for, although we were not badly off, my father bet, spent or lent every penny as soon as he earned it. As a result, if bookings were thin for him, things quickly became difficult for us, and the family had to live on bread and sugar alone for a week.

It took me about three years to learn how to climb. This was a lengthy apprenticeship by the standards of today, when novices start straight away on climbs that we held in high esteem. Modern climbing equipment has made the sport that much safer, and there is also much more knowledge readily available from up-to-date guidebooks and climbing magazines, neither of which were in existence then. There was no guidebook to climbing in West Yorkshire when I started to climb, and most of the information about where to visit and the climbing routes was circulated by word of mouth. We began to visit outcrops throughout our district – Widdop Rocks near Burnley, Rylstone Edge and Crookrise above Skipton and Earl Crag near Keighley. It was at the latter at the age of 14 that I pioneered my first new climb, Erazor Slab, which was much later claimed by a climber from a subsequent generation, Allan Austin. My companions at this time included Peter Greenwood and Tom Cranfield; they didn't believe I had done it and made me repeat the exercise. It is a hard slab route, providing quite delicate climbing, and, although I was small and not very strong, I enjoyed that type of problem. I was pleased when my friends found it difficult, and revelled in the brief reversal of roles, for at that time it was invariably they who shepherded me up the routes we ascended.

I could write at length about our climbing at this period and about the characters involved. Climbing in the 1940s was looked upon as an eccentric pastime and, partly as a self-fulfilling prophecy, some of those who were attracted to the sport were distinctly unconventional and most interesting. By the early 1950s we had begun to travel further and further afield, hitchhiking down to the Peak District, north to the Lake District and Scotland, and west to Snowdonia. There were not many vehicles on the roads, but most of them would usually give you a lift if they had room. Our leading climbers, Arthur Dolphin, Peter Greenwood, Harold Drasdo and Don Hopkin, were pioneering new climbs as hard as anyone else in an exciting period that has not been matched since in Britain. The fabric of British society was changing too, with the introduction of the National Health Service, de-rationing, the nationalisation of many of the basic industries, and (importantly for us) the opening of the countryside with the National Parks and Access to the Countryside Act in 1949. The effect this had upon our climbing was crucial. Before the Act even crags such as Stanage Edge or the Froggatt/Curbar escarpments were only accessible by trespassing, and we climbers had many brushes with the 'keepers'. When I was fourteen, we were on the Marsden to Edale walk on a winter's evening and a keeper actually opened fire on us with his shotgun! Bob Sowden was hit by shot and we ran for our lives through the peat and mud, all except for Tom Cranfield, the oldest amongst us, who had served in the Parachute Brigade during the war. He also ran, but in completely the opposite direction, straight at the keeper.

The man stood stock still, transfixed , pointing his gun straight at Tom. In a trice Tom was on him, fists flying. He left the man lying on the ground and, returning to us, remarked coldly, 'I didn't lose all those good mates at Arnhem to come home and have some bastard shoot at me on my own midden.' Tom never talked to us about his war-time experiences, but he always wore his red beret when he climbed. He was a great climber – only Dolphin could match him.

By about this time I had won a scholarship to Grammar School, but climbing was my whole existence. I spent hours midweek in the Yorkshire Ramblers' Club specialist mountaineering library in the Leeds Reference Building, reading everything to do with climbing, and my school reports began to reflect my disinterest in orthodox study. My parents accepted the inevitable and soon I was away climbing every single weekend and holiday. It was an idyllic time and I revelled in it all. We were not obsessed, as many of today's climbers are, with technical difficulty. The attraction for me was the beauty and the poetry of the hills, and, as I think was the case for my companions too, the adventure.

With de-rationing in 1951, when petrol began to be freely available, and with an increase in general affluence, many of the Bradford Lads were able to purchase (usually *hire*-purchase) motorbikes. As anyone who has had anything to do with these machines will know, they are much more than just a means of transport; motorbikes mean excitement, speed and sport. Soon every one of the Bradford Lads who could afford a motorbike had one, and a fringe member even stole one (unbeknown to us). We would ride from Leeds or Bradford north to the Lake District at breakneck speeds, as if we were taking part in a Grand Prix, and for a few years we kept this up, despite an alarming number of crashes, with quite a tally in broken limbs and damaged machines. We remained enthusiastic until, one Friday night, Bob Sowden, our fastest and safest rider, skidded on a patch of oil on an International Norton 500cc and careered into the bridge at Ingleton. Bob suffered serious injuries, especially to the head, while his bike was a wreck. His life was in danger for days and, although he eventually recovered, he was never the same physically again. After this our preoccupation with motorbikes and speed waned and we focused again on the crags, which seemed much safer.

Travelling to Wales, to the Lake District and to Scotland at the end of the 1940s and the early 1950s I met many young climbers who were to make their mark in the history of the sport, notably Joe Brown, Ron Moseley, Don Whillans, Tom Patey, John Cunningham, Chris Bonington and Hamish MacInnes. Moving from climbing area to climbing area in 1951, you quickly became acquainted with the other keen activists on first-name terms; I doubt if there were more than about 100 such climbers in the whole of Britain at the start of that decade. I was also fortunate to meet some of the great climbers from earlier generations, such as Menlove Edwards, Bill Peascod, Bill Murray, Geoffrey Winthrop Young, Jack Longland, Jim Birkett, Peter Harding and Fred Pigott. Without exception they were all encouraging, although my encounter with Edwards frightened me as he was already showing signs of a serious mental illness. For a fifteen-year-old this was difficult to understand. Nevertheless, it was a significant meeting for me, and inspired an interest in this greatest of pre-war British rock climbers which has stayed with me ever since.

So, I was growing up in the early 1950s, my horizons were expanding, and I was experiencing adventures the memory of which makes me shudder with fright now. My own climbing was slowly but surely improving, and I began to think that life would be – indeed, should be – like this for ever. I was learning about important things from my older, more street-wise friends: about sex, about art, about literature, about jazz and folk music. It was in retrospect a finishing school of an unusual kind, for my tutors were all older climbers from an extraordinary range of backgrounds. One was Harold Drasdo, with whom I made the first ascent of the Extreme North Crag Eliminate on the Castle Rock of Triermain, Thirlmere in 1952. Harold had just returned from a spell in Greece whilst on National Service. He was interested in literature, and able to read French. Although not a naturally gifted climber, being tall but physically slight, he was our most determined leader, and once he had his teeth into a problem he kept on trying until he was successful or exhausted. Later he was to gain entrance to college, then to university, and now he is a distinguished mountain writer with a weighty reputation.

Peter Greenwood was another of the 'Lads' who influenced my thinking at that time. His attitude to life and to climbing was positive and aggressive; motorbikes were to be driven as fast as they could go, bullies, however big they might be, were to be met with head-on challenges, and the hardest climbs had to be attempted whatever the conditions. He was swarthy, almost Mexican in appearance, and possessed great gymnastic strength. Unlike most other climbers of our era he did not serve a long apprenticeship, but headed for the hard climbs almost straight away.

Like me, Peter started climbing by accident, but the circumstances of his introduction to the sport were slightly more bizarre. At that time he was a keen dancer, and one night at a ballroom in Bradford he had enjoyed an argument with a chap who turned out to be a climber. This fellow challenged Peter to come out with him and see how 'real men' take their recreation, instead of pirouetting like a girl around a dance floor. Peter was stung (to say the least) by these words and turned up as directed at the Hangingstones Quarry – in his dancing outfit! Like me, he knew nothing whatever about climbing. Apparently totally fearless, he proceeded to climb up the rock face, and astonishingly ascended a route called Josephine Super-Direct, still a creditable climb for an experienced performer climbing sight solo. His ascent was a considerable achievement, and won him the admiration of his challenger. Much later he confessed that he had found it hard and had been terrified, especially as he was wearing his dancing shoes with thick crepe soles, known to *aficionados* as 'brothel creepers'.

It was difficult for a man with such emotional and physical drive to stay out of trouble, and Peter was often in a fix, crashing motorbikes, taking long leader falls resulting in fractured limbs, and suffering beatings in fights – as a teenager he would take on bigger, older and more experienced antagonists. He was never down for long, however, and always bounced back. He pioneered or helped to pioneer some of the hardest and best climbs of his era, and with Arthur Dolphin he formed for a short period one of the strongest partnerships in climbing, a perfect blend of sage experience and driving youth. They climbed some impressive new routes together including Hell's Groove and Pegasus on Scafell, and the Sword of Damocles

Arthur Dolphin (left) and John Lockwood at the Tour Rouge bivouac shelter, Chamonix Aiguilles. (Photo: Dennis Gray Collection)

on Bowfell. The death of Dolphin and a move to Carlisle rather cut short Peter's climbing career, and I was truly fortunate to have done some of my earliest climbing with him.

Alfie Beanland was another of my mentors. He suffered from asthma and TB (at a time when that disease was regarded in the same way as cancer is today), but his tall, emaciated frame often led me over a winter's landscape, never putting a foot wrong with his navigation, or took me up some first-class rock climb. I never knew how old he was, just that he was much older than me. He had grown up in the slums of Bradford and, despite ill health and little schooling, had used his artistic ability to win entry into a leading college. In the winter of 1958 he was leading the second ascent of Zero Gully on Ben Nevis. With all the difficulties behind them he and two companions were caught in an avalanche and killed. His death caused us great grief.

Although I formed many memorable relationships at this time, the greatest influence of my youth was Arthur Dolphin. I was drawn more and more to him as I grew up and he would take me with him climbing in the Lake District and on midweek evenings on Yorkshire gritstone. In retrospect, he was a better climber than even he, I think, realised. He was inhibited by having begun to climb in another, pre-war era, but his best new climbs, such as Dier Bield Buttress in the Lake District, were as hard as any leads being pioneered at that time by Joe Brown in Wales and John Cunningham in Scotland. He was a mite more cautious than these two because, I believe, he was older and more traditional, yet I know from bouldering with him that he was technically capable of surpassing anything that had then been achieved. Perhaps if he had lived, the story of British rock climbing might now be different.

I well remember one weekend that I spent with him at Malham in the winter of 1952. We inspected the Cove and then walked over to Gordale Scar. There we did some bouldering about the base of the cliffs, then cut steps with our ice axes up the frozen waterfall at the back of the gorge, and climbed it to its top. On the Saturday evening we stayed in the Youth Hostel near the cove with other outdoor groups: some climbers and walkers, but mainly potholers, whom Arthur knew well, for he was also very active underground. Arthur did not drink or smoke, and he kept up a high level of fitness with cross country running (at which he represented the county). He was also mad keen on party games, when his fitness, agility and strength came into their own. That night in the hostel, when the inevitable games session was held in the common room after supper, Arthur was in his element. He was very competitive, but always contained and controlled, quiet but friendly. His unusual appearance, tall and gangly, with white hair and a white complexion (perhaps best described as 'albino'), meant that those who did not know him thought him a good bet for a challenge. Unfortunately for them, this slightly sickly look belied his abilities. In a fingertip pull-up competition that evening he managed seventeen pulls, while his nearest rival could not even reach half that number. This fingertip strength served him well when out on the rocks.

Arthur was killed while climbing in the Alps in July 1953. His death deeply affected all who knew him and especially the Bradford Lads. Because I was so young at the time of his death, and because he was the first of my friends to be killed in this way, his demise has remained with me as one of the significant events of my own life. How I missed him. In his last months I had been with him a lot, and he had become a special person for me. He was never superior, always encouraging. If I did not know how the gears worked on a Triumph twin, or did not understand some climbing technique, he would spend however long it took until I grasped what he was demonstrating. I cannot recall him swearing, and I never knew him to exaggerate, or to lie or to say an unkind word of anyone else. His death at the early age of 28 was a tragedy, but his example is still there for me and other climbers to live up to. He was a truly good influence and, as I have written before, a 'knight in shining white armour'.

Shortly after the death of Arthur Dolphin I was forced to register for National Service. By that time I was both studying and working in the printing industry in Leeds, and the Principal of the Leeds College of Printing advised me to 'go into the Services and get it over with'. In retrospect this turned out to be a poor suggestion, for if I had taken deferment, which I was entitled to do until my studies were completed, I would not have had to bother. In a few years conscription had ended.

I had left school in some despair. Although I was reasonably good both at games and academically, I had been too alienated to try hard. At weekends I spent my time in the company of grown-ups, discussing every topic under the sun. Influenced by their attitude, I was still anti-rule, anti-authority and I felt, however misguidedly, that whilst away climbing I was free from society's constraints. The return to a classroom on Monday mornings was frightful – boring, stifling, maddening. However, as soon as I left school and started studying and working, my attitude changed. I was fascinated by the graphic arts, by printing processes and fine art reproduction and working in these fields I was happy and fulfilled and my conflicts were resolved. Like many young people I had strong political and moral views on certain issues, and I was a confirmed pacifist. I wanted to be a conscientious objector when I registered for National Service, but I was still only seventeen, and I

Joe Brown, the Grand Master Flash. (Photo: John Cleare)

could not have presented a coherent case or passed through any examination board, which based exemption mainly on the grounds of religious conviction. My only recourse was to register as a non-combatant, with the prospect of serving in one of the service arms of the Army: the Educational, Medical or Dental Corps. By this date the Bradford Lads were breaking up, moving to other parts of the country either to study as mature students or to better their opportunities, or for other good reasons – two were in prison! Harold Drasdo commiserated with me about my National Service, but, ever positive, he commented, 'It will teach you how to hate properly!'

Call-up came in January 1954 when I was just eighteen, and after a short spell of training (which confirmed Harold's prediction), I was posted to the Army Pay Office in Manchester. From here all British Army Officers were paid and it was, without question a non-combatant unit, staffed in the main by civil servants, soldiers who had been invalided out of infantry regiments and National Servicemen who had passed their medicals at the lowest possible acceptable grade, many of whom were excused wearing boots! Most of the time, thank goodness, it was possible to get by wearing civilian apparel. We were situated in Pownhall's Daisy Works, a large, red-brick former textile factory in Stockport Road, Longsight, Manchester, and we were known as 'Daisy's Commandos'.

I now exchanged living in the slums of Leeds for living in the slums of Manchester, around the districts of Ardwick, Longsight and Levenshulme. Despite the squalor, I knew I was in good climbing territory for here was the home ground of many of my friends of the Rock and Ice Climbing Club. Spearheaded by Joe Brown and Don Whillans, this group was, in 1954, changing the face of British climbing. I knew several of them well, having met them originally at the Wall End Barn, the climbers' den in Great Langdale, and soon I had made contact with them. I began to be out climbing at weekends and spent midweek evenings drinking copious amounts of tea (on which they seemed almost to live) at the various meeting sites they had set up around the city.

Unlike the Bradford Lads, the Rock and Ice was a properly constituted club, affiliated to the British Mountaineering Council. In many ways it was typical of the small climbing clubs that sprang up in almost every town and city after the last war. There are now hundreds of such groups in existence.

Joe Brown, one of the leading lights, lived at that time at his mother's house in Longsight, and earned a living as a self-employed property repairer. Don Whillans, the other 'main man', was a plumber from Salford, and many other members of the group were tradesmen. The exception was Ron Moseley, who was a Scraper Board artist. Surprisingly, I found the Rock and Ice conformist and traditional compared to the Bradford Lads, but by today's standards they were iconoclasts, and by 1954 they were the leading climbing group in this country. It is perhaps hard to appreciate now how the Rock and Ice dominated British climbing in the 1950s, but nothing similar has been seen since. The club never exceeded thirty members and, whilst Brown and Whillans were the arrow's tip, the weight behind their performances was contributed by a galaxy of talent in the other club members like Nat Allen, Joe Smith and Ron Moseley.

Joe Brown is still *the* outstanding climber of my experience. It is only possible to judge people by comparing them with their times and contemporaries, and with the death of Dolphin and the temporary emigration of John Cunningham, Brown and Whillans were without peers in this country. On my arrival in Manchester Joe decided that as he was now becoming famous he needed a 'gentleman's gentleman', and that I was the ideal person for this role! Exactly what I was supposed to do I never really found out, but I did make a lot of tea, carry a lot of ropes, and act discreetly over several affairs of the heart. I also almost dealt a death blow to his property repairing business by acting as a labourer on one occasion and a tax adviser on another.

I had many adventures with the Rock and Ice over the next few years, for even after my demobilisation and my return to Leeds, I continued to climb with the club until its disbandment in July 1958. In the winter of 1954, I witnessed what remains for me the single most outstanding climbing performance I have ever seen, illustrating I hope in part Joe Brown's tremendous climbing abilities.

On the weekend in question Joe, Ron Moseley and I left Manchester one Saturday morning. It was a cold, grey day and we caught a train to Greenfield in the Pennines and then walked in worsening weather up the hill above the town, to the unfashionable outcrop of Wimberry Rocks, a series of jutting gritstone buttresses, smooth but seamed with impressive cracks. As soon as we arrived at the Rocks, situated on the crest of a hill and totally exposed to the weather, it started to snow. However, it was still impressively cold. 'Good,' I thought, 'no climbing today.' On this, my first visit to the crag, the climbs looked in the prevailing conditions to be ridiculously hard.

The Rock and Ice had much better equipment than my earlier climbing companions, and Joe in particular spent all he earned making sure he had the best available at that time. He climbed on over-weight hawser-laid nylon ropes which had long since replaced ropes made from the natural fibres of hemp and manilla. However, his footgear on this occasion was makeshift. He was still wearing nailed boots then, but his own were away being repaired, and he was shod in a borrowed pair of Eric Price's. These old things had only about four tricouni nails in each. The majority of us had by this time discarded such footgear in favour of rubber-soled vibram boots, but Joe preferred to climb in nailed boots in bad weather, whilst for good conditions he had a pair of the new lightweight rock boots (PAs) from France which were to revolutionise climbers' thinking on footgear.

We had all our equipment with us, and soon we had a primus stove roaring away in a crevice in the rocks and the inevitable tea was being made. Crouching against the wind, trying to make this tea, I thought it a miserable place to be, but Ronnie, perhaps the keenest climber in the Rock and Ice and very fit, was determined that we should try a climb. He decided to have a go at 'Freddie's Finale' and persuaded a grumbling Joe to hold his rope. The wind was rising, the snow whipping into our faces and bodies, and the whole enterprise seemed to me to be ridiculous. Ron set off up the route and managed to get to a chockstone at an overhang about 20 feet from the ground. He managed to get a sling over the jammed stone to protect him, but try as he might he could not get over the bulge in the crack. His vibram boots kept slipping off the rock and in the end he was forced to resort to grabbing the sling. Over the roof 'Freddie's' takes the form of a wide crack slanting upwards from right to left, and it was obvious from Ron's efforts that the jamming was extremely awkward over the bulge. Off he shot again to grab the sling, and Joe had to hold him on the rope.

'Let me down! Let me down!' gasped Ron, hanging by his waist and almost suffocating. Joe lowered him and as he reached us he said, 'It's bloody cold, and there's ice in the crack. You give it a try, Joe, and see if you can crack it!' I was appointed rope-holder in Joe's place, whilst he tied directly on to the rope with a bowline around his middle – this was long before harnesses had been developed by Don Whillans. Joe set off and, although Ron Moseley was a good climber, indeed one of the very best of his era, here was the true authentic genius of rock climbing. Up Brown climbed to the roof, hung there for a moment, then he was over and into the crack above. The wind howled and the snow pattered down, but slowly he shuffled up the awkward jamming crack above, hanging from fist jams, his feet marking time on the smooth wall as he ascended, showering sparks from off the tricouni nails. A fag end drooping from his lips, a balaclava pulled down over his head, wearing an old torn anorak over endless numbers of woollen jerseys on his back, and camouflaged windproofs on his legs he was a sight to remember. 'Oops' I heard him mutter as his feet shot off the rock again to leave him hanging by a single fist; then, incredibly, as we looked anxiously up through the snow, we saw him reach the top.

Neither Ron nor I could follow this lead, but it had galvanised Joe and he was now enjoying himself. He climbed up solo to retrieve Ron's sling from off the chockstone, then he proceeded to lead first 'The Trident', then 'Coffin Crack' and finally the horrible off-width corner of the 'Blue Lights Crack', all climbs of which he had made the first ascent in the late 1940s. Ron managed to second 'The Trident' and I 'Coffin Crack', but neither of us could manage the latter, which not only had a bank of snow at the top, but also ice on its walls.

I observed Brown and Whillans make many fine leads in subsequent years, and I have seen others make equally impressive climbs, but none of these were ever so memorable as those that day at Wimberry Rocks. It was almost as if Joe had wanted to handicap himself, climbing in inferior footgear, in extreme conditions, a world away from today's sun-kissed French scene with lycra tights and chalk bags. Brown remains the finest bad-weather climber I have known. Others have since surpassed his standards of climbing on dry rock but no one has yet managed to do the same in inclement weather.

Two years on from that snowy winter weekend this small group of Manchester-based climbers had become a legend in the sport in Britain. Joe Brown had climbed to the summit of Kangchenjunga in 1955, and he and Don Whillans and other Rock and Ice members had made some fine ascents in the Alps before this event, spearheading the British Alpine revival. The most notable of these was the first ascent of the West Face of the Blaitière by Joe and Don in 1954. At this time Brown was definitely the senior partner in the duo, being older and more experienced than Whillans, but from the mid-1950s onwards there was little to choose between them in terms of performance. Whillans was outstanding on bold and strenuous climbing, whilst Brown remained the master on technical ground.

Don Whillans was the most talked-about climber of his generation, and stories abound of his dry wit, his uncompromising character and his climbing feats and physical prowess. In his twenties he was a pocket Hercules, small but immensely powerful, with wide shoulders and over-large forearms for his size. His facial features spoke of northern realism, and were crowned by a quiff of fair hair. Over the next thirty years he was to live through an unprecedented series of mountain adventures, where often his judgement and strength proved to be the decisive factor in ensuring either a summit won or a safe retreat. During my days in Manchester he was a difficult person to live with, and I well remember how uncompromising he could be with anyone who he felt was not giving it their best shot! One of my

Out of the west there came a hard man – Don Whillans!
(Photo: courtesy of Mrs Audrey Whillans)

keenest memories concerning him is of the time in 1958 when he and I were descending a couloir in the Mont Blanc range as it was getting dark and a storm was setting in. Gingerly I climbed down from hold to hold, testing the rock, blowing on my fingers, facing inwards to shelter as the storm grew in intensity. I stopped and peered down into the gloom searching for my companion, of whom there was no sign. I climbed down a bit further, totally absorbed and gripped, and stopped again to try to pick out a route down. To my surprise, climbing up through the gloom came the 'Villain', as he was known to us then. He soon reached me and yelled, 'What's bloody wrong?' 'I'm finding it hard to climb down Don,' I stammered, at which he almost exploded. 'Climb down, climb down? You can fall down this bleeding lot,' he retorted, and shot off again, bounding from hold to hold. With such an example I had to follow suit, for the truth is that I was more frightened then of Whillans than I was of the elements.

I could write a whole book of anecdotes and stories about Don Whillans, for he was the most singular character in all our climbing lives, and (for some reason that I cannot explain) the older we grew the more outrageous many of the stories become … There was the rumble with Big Jim at Ruthin, the most enormous man any of us had ever seen, who nearly strangled me, and who gave even Don a hard battle. There was the night we fought the Sheffield Chapter of the Hell's Angels (or at least Whillans did, whilst I and others hid under a table), and there was the incredible party the night we left for Gauri Sankar in 1964, when we rolled huge wooden metal-hooped barrels with 216 pints in each from Don's local after closing time, up the steep hill to his and his wife Audrey's cottage at Crawshaw Booth in Lancashire. However, I do not wish here to indulge in such story-telling. Although the tales are true, they are not the greatest feature of Don Whillans' life. What I wish to remember is his climbing record, world-wide from Patagonia to the Himalaya, which marks him out as the single most outstanding mountaineer Britain has ever produced. He and Joe Brown were equally brilliant on every type of terrain, as good on ice and mixed ground as on the rock. In the end Don became the victim of his own legend. The drinking bouts, with less and less climbing in between, undermined even his iron constitution, and he died of a heart attack in 1985 at the early age of 52. He was on his way home, on a solo motorbike ride from the Dolomites – a fitting but tragic end to this greatest of mountaineers.

When the original Rock and Ice club disbanded in July 1958 (it was re-formed in 1959) I was in the Alps with Joe Brown, Joe Smith and Don Whillans. Looking back now the disbandment marked the end of seven years of unparalleled success. No such small group of climbers has since surpassed the Rock and Ice's achievements, the range of which, from the Peak District to the Himalaya, is remarkable. This success is even more notable when you consider that the group was solidly working class; without the benefit of social position or secure finance, their life-styles and physical work kept the members in trim. Most were inured to working outdoors, so thought nothing of sleeping rough and bivouacking out even in winter.

British climbing almost seems now to have gone full circle. It started with the well-heeled middle classes, then experienced, like society itself, a social revolution with the participation of working class groups such as the Creagh Dhu, the Bradford Lads and the Rock and Ice in the 1930s, 1940s and 1950s. Now it is safe, respectable and middle class once more.

Oh, to see a phoenix rise from the Leeds 6 area of Harehills and Woodhouse, or from Manchester's Longsight again in the form of some of today's unemployed, particularly our young Blacks and Asians. Then that fire originally set alight by groups like the Creagh Dhu, the Bradford Lads, and the Rock and Ice might truly be rekindled!

Rock Face

Perfect monsters are bred on crags.
W. H. Auden

Although an integral part of mountaineering, rock climbing is a specialised and highly developed sport. During the last 40 years it has undergone a revolution in style, equipment and attitudes. When I started to climb very few, if any, climbers would own up to being 'rock gymnasts'; rather, this was a term used in derision of those who were only interested in this single branch of the sport. Among my own friends only Peter Greenwood fitted into this category. Today the situation is totally reversed, so much so that rock climbing is now further compartmentalised, with activity on artificial climbing walls, bouldering, crag or big wall climbing being in some cases followed as separate activities.

Rock climbing remains for me an intensely enjoyable, absorbing, physical and mental exercise. I enjoy its whole gamut; its kinship with dance, and with gymnastics, and its problem solving. British rock climbing is unique, with its long history, and its boldness and variability. In Britain we can climb on every type of rock – the volcanic series, limestone, gritstone and sandstone – free climbing standards are high, ethics complicated, and the setting of outcrops, sea cliffs and mountain crags beautiful. Compounded with this is the variable British weather. All this means that if you rock climb the length and breadth of the British Isles at all seasons of the year, you will find sufficient of interest and enough challenges to keep you engaged for a lifetime. There can be as much fun and satisfaction in solving a short boulder problem as in leading a major granite climb.

Rock climbing has a different type of appeal for different people. To some, particularly the young, it may have a purely physical attraction. There is certainly a sensuous side to modern rock climbing, much hyped by designer clothing and specialised equipment, an emphasis on physical appearance, and a narcissistic trend of reporting by the climbing media. But in truth there has always been this physical aspect to this sport where you move your body into unfamiliar postures, feeling the rock and the sense of space, and experiencing a sense of timelessness.

One great thrill in rock climbing is to pioneer new routes, and even on small outcrops there is always the feeling of going into the unknown, and of being where no one has been before. My own introduction to new routing began with Peter Greenwood in the Lake District, and with him I took part in first ascents in Langdale and Easedale. One climb from this period stands out in my memory above all others: when I supported Harold Drasdo on the first ascent in 1952 of the North Crag Eliminate of Castle Rock in St John's Vale, Thirlmere. At that time I was very much an apprentice, but the rest of my friends within the Bradford Lads were at the height of their creative powers and were combing the whole of the Lake District seeking out new climbs.

The North Crag of Castle Rock is approximately 200 feet in height. Shortly before we climbed the Eliminate, Harold Drasdo and Don Hopkin had pioneered on the face a fine and intricate new traversing climb which they had called 'The Barbican'. It was during this climb that Harold had noticed the possibility of a direct route up the steepest section of the face. Harold was not physically powerful nor endowed with great natural ability, but he was the best technician and most tenacious leader among the 'Lads'. He was also a master of the new and revolutionary protection techniques of utilising carefully placed and contrived running belays. Secretly, Harold made plans for the new direct route on Castle Rock. He and his brother Neville gardened part of the climb and got up the first pitches, and then he took me into his confidence and asked me to second him on the actual ascent, mainly because one of the first items I had bought with my earnings at work had been a nylon rope! It was only medium weight but it was 150 feet long, and the new climb would obviously need what was then an unusual length of rope.

We hitch-hiked separately to Thirlmere, keeping our plans secret in the best climbing tradition, and spent the night in a barn near the crag. From the scree leading to the base of the cliff, Harold pointed out the line he hoped to take; I was impressed. The morning was unusually bright, with autumn beginning to show over the Vale of St John and away down the valley into Thirlmere. We tied on under the North Crag, the largest face of Castle Rock, and Harold set out. Looking up the face I secretly hoped that his enthusiasm would be thwarted before he got too high. He climbed quickly, first across a small slab, then bridging up a steep groove where he placed several running belays with his usual expertise. Soon the first lead was accomplished, with Harold already high up the face and belaying himself to a fine yew tree. The North Crag is uniformly steep and overhanging; its bold aspect is barely equalled in Lakeland. However, Castle Rock is a most deceptive cliff. Its overhangs and the gangways which cut through them often give the feeling of extreme climbing even when the standard is relatively easy. There are often large incut holds, as I discovered when I followed Harold and joined him at the tree.

'From here,' he proudly announced, 'we employ an unusual method. First we climb the tree to its top branch, then we launch ourselves at the overhang above, and climb it direct.'

'No kidding!' I gasped.

'Actually it's easy. We came this far the other week and our kid romped up it!' Harold assured me.

I hastily belayed and watched Harold shin up the tree and then, from its topmost limb, do exactly what he had said he would do – launch himself from the swaying mass on to the overhang. A short struggle and he was on a ledge in the middle of the overhanging upper face of the cliff. Here out of another fissure in the rock grew a second tree to which Harold made fast. The trees on Castle Rock grow in the most unusual places; I reflected on this as I struggled with the yew. I was still only sixteen and rather undersized, and from the highest branch I couldn't reach any handholds on the overhang above my head.

'Get the tree moving,' commanded Harold. Obediently I got the tree swaying out from the rock face, arched under my body. I hadn't intended to move straight away, but suddenly I catapulted upwards from the tree and found myself clutching the overhang, my fingers curled on incut holds.

'Give me a tight rope!' I yelled.

'Can't. It'll pull you off, it's running sideways,' came the reply. 'Get a knee on.'

I scrabbled at the rock, hanging out over a hundred feet of space. Just as my strength gave out, I swung right on to better holds and managed to get a knee on a ledge.

'Phew! I nearly came off,' I croaked as I joined Harold. 'Where to now?'

'Up there.' Harold pointed to a narrowing gangway which disappeared on the overhanging face to our left. 'Then round the corner, on the other side of the overhang. It's only vertical round there,' he added, tongue in cheek. He was always the optimist, capable of convincing himself and everyone else of the feasibility of any plan, especially in bad weather. A great man for the melodramatic, he was savouring every moment of our struggles.

Looking up the proposed finale, I wished again that my leader might be turned back – roping off appeared infinitely preferable to what was above our heads. But Harold had reconnoitred carefully on his previous visits and he set off again with confidence. He went up the gangway in good style, and where it merged into the face reached the base of a flake; this appeared loose but Harold confounded my opinion by lay-backing up its edge and then fixing a running belay round its whole girth. He jammed himself behind the flake for a rest, looking down on me like a bird of prey, then swung round the corner of the overhang and on to the vertical face out of sight. Communication became difficult. First the rope was dragging at him, then it moved more freely through my hands, then it stopped. He had come to a niche, perhaps 70 feet above, and was trying to rest. I could hear him shouting something about 'no alternative', then the 'bang, bang, bang' as he placed a piton; another shout, 'Watch the rope!', and he was moving again. Inch by inch the coils ran out, then the last few feet went at a gallop and he was on top.

I followed with great difficulty and arrived at the top full of admiration. 'Dras' later had the satisfaction of seeing his new climb, which we named the North Crag Eliminate, become a classic of the Lake District.

Looking back now at the above incident I realise not only how impressionable and romantic about climbing I was, but also how little I knew about life itself. I had been much influenced in my attitudes by reading climbing books such as *Always a Little Further* by Alistair Borthwick, about the pre-war working class climbers of Glasgow with whom we all identified, and similar books like John Steinbeck's *Cannery Row* and W. H. Davies' *Autobiography of a Super Tramp*. It seemed to me in reading these that to be free from society's demands all a man had to do was renounce its values, to eschew material possessions and to get out on to the hills and the rock-faces. However, even my young immature mind was beginning to suspect that other things mattered too – my family, my friends, compassion, love. In a search for knowledge I started to read voraciously: *Crime and Punishment* by Dostoevsky made a great impact upon my thinking, as did books by Schweitzer and Bertrand Russell, but the most influential of all were works by Einstein. It was his essays that converted me to being both an agnostic and a pacifist. To all outward appearances I was a round-faced, extrovert, cheerful lad but, like nearly all adolescents, inwardly I was in turmoil. I placed my trust and affection in my older climbing companions; growing up within and influenced by this all-male society, I tried to make sense of the world and to come to terms with myself and my own needs. This was the beginning of a quest which has influenced my subsequent life and the paths I have taken.

When I started to climb on the outcrops of West Yorkshire they had already enjoyed a long history of development. The first climbs had been pioneered by people like Cecil Slingsby, who had started climbing in the district in 1864, before any outcrop climbing in other regions of Britain. Although there were no guidebooks in existence to edges such as Crookrise (above Skipton), some of the climbs were already well known and the holds were well worn by the use of nailed boots.

The author leading the first ascent of Minion's Way, Brimham Rocks, West Yorkshire, October 1957. (Photo: Dennis Gray Collection)

Throughout the 1950s my rock climbing activities were intense by the standards of the day. I climbed many new routes, some of which were memorable for being at the top technical standards of the time (equivalent to today's 5A or 5B), and some of which stand out in the memory because of incidents which occurred during their ascents.

I particularly remember a new route on the Chevin Buttress in 1957. This is a part of the outcrop system on Otley Chevin, the hillside above Otley town, which includes Caley Crags. Chevin Buttress is a small isolated buttress about 50 feet high, at the western edge of the area, set in pastureland and adjacent to a small wood. It is now a country park owned by Leeds City Council but then it was private farmland, zealously guarded by barbed wire, dogs and an irate farmer.

One of my climbing companions at this time was Doug Verity, an amiable giant of a man, a great cricketer and rock climber, and son of Hedley, a Yorkshire legend. We had decided to brave the hazards and visit the largely uncharted Buttress. I had been there before, sneaking in and out under the farmer's nose, and had ascended the easy left-hand crack line up the centre of the crag, but my heart was set on climbing the more difficult right-hand crack directly up from where the first route moved left at half height. One summer's evening found Doug and I, therefore, creeping in silence towards the buttress as if we were treading across a minefield. We climbed barbed wire fences to arrive nervously at the base of the rock where we roped up after donning our PAs (the universal rock boot by 1957).

I set off up the easy first part of the climb and, at the small roof which bars entry into the right-hand crack, I placed a chockstone, looped a sling and karabiner over it and set up a running belay. A strenuous pull brought me into the upper crack, and then I stuck. I hung by a good hand jam, my body arched against the rock, and started cleaning away at the crack with a stick I had carried up with me. Suddenly a loud shout startled me: 'What the bloody hell are you up to?'

'Oh no!' I shouted down to my partner. 'Watch out, it's the farmer!'

Doug had been holding my rope in a sitting position tied down to a low belay. Now he stood up. 'Climbing,' he replied defiantly, eyeing the farmer, who was enormous and carrying a double-barrelled shotgun.

'Get off me bloody land and don't come back!' was the swift response. 'Come on, get down here, quick!'

'I can't,' I replied truthfully. 'I'm stuck.'

'Stuck? Stuck? We'll soon see about that!' With this he pointed his gun up at me. 'I'll give tha' a minute to get off and then I'll blast thee,' he shouted up at me, purple with rage. Knowing the locals well in this area, I was convinced that he meant it.

'My father's people own the next farm to you. They're called Jennings,' I cried down to him in desperation, hoping that he might be on good terms with his neighbours. Obviously he was not.

'I don't care if you're related to the bleeding Queen herself, you get off me land, and don't come back. You're bleeding trespassing! What's your name?' He turned his attention to Doug, still pointing his gun at me.

'Verity, Doug Verity.'

'Where's tha' from?'

'Yeadon,' said Doug.

'Tha's never Hedley's lad?' demanded the farmer.

'Yes,' was Doug's embarrassed reply. Non-Yorkshire folk might just be forgiven for not knowing about Hedley Verity, an extraordinary popular figure in county cricketing circles, and the greatest spin bowler of his era. He had perished tragically in the war.

'Bloody hell. Deadly Hedley's lad on my land? Well, that's different! Finish thee climb lads, and stay as long as you like!' I almost sobbed with relief as the gun was lowered. We did finish the climb and ended up shaking the farmer by the hand, but not before he had warned us what would happen if he ever caught us on his land again. Even the best cricketing connections would not save us next time!

One significant first ascent in North Wales in which I took part was Grond on Dinas Cromlech. This is perhaps the most impressive of the cliffs in the Llanberis Pass, situated on the north side of the valley, and a natural architectural master-piece, with steep rock walls, angled corners and superb cracks. It is the site of classic climbs such as the Cenotaph Corner, and the Left and Right Walls, as well as such modern test pieces as Lord of the Flies. Grond is actually only a slight route in comparison to these, and yet it is a fearsome pitch, a ferocious crack which, when first climbed by Brown and Whillans, was the hardest route of its type in Britain.

In September 1958 Joe Brown, Don Whillans, Joe Smith (Mortimer) and I arrived by diverse means at the ledge known as The Valley, where routes such as Cenotaph Corner finish. Above this is a short section of cliff seamed with cracks. To that date only easy climbs had been pioneered on this section, including the normal way to the top, graded in the latest guidebook as Difficult. We traversed about looking at new route possibilities until Joe Brown called us across to look at a vicious crack he had discovered. We all four stood looking up it: 60 feet of unrelenting rock with no apparent means of protection. It slanted a little from left to right, was narrower at its base than at its top, and looked like it would be possible to jam the first section but that the final section might have to be overcome by laybacking. Just looking up at it was enough to dry your saliva out!

'Find me a stone,' commanded Brown. Morty and I began to look for something big enough to jam in the crack. Soon we had unearthed a fair-sized boulder, and Joe stuck it down inside his jumper. Whilst Whillans prepared to belay him, he tied on to two double over-weight nylon ropes. Brown was the best crack climber I have ever witnessed in action, and his performance was impressive as he jammed up the crack until he was at about 30 feet then hung by a knee and a hand jam whilst he carefully placed the stone into the crack. Soon he had a sling over this well-jammed chockstone, then to our surprise he announced that he was coming down! It looked difficult above him and it had obviously tired him carrying up such a heavy weight; still, if Brown was climbing down then it must be very hard above indeed.

Carefully he descended to join us, protected by the rope around the stone, and when he reached the base of the crack we all hung off the rope to make sure it was safe. It was – typical of the Baron! 'Belay me!' demanded Whillans, looking like this was war. 'When I get up both Morty and you can lead it!' he said pointedly, looking at me. 'It's only a bleeding boulder problem!'

Off Don started, with Joe belaying him, and with a little grunting he arrived at the chockstone. His flat cap set jauntily on his head, wearing Alpine breeches, long socks and a smart jersey, he looked dapper compared to the rest of us. Morty and I were in the jeans and very tattered sweaters which were *de rigueur* in 1958, whilst Brown sported the same except for the inevitable addition of camouflaged wind-proof trousers.

Anxiously we watched as the Villain swung into a layback. This strenuous technique was his forte, and he had been known to claim to rest in such a position! His strength certainly was impressive. Feet against the rock, hands on the edge of the crack, he just kept on climbing upwards. After 30 feet of laybacking, and without any undue fuss or apparent excess of effort, he arrived at the top. Turning round, balanced on the edge, he untied and threw the ropes down. 'Your turn, Morty,' he shouted.

Joe Smith had the greatest strength in proportion to his weight of any person I have ever met climbing and, though he had not the technique of Brown or Whillans, he was physically more powerful than either of them. Unluckily, a short while after the ascent of Grond, he had a particularly serious motorcycle accident, and as a result was never able to fulfil his promise as a climber. In 1958, however, he was formidable. Protected by the rope as far as the chockstone he struggled a little to reach that point, but once into a layback position he just walked up the rock face as if it was a stroll.

'How hard is it Morty?' I shouted up anxiously.

'It's a piece of duff. You'll be OK!' he assured me, and untied off the rope. Hesitantly, I put the ropes around me, and with Brown holding them I set out.

Whillans was determined that I would succeed. Despite his fearsome reputation for sarcasm, as long as you were prepared to give it your all, he was as encouraging as the others. I have always been reasonable at hand jamming, and I reached the chockstone successfully, but bridging across the crack looking up at the top section I wanted to quit! A fall from higher up was not to be countenanced, but I thought I might just go up a few feet and see what it was like; that way I could retreat if necessary to the chockstone, which I knew to be safe.

I started to layback and, before I realised it, found myself committed. Laybacking up was difficult enough, but laybacking back down the slanting crack was impossible! I closed my eyes and went for it. It was the most strenuous pitch I had ever climbed; as I neared the top my arms were throbbing to burst, and I was nearly off. Evenutally, with an overwhelming feeling of relief, I crawled over the top to the shouts of the three strong men. Brown then led the pitch in immaculate style, jamming and bridging the whole way, and talking as he climbed. 'Just as I told you, you don't need to layback it at all,' he chuckled at us.

Grond was a typical Rock and Ice piece of teamwork. Some of those outside the 'magic circle' were envious and made critical statements about over-competitiveness, secrecy and even ruthlessness. Nothing could be further from the truth – they were simply the best around. The Grond climb illustrates this. Although today it is no big deal with modern equipment, in 1958 it was the hardest crack climb in Wales, and the ascent was made without any fuss and with a minimum of comment afterwards.

I have now been climbing for over forty years and, although I have rock climbed on cliffs in many parts of the world, two of my most significant first ascents were made in Yorkshire, my home county.

I first met Robin Barley at Caley Crags early in 1963 and we struck up an immediate friendship that has remained intact to this day. He has lived most of his adult life abroad, so has never enjoyed the reputation or plaudits he deserves, but during the mid-sixties Robin and his brother Tony were pioneering some of the hardest rock climbs in this country. On my first meeting with Robin I was impressed by his courtesy and gentleness. Dark, good-looking and lithe, he was very self-assured, and spoke quietly but knowledgeably. Climbing meant a lot to him but it was obvious that his career in medicine was where his real commitment lay. Tony, then still a schoolboy, was so unlike his elder brother that it was hard to credit that they were of the same family. He was powerful, bespectacled, gingery, outspoken but not brash, and a good sportsman – a runner, long jumper and rugby player. Climbing together, they soon emerged as the strongest team of their era, but even before this, in 1963, Robin, at 18, had solo climbed the first ascent of The Beatnik at Brimham Rocks, perhaps the hardest route on gritstone at that date.

Robin and I climbed together often at that time and made many early repeats of routes in Wales, including Pellagra at Tremadog, the Cromlech Girdle at Dinas Cromlech and Shrike on Clogwyn d'ur Arddu. The latter was climbed in bad conditions and, before any modern climber demands 'so what?', they should remember that it was led with little in the way of protection. Although we knew about 'nuts' as protection devices, we, like most others active at that time, felt they were unsporting. They did not really gain universal acceptance until around 1966.

In 1964 Robin and I decided to explore Malham Cove for free climbing possibilities. A limestone bastion set in the Yorkshire Dales, it is an impressive place. It is over 300 feet in height and its arching walls, in the form of a huge semi-circle, make it a natural amphitheatre and a sun trap. It is now a climbing area of international repute, but before 1964 the free rock climbs which had been pioneered there were mainly timid affairs avoiding the major challenges of the cliffs, still thought of then as fair game for artificial methods of aid climbing. Free rock climbing on limestone before modern protection methods were developed was a serious affair. We were against pitons and never used bolts, and relied on slings looped over spikes, on chockstones jammed in cracks, or on natural thread runners. If we could not gain protection by these methods we either committed ourselves totally or backed off and retreated.

That June, Robin and I elected to try the line of what was to become the route of Wombat. This was on the right wing of the Cove following an obvious line of weaknesses. The line commenced with a boulder problem fingery start to reach a small tree, followed by a short groove, then a rib which led to a crack and a roof. A move right from here and then some moves back left led to a steep finishing wall which we guessed would be the crux.

The author pioneering at Malham Cove in 1960. (Photo: Dennis Gray Collection)

The day of our attempt was hot and humid. After I had led the 15-foot wall at the start to the tree and belayed, Robin set out up the groove, weighed down by a large chockstone stuck down inside his shirt. He had great difficulty placing this in the crack at the roof. Hard climbs of today are often 'pre-inspected', 'cleaned', or even 'practised' before leading, on the safety of ropes from above. In 1964 we thought such tactics unfair; not only had Robin no idea of how hard technically the climb might turn out to be, but he also had to clean the route as he climbed. As he poked about in the crack in order to place the chockstone, he showered me with bits of earth and rock. Soon the deed was done and the stone was placed in the crack, with a sling around it. The rope was then clipped through a karabiner, which by that date were fairly reliable even though they were made of impractically heavy steel. Robin swung right and reached a niche, but there he stuck.

It began to spit large raindrops. *Zip. Crash.* A flash of lightning was followed by a large thunderclap, and the rain suddenly became a deluge.

Frantic shouts were exchanged between us and then my leader shouted down, 'No alternative' and *bang, bang, bang*, in went a piton! You might wonder why we who were anti-piton were even carrying such equipment, but we had to be realistic and even purists realised that in emergency situations some kind of insurance policy was needed! Robin was now in just such an emergency situation, 60 feet above me with a fall not to be contemplated. Above him was an ear of rock and at the top of this he placed a piton then somehow, despite the deluge, managed to climb rightways off our intended climb to easier ground and the top. Surprisingly, two other climbers were at the cove and they had run round to the top of the crag to try to help Robin, but the 'Lemon', as I sometimes called him, was crawling over the top as they arrived.

Wet limestone is impossible to climb well, and Robin almost had to winch me up as I ascended, but I did manage to climb the final wall from where Robin had been forced to traverse right. A wild swing left was followed by a difficult reach to gain some good finishing holds but in the rain I developed a very exaggerated opinion as to the difficulties. Soaked to the skin, I joined up with Robin to be greeted by Mike Mortimer, an old friend from Leeds University, and one of the would-be helpers.

'What route is it?' he demanded.

'It isn't, it's a new route!' we explained proudly.

Limestone dries out very quickly and an hour later the storm had passed and the sun had begun to shine. We lay on a flat boulder under the rock face with our clothes strewn around, steaming in the sun, and decided we could not leave this place with the problem unresolved. The rock dried visibly as we sat talking our way back up the climb and then, as the evening sun lit up the rock walls, we set out once more to try to finish it.

This time with a chockstone in place, and a piton higher up for protection, Robin soon reached the final headwall. The swing left was accomplished, but then he hung for a long moment over the final moves, whilst I anxiously clung to the single over-weight nylon rope we were climbing on. I need not have worried, for he was hanging there simply to savour the position; soon he was up, and it was my turn to follow.

The rock had dried out totally, except at the overhang, and it was warm and exciting to the touch. Having climbed up it once already I knew the moves, but how much easier it all was when dry. I reached the top: 'A good little pitch' I conceded, 'but a pity about the piton! You'll be getting a reputation as a man of steel.' He just stood and grinned happily. We called the route 'Wombat', and it was the hardest route on limestone at that date in the country

A short while later we returned to the Right Wing of Malham Cove with an even more ambitious new route in mind. This was to be my last big effort of the year in Britain – I was leaving for the Gauri Sankar expedition that weekend, and I would be away until the New Year. We had named the climb before we set out – 'Macabre'. As it turned out this was an apt title, for, unlike Wombat, the rock was incredibly loose and the route badly protected for both leader and second. It was, we recognised, a serious project, for the climb ascended a huge wall, traversing from right to left to reach a corner and crack at two-thirds height. The rock is black and crumbly and this should have forewarned us how dangerous it would be, but youth brushes aside such considerations. The line was Robin's idea and he had his heart set on it.

At that time I owned two hawser laid ropes, one of 120 feet, the other an unusual 150 feet in length, both of over-weight nylon. As we roped up I reassured Robin that we were using the longer rope, and I then tied myself to a large tree at the base of the wall and Robin started out. He climbed up to the first barrier, and arranged some sketchy protection, then he began a series of traversing moves leftwards. From there he climbed down a little – the hardest part technically of the climb.

However, it was the loose rock which posed the major challenge. Somehow, despite handholds breaking and footholds snapping, Robin reached the overhang at about 80 feet which barred entrance into the corner leading to a crack line. There, with no other real protection, Robin placed a piton, and from that position he began to bridge across into the corner. Suddenly, the rock pillar, which barred his way and to which he clung for balance, simply dropped out from between his arms, hitting the ground away to my left and shattering into pieces.

He managed to stay in contact to reach the crack, up which he started lay-backing. At this crucial juncture we found out (rather too late) that I had made a mistake and that we were using the 120-foot rope. Crisis!

I quickly untied my belay and ran in to the foot of the face, which enabled Robin to reach a spot where he could bridge across the crack. He dealt coolly with the desperate situation by untying off the rope, tying all his slings together, joining them to the rope and then tying them back into a sling around his waist. I mumbled my apologies, realising how serious his situation was, but he seemed completely in control. He carefully climbed the rest of the crack with a precision and concentration worthy of major surgery, reached a large ledge at the top of the pitch and belayed to a superb fir tree. My relief was indescribable and on seconding the pitch I was awestruck with its seriousness. If Robin had fallen from the upper section of the wall he would have been killed, and at the overhang I was able to remove the piton he had placed by hand, so rotten was the rock. If I had fallen off the first traversing sections I too would have hit the ground hard.

The top pitch turned out to be a sheer joy, and we climbed a steep groove immediately behind the tree, situated on perfect rock. Robin pleaded with me to let him lead it, and I had to agree after his efforts on the first pitch, which had so frightened me. When I came up that, for once there had been no mickey-taking. Soon the groove had been climbed and I followed. By common consent that first pitch was then the boldest lead in the country and it is still, decades later, graded E3 despite the presence on first section of a ring piton (actually on an adjacent climb, Carnage).

Wombat and Macabre were in retrospect historically significant ascents, for they were a part of that limestone free climbing revolution which has had such an effect on rock climbing world-wide. Back in 1964 climbers were still feeling their way on a type of rock that many felt was best left to be climbed by artificial means. Other climbers before us had shown what might be possible, but by his two superb leads at Malham Robin he had broken new barriers of technical and serious climbing on limestone. Where one climber leads others quickly follow, and they soon surpass the first man's efforts, but I do feel fortunate to have been in at the beginning with Robin.

This period in the mid-sixties was crucial in pointing the direction that rock climbing was subsequently to take. The first modern indoor climbing wall was built at Leeds University the year we climbed Wombat. Artificial walls allow practice to be kept up even in midwinter, and by the end of the decade the rapid spread of fitness training and climbing wall practice meant that climbing standards rocketed. I studied a course in psychology at Leeds during these years and, although initially none of us realised just how important wall training could be, we soon saw what could be achieved by these methods in the example of John Syrett. When John had arrived at the university he was almost a novice, but within six months, after hundreds of hours of wall training, he was able to start pioneering new routes on the local crags at the highest standards of the day.

Another crucial feature which changed rock climbing practice in the 1960s was the acceptance and development of nut protection. I have recently read in Continental magazines that *coinceurs*, as the French call them, were developed in the USA. This is not true; we had known about them from the early 1950s but had always felt it unethical to carry machine nuts, with the thread reamed out, on slings to stick into cracks or holes in the rock. To us, they gave an unfair advantage which cut down on the adventure potential. By the mid-1960s, however, with the rise in standards, leaders needed to improve their protection so that falls could be taken if necessary when trying to break through and take on the steeper, more holdless challenges. Nut protection became acceptable and during the 1970s the methods developed rapidly world-wide, so that now there is a bewildering array of devices.

Rock climbing is still, despite such devices, challenging and dangerous. Twice I have hurt myself on British cliffs, and many times helped to rescue others who had been similarly injured. On one occasion I was with the late Eric Beard when two climbers fell on Cyrn Las in Snowdonia. The woman climber was killed outright, and I was left with her seriously injured male companion while Eric ran for the rescue team. Despite our efforts to help him he died on the way to hospital. It was a harrowing experience for me.

The first of my own accidents happened on the sea cliffs at Swanage on Britain's south coast in 1967 whilst climbing at Boulder Ruckle. We were climbing on a single new hawser laid rope and my companion fell. In stopping his fall I burnt my hands so badly that I had to wear dressings for almost a month afterwards. The pain during the first week after that accident was indescribable, and so bad at one point that I involuntarily danced round my parents' lounge one night, to the amazement of some visiting musicians. Modern belaying devices are a great step forward in climbing safely. Before they were developed, the only way of stopping someone who fell was by the friction of your body and the strength of your grip on the rope.

I used to be very proud that I had never fallen whilst leading on a rock climb – until 1984! In March I was leading a climb called Lime Street Direct, a limestone route on a cliff at Willersley, near Cromford in Derbyshire. I had overcome the difficult lower section (graded 5c), and was on the last part of the long first pitch, nearing the top. I was finding it relatively easy so I had not placed much in the way of protection. Nearing the end, I swung into a layback using the edge of a crack. Suddenly, with an explosive *bang*, a sound I had never heard on a cliff before, the rock broke in my hands and I was falling. I fell for 30 feet, passing all the protection possibilities where I could have sewn myself to the crag. As my weight came on to the rope my left foot struck a small ledge and this time it was my ankle which gave out a loud *crack*. The pain was excruciating and I had to be lowered off immediately. My companion, Tim Clifford, was then too young to drive and had real difficulty getting me to my own car, despite the help of another climber. I drove the 70 miles home before visiting the hospital – each gear change was an agony, and I came close to passing out. I learnt a severe lesson that day and now never pass good protection placements on hard climbs. These days my rope resembles a cat's cradle on such routes.

Despite all the risks, rock climbing is a truly rewarding and challenging enterprise. I have taken part in no other physical sporting activity that is so varied or so thought-provoking, and which can be pursued in such beautiful settings. The extraordinary rock architecture never fails to fascinate, while all around is the wondrous scenery of the sea cliffs, outcrops and mountains.

Bens and Alps

I look upon Switzerland as an inferior sort of Scotland.
Sydney Smith

I stood balanced on the front points of my Grivel crampons, the narrow snow band we were following swung away to my right, made up of perfect névé. I felt sick and hungover after over-indulgence in Glenmorangie whisky in the bar of the Loch Laggan Inn the previous night. Before starting to climb I had thrown up, an act which my youthful Scots companion, Alastair 'Bugs' McKeith, had attributed to English weakness. Perched over a drop of Dolomitic proportions, in the lead with about 60 feet of rope out, I had to reach a safe belay. I moved along crab-wise, a dagger in one hand, a short axe in the other, and cursed myself bitterly for the fool I had been – drinking, singing, and playing the banjo until the wee small hours. I reached a suitable spot and brought Bugs across to me. His face creased with a grin as he handed me a bar of chocolate. 'Here mon, eat this.' I did and immediately began to feel better.

Perched high on the cliffs of Creag Meaghaidh, at last we were getting to grips with our objective – to complete the first winter crossing of the buttresses of Coire Ardair on this mountain immediately north of Loch Laggan. The faces are second only to Ben Nevis itself in scale and grandeur; a mile and a half in extent, they provide some of the finest climbing in Scotland, with walls of over 1,500 feet. Across this intricate face is a natural traversing line which follows a horizontal fault for about 8,500 feet, broken by ice flows, rock walls and deep gullies. Winter ascents on Creagh Meaghaidh have a remoteness and scale which make them a serious proposition. The base of the cliffs can be reached in two hours' walk from the nearest farm at Aberdair, above the Newtonmore–Spean Bridge road but, as quite a few climbers have discovered, in bad weather route-finding on or off the mountain is difficult, and getting back to the valley can be a fight for life in a blizzard.

The date was January 1966 and I had moved to Edinburgh, and was well attuned to Scottish attitudes and opinions. Friends in Glasgow regarded my living in the capital and associating with its climbers as unpardonable – 'Sassenachs are nae sae bad as the denizens of Auld Reekie!' they warned me – but I had been drawn there by an affair of the heart. The previous winter on Cairngorm I had met and fallen in love with a beautiful girl from the city.

Edinburgh is a mountaineer's town, within easy reach of the Highlands, and has produced an impressive line of climbers – the Marshall brothers, Robin Smith, Dougal Haston and, in the 1960s, the Edinburgh Squirrels, a non-comformist climbing group very much in tune with my own attitude to climbing. Despite Glaswegian forecasts, the Squirrels greeted me with open arms and I soon struck up a close friendship with one of their younger members, known to everyone as 'Bugs' because of his prominent front teeth. He wasn't sure of his own ability yet, but there burned within him a fire, and an enthusiasm for everything to do with mountains, which were to make him an outstanding mountaineer.

Alastair 'Bugs' McKeith.
(Photo: *The Glasgow Herald*)

By 1966 I was a devoted adherent of Scottish winter climbing. I had made my first such climbs in Glencoe in 1950 as a very young boy, and during my journeys in the Highlands I had been lucky to make many good friends in the Scottish climbing fraternity, particularly Tom Patey, Dougal Haston and Pat Walsh. I had also climbed north of the border in summer, on Skye, in Applecross, at Ben Nevis, Glencoe, the Cobbler and many other areas, but for me the winter season in Scotland is unique. No place I have seen in the world is more beautiful than the north-west of Scotland in winter, with its interplay of mountain, moor and sea and loch. It is often compared by the not-so-discerning to the western Alps in summer, but this is misleading; the northern Bens are in that sense more accurately Arctic, and because of this they offer the most demanding, fatiguing and variable mountaineering in the British Isles. This mountaineering has several special features: short days which demand speed, generally harsh weather, sudden changes in temperature which can severely alter the snow and ice conditions, and storms which can test to the limit even the most competent. The scale and isolation of many of the Scottish mountains mean that any winter ascent on their flanks has a spice and flavour of adventure that is lacking in summer crag climbing, and put such routes in the realms of greater mountaineering.

The author singing the night away at a Ceilidh. (Photo: Dennis Gray Collection)

The development of winter climbing north of the border has been mainly the product of the sturdy individualism and parochialism of the local Scots, with small enthusiastic groups working out their own methods and climbing philosophies, and solving the problems presented by the terrain. Climbers from other areas of the country have inevitably contributed, and this has been increasingly the case in recent years with the improvement in communications, but it is possible to argue that there is still a school of Scottish winter climbing with its own distinctive traditions.

There were other attractions for me living in Scotland in the 1960s, not least a thriving music scene, both folk and classical, which spilled over into the climbing world. At its head was Tom Patey, writing brilliantly witty acerbic ditties about the contemporary mountaineering scene, and we also knew many non-climbing musicians who joined in at some of our Ceilidhs, including Alex Campbell, Jimmie Ross and Hamish Imlach. I was able to indulge my love of poetry too, for Edinburgh was abuzz with readings almost every night, in some of which I took part. I also had my girlfriend, although both of us recognised it would not last for she was, like myself, too independent to want to be tied down. We had a wonderful time and it did hurt when we parted in the early spring.

There is something infectious about Scottish nationalism. They're all like that, it seems, and nothing annoys them more than criticism of their attitude. It is surprising how quickly the Sassenach living in Scotland is won over, becoming almost more 'Scotch' than the Scots themselves. I soon fell in with their habit of plans and plots veiled in secrecy, an essential part of mountaineering in Scotland. The telephone calls in the middle of the night to ask about conditions, the mad drive along icy roads, and the long plod in the dark to reach an objective ahead of rivals, real or imaginary, leant an air of excitement and derring-do to our exploits. There is room in Scotland for innumerable first ascents in winter but, as with climbing elsewhere, a little publicity makes one route seem more desirable than any other, at least until it is climbed. And that was the background to Bugs and I finding ourselves on the girdle traverse of Creag Meaghaidh, for it seemed to us that it was then the outstanding first ascent awaiting completion. We were not the only ones interested in the project, and Tom Patey had a proprietary interest having already climbed what would be the middle section of the traverse on his aptly named 'Posthorn Gallop'. In typical Patey fashion he of course denied any interest in what he described as a 'worthless outing'. Being well versed in such matters, we knew that this meant just the opposite, but the rules of the game decreed that we must appear to believe him!

We spent many weekends at Laggan examining the face, working out the route, usually in atrocious conditions, and up to January we had accomplished nothing more than a new route on a lowly valley crag, and nearly meeting our end in a frightening encounter with a blizzard. Now we were here in perfect conditions and at last on our climb. The first problem, moving from left to right across the cliffs, was the Bellevue Buttress, but running across it was a gangway or band, steeped in snow, which finished on the edge of Raeburn's Gulley. The first ten feet had proved awkward, but thereafter it had been relatively simple. Each pitch offered something new, but the climbing was never too demanding (about Grade 2). At one point there was a pinnacle to climb, and at another the band of snow narrowed to a mere sliver, and the exposure was tremendous, but by midday we stood in Raeburn's Gully with an easy but magnificent traverse behind us which Bugs decided we should call 'The Scene'. Eagerly we crossed Raeburn's towards what we considered would be the crux of the girdle, the Pinnacle Buttress, largest on the Ardair Cliffs. From our explorations we knew there were two possible crossing-places, a low and a high line. We decided to look first at the lower one. Just as Bugs was about to launch himself at an improbable ice-fall which barred our way, it began to snow. After a few moments' hesitation he got to work with his axe and then placed an ice piton as he moved out on to an almost vertical wall of ice. His progress became painfully slow and the falling snow steadily increased in density. 'It's brewing up!' I observed.

'I'm coming back. Watch the rope!' Bugs' ice piton popped out as soon as he moved sideways to it, and he slithered back to my stance.

'Let's take a look higher up,' I suggested and, moving together with rope coils, we cramponed up to the second possible crossing-place. It looked difficult and entailed traversing Smith's Gully, one of the hardest existing Scottish ice climbs. However, it did appear more likely than the lower line, as far as we could see through the falling snow. Indecision gripped us and we hung around waiting and waiting until it was obviously too late to make an attempt on the Pinnacle that day. Finally, we climbed the top sections of Raeburn's Gully and exited on to the summit plateau of the mountain. From there, aided by our knowledge of its topography, we hurried back to the spartan comfort of the barn. Staying in the barn with us was a

The author on the first ascent of
The Scene, Creag Meaghaidh.
(Photo: Bugs McKeith)

crowd of Aberdonian climbers, including the legendary Jim McArtney, who a short while later became a close friend and with whom I visited the Tatra mountains in 1967. Later that evening in the Laggan Bar, above the noise of the singing, I ventured to question McArtney about his climbing activities. 'What climbs did you make today?'

'Och, just a couple of the Post routes. And what did ye climb mon?'

Bugs' eyes narrowed and his brow furrowed more than usual, and before I had time to reply he named some climb I had never heard of, let alone ascended. 'Och, ye can nae trust the Aberdonians,' Bugs confided over a 'Morangie when we reached the bar. 'It might be they're nae interested in the girdle, but Patey is and he's Aberdonian, dinna forget!'

I found all this highly amusing and it certainly gave a spice to our doings. There was never anything unfriendly in the jockeying; I climbed with Tom Patey a short while later in Applecross, and when I mentioned our attempts on the Ardair girdle he gave his honest opinion on what he considered the best route for tackling it. Of course, he wasn't interested in it himself.

Next morning the weather was fine and, rising early again, we retraced our steps and cramponed down Raeburn's Gully to our point of retreat. The sun was shining and the sky was blue. The view as we climbed higher was breathtaking: at our feet the Loch Laggan valley, dark and brooding, away to the west mountain and sea, and above us the dazzling white snow slopes of our dreams. On reaching the highest of the two possible crossing-points Bugs led the first rope-length to a belay on the edge of Smith's Gully, then I took over the lead. Our equipment by today's standards was primitive, for this was before the development of the curve picks on ice-axes, snap-on crampons, and plastic double boots. Still, we did have the best available at that time – 12-point Grivel crampons, double leather boots, and various lengths of ice-axe, depending on the amount and type of step cutting we thought a climb might demand.

The steep black ice in the couloir looked difficult and I moved gingerly down after cutting steps with my longest axe. That day I had brought two axes, one a medium-sized Charlet, the other a short axe with a fourteen-inch shaft, shaped from an ex-WD model which had once been Robin Smith's. I cut out into the bed of the gully with the Charlet and, balanced only on front points of the crampons in the ice, looked up the fissure above my head. Whoever called it a gully was an optimist; it was more of a hanging chimney chockful of ice. Jimmy Marshall had pioneered the climb, and gazing up at it I could understand his reputation for ice climbing.

I stopped staring upwards and continued cutting. The gully here was like a bowl, below which the bed steepened, and it was quite a long way across. The ice was peculiar, with a black, shiny, very hard surface of which when broken revealed a myriad of small crystals like diamonds. 'Damn!' The head of the Charlet flew off and disappeared with a clutter down the ice; the shaft had broken. (Today's ice climber rarely has to worry about this as axes are now made from special steel and not wood!) Just then from Raeburn's on our left came a hail, and Jim McArtney appeared, climbing solo at an incredible speed. He was quickly gone again with a farewell wave, leaving me marvelling at a beautiful display of front-point crampon technique. A few minutes later two more Aberdonians followed in his wake; the difference between their movement and McArtney's was the difference between chalk and cheese.

Luckily I still had my second axe in reserve. I cut my way up to a ledge, fashioned a stance in the banked snow and brought Bugs across. 'Did ye see McArtney watching us?' he asked.

'Oh, you Scots are awful suspicious men!' I remonstrated as he led off on the next rope-length.

This proved reminiscent of our traverse of the Scene. It was not too difficult, but its position and great exposure gave it a feeling of openness as we balanced along a ribbon of hard snow. I joined Bugs, well tied to a rock pinnacle; looking across the face to our right, it was obvious that the next lead would be the crux. The fault we had been following finished dramatically with steep rock and shale but below and to the right I could see a horizontal fissure trending away from us; the problem would be to join the two up by climbing the bare sections of thirty feet or more in between.

From the end of our gangway I stepped on to steep rock with my Grivels rasping, balanced across some shale, moved a few feet further right and found myself stuck on nearly vertical earth. 'What to do?' I kept muttering to myself. Half an hour passed as I hopped first on one leg then the other. 'Why not cut steps in the shale?' I poked rather feebly with the axe spike and then the adze. 'No good!' The ground was firmer than it looked. Above my head was a large ice boss so I climbed up to this and carefully fashioned a channel round which I fastened a sling. Protected by my running belay I climbed cautiously down the shale for about fifteen feet, then made a difficult rock move to the right, with crampons sparking, to swing into the horizontal crack.

I managed a kind of mantleshelf and, placing my right leg and thigh inside the crack and using the upper lip as an undercut, I shuffled slowly along the face. The position was wildly exposed with nothing underneath for hundreds of feet, but after a few moves I found another ice formation which I succeeded in converting into a second running belay. These shuffling antics were most painful and I began to get cramp in my leg, but luckily the crack finished with huge handholds and swinging down on these I was able to get to a ledge. Thereafter followed some step cutting over hard snow, then easy cramponing to reach, at the very limit of a hundred and fifty feet of rope, a perfect vertical crack in the rock face into which I banged a twelve-inch channel ice piton to the hilt. 'Clip in! Relax!'

I decided it had been quite a pitch and this was confirmed by the difficulty Bugs had in following. He arrived with a grin as wide as a banana but all the same dropped his Edinburgh reserve to exclaim, 'Mon, that was a hairy lead! Jeez! I've never seen such unusual winter climbing.'

The rest of the Pinnacle Buttress proved an anti-climax; after one more rope-length we could amble solo over perfect snow banked on to large terraces until we reached Easy Gully, the next main feature of the cliffs. We rested there and looked at the way ahead. Behind us lay over 3,000 feet of climbing, and before us was another 5,500 feet. The Appolyon Ledge which we had just climbed might prove to be the crux, at Grade IV, but there were many more sections of hard climbing remaining. It was now late on Sunday afternoon and we both had to return to Edinburgh; either we had to miss work, continue climbing and bivouac, or call it a day and climb up Easy Gully to the summit. We wavered for quite some time but in the end, saying 'We'll come back next weekend,' we raced to the top of Meaghaidh and home.

We never got back together on the girdle. Although Bugs completed all its sections in separate forays, the complete unbroken traverse, which we had meant to do once we knew the whole route, had to wait for several years. Shortly after the crossing of the Pinnacle Buttress I went back to live in Yorkshire. My love affair in Edinburgh had broken up, and I also had to prepare for the Alpamayo Expedition. Bugs left Scotland for the sterner joys of Antarctica. For me the weather was the problem; I did travel up from England on a couple of occasions, but each time the conditions were no good. In the end the climb, 8,500 feet of serious climbing with many difficult sections, was accomplished in a single day, solo by the man then most versed in Scottish winter tactics, on or off the Bens, Tom Patey! Maintaining his disinterest to the last, one day in the winter of 1969 he raced across the whole of the Coire Ardair precipices. His write-up of this climb, 'Creagh Meaghaidh Crab-Crawl', is included in his posthumously published book *One Man's Mountains*, and has become a classic of mountaineering literature.

Only a decade after these events all the above players but myself were dead. Jim McArtney was to die tragically in an avalanche on Ben Nevis in January 1970, and thus Scotland lost its most powerful ice climber of his generation. Tom Patey was killed in a freak abseiling incident a few months later, after climbing a sea-stack, The Maiden, off the north-west coast. For all of us who were his friends his death marked the end of an era, and my only consolation was that I had been in-strumental in making some of the arrangements which eventually led to the publication of his writings. There is a dark side to modern climbing, for the growth of our activity into a mass sport has meant that some of the magic, the myth and the legends no longer thrive. There is a degree of unhealthy cynicism, and it is hard for many young climbers now to appreciate not only the climbing achievements of earlier generations, but the sheer joy that we could find in, for instance, the accomplished musicianship of Tom Patey, playing his accordian in a bar in the Highlands, backed by a team of other instruments, singing some of his own songs, and many others from Brahms to a Hebridean love lilt. It was a simple but extraordinarily profound pleasure and enlivened the days on the hill. A visit to Scotland in that era just to be in Tom's company was truly worthwhile.

Bugs was to survive Jim and Tom by a further eight years, by which time he had become one of the most accomplished mountaineers in the world. His climbing career was broken into two distinct parts: the first as a young man in Scotland, the second in maturity in Canada, where he brought Scottish winter climbing techniques and know-how. During the first phase he made many first ascents in his native country in both winter and summer, and also many outstanding climbs in the Alps, such as the North Pillar of the Eiger in 1970. In between the first and second part of his life came the time he spent in Antarctica, following many other leading Scottish climbers before him, including John Cunningham. I have already intimated that Bugs was an unusual character – restless, full of driving energy, sometimes moody – but it was not easy to appreciate immediately the range of his talents. He had many strings to his bow besides his climbing. Self-exploration drew him to Antarctica and, although I did act as his referee, I mistakenly tried to dissuade him from committing a part of his young life to what I felt was not the best use he could make of his time. How wrong he proved me to be, for in a short time he refined his ice technique, learned to touch-type, and to play the guitar, and mastered the subtleties of black and white photographic techniques.

After trips to climb in the Andes and further new routes in the Alps, he emigrated to Canada, and it was there that he really found himself, and that his climbing really developed. He specialised in ice climbing, making the first winter ascent of the Tatakakken Falls, over 1,000 feet of steep ice and the first such climb anywhere to be graded VI. His rock climbing prowess remained and at the time of his death he had probably done more big wall climbing in Yosemite Valley than any other British climber.

Bugs was killed on Mount Assiniboine in the Canadian Rockies in June 1978 when, after he had completed a major face climb, a cornice collapsed. Typically unselfish, caught in a storm, he had gone down the descent ridge ahead of his companions looking for the easiest way off. He was carried off to an untimely death at 33 years of age, but not before he had completed a degree in fine art at Calgary University, and become the father of a baby girl.

A sad group of us, including several people from Canada who had come especially for the event, gathered in Glencoe over the weekend of 8–9 July 1978 to scatter his ashes and, in the manner of our forebears, to hold a wake. The wake lasted all night and we all said farewell to a true friend. We had been privileged to witness, and to help, an awkward youth become, by dint of sheer persistence, one of the most potent climbing forces of his or any other generation.

Alpine climbing is a totally different game from British climbing, made so by one single factor – the mountains are glaciated. There are parts of the range where this is hardly significant, but even in those areas the climber is conscious of a difference in scale, additional objective dangers such as more stone fall, and increased weather hazards.

My own first visit to the Alps was an unusual one. In 1954 I visited Austria while it was still occupied, when I went to run during my National Service. On that visit I also climbed in the Wilder Kaiser mountains and the Dolomites, and since then I have been to the Alps at least twenty times, on two occasions for as long as twelve weeks at a time, on others for short trips of a mere few days. I have made over 100 ascents there, some major climbs such as routes on the South Face of Mont Blanc, others short climbs in areas that are not so well known. I have also delighted in introducing friends either to areas off the beaten track, or Alpine novices to their first routes.

Of my Alpine climbs only a few remain clearly etched in the memory, either because of unusual conditions, the quality of the climbing, storms resulting in epics, or the personalities of my climbing companions. One climb which qualifies on every count was the East Face of the Sass Maor, a huge and complex face in a rarely visited area of the Dolomites, which I climbed with Ian Howell in 1965.

The Sass Maor is situated in the southern part of the Dolomites in the wild and beautiful San Martino group. The eastern side of the mountain has as bold an aspect as any in the range, but because it is very remote, reached via a deep valley, the Val Pradidali, it is rarely climbed. One of the greatest climbers of all time, Emil Solleder, had made its first ascent in 1926, but he had avoided the true challenge of the 3,500-foot face. He had traversed on to it half-way up by a line of easy slanting chimneys which lead diagonally into the centre from the south side. Inevitably, the face was climbed direct later, by way of a prominent rib of compact grey rock. Looking up the Pradidali valley, I could follow the route up the whole height of this enormous bastion. Beginning with the rib, it runs through a zone of terraces interspersed with steep walls, a line of chimneys (the original route), a series of roofs – presumably overcome by the famous traversing pitches – then a series of corners and finally the finishing wall to the tip of the giant dagger which is the Sass Maor. I had been to look at it before, several years previously, and Ian Howell and I had come there now, driving south by terrible weather conditions, in the hope that this face would be in condition. 'Well, what do you make of it?' I asked with a proprietary air.

'Absolutely spiffing!' replied Ian with a grin, in his best public school accent. Ian, a power-house striding from hard climb to climb, hides his determined drive behind a Greyfriars school manner which matches his background and his natural good humour.

At sunset the sky was clear, without a trace of cloud on the horizon, demonstrating, as I pointed out to Ian, what a good idea of mine it had been to come. I spoke too soon.

Seven o'clock next morning found us moving up the rock rib with the confidence born of success on other climbs. When the route description almost at once proved wildly inaccurate, we cheerfully picked our own way, admitting that the steep and compact rock was perhaps harder than we had expected. We had nearly always improved on guidebook times, so, as the forecast for this ascent was eight to ten hours, we carried no bivouac equipment. Our food supplies consisted of oranges and boiled sweets and we carried some water and four pitons each, having been led to expect free climbing. Our piton allowances soon began to worry us as we discovered few in place, and the compact rock provided no natural running belays.

I have rarely climbed with so little protection. We made good progress, however, completely absorbed by the climbing; so absorbed, in fact, that we didn't notice the first black clouds boiling up on the horizon in spite of the clear sky at dawn. Suddenly, with a roar, a large rock-fall swept over the rib below us. 'Thank goodness we're not down there,' I muttered.

'I don't like the look of those clouds,' Ian rejoined, 'But we'd better go on. We couldn't go back down the rib if we wanted to, I don't fancy being under the next rock-fall.'

We climbed up and up the never-ending rib, and slowly the clouds came up until tentacles of mist crawled over us and our mountain. Soon we couldn't see 100 feet up or down, and it grew thicker all the time. The first distant rolls of thunder put us on edge. 'We're in for it this time!' I observed, as I started to climb a steep crack of perfect but compact rock.

Forty feet up I stuck; I couldn't move out of the crack, which ended in an overhanging bulge. At that instant the rain began; within minutes it was torrential and I was soaked and almost washed off the rock. I had to do something and quickly, with a hand jam, I reached up and under the bulge and a frenzied glance revealed a possible running belay – a thread round a jammed chockstone. How I struggled to thread that stone! It was my whole life, existence itself. When my hands became frozen I used my teeth; I jammed my knee against the bulge and almost fell. Finally, gasping and shaking, I got the sling threaded, clipped a karabiner in, pushed in my rope, and hung on it. The rain was beating on my head so hard that I didn't dare look upwards. 'Go down!' came a voice from within, and, as if it were an unchallengeable command, I cast-off and climbed down to Ian, sheltering in the bottom of the crack. We huddled together.

'We must get up before it gets any worse,' Ian declared as we pulled our cagoules over our soaking bodies. 'I'll have a try.'

He changed places with me to climb up to the thread runner. It was no time for niceties. Ian clipped another loop into the sling and standing in this reached round the bulge, then swung out and over the top. The temperature was dropping and the rain turned to snow. Shivering, I climbed up to Ian on a small ledge beneath a vertical crack. Whoever gave the description for the English guide was an idiot, we decided uncharitably; it bore little resemblance to reality. I had to ask Ian to lead the crack; my hands were numb and I knew I wouldn't succeed without taking time to warm them. Our world had shrunk to a few feet of wet rock. It is hard to re-experience the anxiety of such moments, but I have never been more frightened in my life. Ian's determination was unflagging; teeth clenched he set off again without a word, to the accompaniment of reverberating thunder. He struggled with the crack for what seemed hours; it became colder and colder and he had to stop in a small cave near the top of the pitch, blowing on his hands to get some feeling into them for the last few feet of laybacking. With a desperate thrust he succeeded in reaching a stance fifteen feet higher. As he took in my rope, the blizzard swirled with increasing fury.

I joined Ian with difficulty and found him on a little shelf with no possibility of shelter. 'Shall we sit it out here or press on?' I yelled through the gale.

'We must keep going,' Ian declared emphatically. My hands were dead and I feared frost-bite. I have never been in a storm of such violence in the Alps before or since, and its ferocity completely undermined me. I was for bivouacking on that small platform, but Ian moved off again to tackle the steep wall above our heads. I could see he was as worried as I was. Two rope-lengths of desperate climbing with icy holds and occasional stones peppering us brought us to an even more serious situation. Night was almost upon us as Ian brought me up to join him, both of us suspended from indifferent pitons with no ledge or shelter from the storm. 'Oh God, what a place!' I moaned.

'I think there's a cave above and to our right if only we can reach it,' Ian said, pointing up through the snowy dusk. 'We must get out of this!'

I forced myself to lead and hesitantly climbed towards the promised haven. My hands were frozen and I was desperate, yet somehow in the darkness, at the end of the rope, my experience, luck and reserves got me up. What a disappointment! Our refuge was a mere depression in the rock, like a saucer, perhaps a melt-hole, but certainly no cave. I hammered in a piton and brought Ian up; for better or worse this curved hollow was our shelter for the night.

I shall never forget that night. We had nothing to protect us, although we did manage to take off our boots and get our feet into rucksacks. Feeling returned to my hands and the subsequent hot-aches kept my mind occupied for quite a time. We rationed our boiled sweets to one an hour and I began to look forward to this treat in a quite unreasonable way. Stones whistled down the face; under the lip of our depression we felt safe, until one hit me in the back with a resounding thud. 'It's nothing,' I reassured Ian. 'Only a little one.' We were surprised next day to find that it had cut through my clothes and drawn blood.

'I think we've had it!' whispered Ian in half-spoken thought, during a slight lull. 'Certainly if it doesn't stop snowing soon.'

'Let's sing,' I suggested, but we soon tired of howling into the wind. The snow continued to pile up round us. I felt myself suspended in time and space, full of my own suffering, as if I was caught inside a never-ending nightmare. A jerk brought me to full awareness; I was hanging on the ropes that tied us on. Peering through iced eyelashes I glimpsed stars. 'Ian, Ian we're OK! It's stopped snowing!' Ian too had been locked in his own world of misery, but greeted this critical news with a characteristic 'Super!' and handed me a boiled sweet to celebrate.

Climbers are quite often asked how they cope with the calls of nature in such a situation. Usually the body, pushed to its limits and short of liquid, is kind in its demands in this direction and you can usually avoid having to act until a more convenient place and time. But if there is no alternative you simply get on with it while your partner turns his head. Inevitably things can go wrong but it is no time for false modesty or squeamishness.

In the last hour before dawn the intense cold had us writhing as if trying to escape from probing needles. Cloud covered the stars again and what the first light, heralded by fine driven snow, revealed made my heart sink. The steep rock was so plastered with verglas and snow it looked hopeless. I was for sitting it out, but Ian was unwilling to stay put for another second and struggled into his boots.

Somehow he inched his way upwards; slowly and interminably the rope jerked out. 'Come on!' It was so like winter climbing in Scotland that I had to keep reminding myself that this was the Dolomites in summer at a mere 8,000 feet. I took over the lead and immediately felt better. There is something about leading which, despite the added danger and responsibility, makes you concentrate far harder than if seconding. I could not have led the first rope-length for my life but now I felt that nothing could stop us. We should have been somewhere near to Solleder's traverse on to the face; if we could find that we would know where we were and have an easy descent to the valley. Peering through the mist we could see nothing to tell us our position.

Around lunch-time, I came upon a big ledge while leading, and at the same time realised it was becoming warmer. The snow ceased abruptly, but thick mist blotted everything out. 'This must be the junction with the original route,' Ian suggested, and I nodded agreement. We walked along the terrace to the south; it became wider then disappeared into a deep chimney. A rusty piton told us this was Solleder's route. At once our tension dispersed; our worries were over and we unroped and sat happily on the edge of the chimney, knowing we had got away with it. A lot of rubbish has been written about the spirit and comradeship of the hills, but Ian and I looked at each other sheepishly and grinned. We had been to the edge and escaped by a combination of teamwork and luck.

It was late in the evening before we were completely off the hook, after slithering down Solleder's chimneys and climbing down 1,000 feet of loose and broken ground. We crawled into a cow shed at the foot of the face, feeling as virtuous as gods. The direct start to the east face of the Sass Maor had provided enough adventure to frighten and satiate us, and we lay sleeping while it rained and rained.

Three days later, on the first fine morning, we completed the ascent using the Solleder start. The climbing was classic, especially the famous traversing pitches, but it was an anti-climax after our involvement with the direct start. This time the route description proved accurate, and we even restored faith in ourselves by being several hours ahead of the guidebook time. Drinking tea as evening shadows dramatised the face, I decided we could still count our ascent as a correct, orthodox climb, even though we had been almost a week in completing it. Famous words come to mind – the late Robin Smith's, I believe, about one of his own quixotic adventures: 'Unpremeditated bivouacs before, during and after the climb.' This more or less sums up our escapade.

A short while after these events my life changed dramatically. I enrolled as a mature student on a 3-year course studying psychology at Leeds University. In my first year there my mother died of a brain tumour, her suffering mercifully over a few months after the diagnosis. And at the end of the three years' I got married. Inevitably, Leni belonged to the climbing world. A climber and skier from Nottingham, she was a member of the Oread Club and ten years younger than me. We had met when I had given a lecture to her club on our Andean expedition of 1966, and our wedding was very much a climbing event. Ned Kelly was our best man, and many members of our respective clubs, the Oread and the Rock and Ice, were present. We managed by scraping and bowing to purchase a run-down, former weaver's cottage in a terrace in Guiseley, near Leeds and soon we began our family. Stephen was born in 1969, Robin in 1972, and Helen in 1975.

I have known people who have stopped serious climbing activities as soon as they have got married, and even one bizarre case of a climber ceasing to climb, saying it was 'too dangerous and risky for a married man with responsibilities', who fell down his stairs at home and broke his neck. I have never changed my own attitude to risk-taking. Climbing is risky, but then so is life itself, and it is more or less possible to set levels on how much risk you want to take. Himalayan mountaineering is bloody dangerous, the statistics prove that; Alpine climbing is not as dangerous, British mountaineering is safer still, and pure rock climbing even more so. There is always the chance that things will go wrong, it is true, but none of us

Robin and Stephen Gray as young boys at Kinder Downfall.
(Photo: Dennis Gray)

climb either to hurt or kill ourselves. We do it to know life the fuller, and to experience a richer and more fulfilling existence.

We introduced our children to climbing at an early age. It is no use forcing them, and so far Helen has shown little or no enthusiasm for the sport whilst both Stephen and Robin enjoy the environment. Stephen is keen on rock climbing but Robin is happier hill walking and Alpine climbing, and at fifteen he completed the Plan-Midi traverse in the Mont Blanc range, partnered by a fourteen-year-old French boy! Their preference is partly explained by their physiology; whilst Stephen is like a stick, Robin is like a tank, being, as Joe Brown recently remarked, 'at least one and a half people!'

When Stephen was twelve, I decided to take him up his first real Alpine route and peak. For this we went to the Mont Blanc range, a mecca for climbers from all over the world with its superb rock climbing on reddish granite, its wonderful mixed climbs, its demanding ice routes and its jagged summits. Stephen's 'initiation' was to take place on an easy route up the Aiguille du Moine which, at 11,194 feet, is high enough to provide impressive scenery, but has a swift and easy descent route, and only a small glacier to cross in case of difficulties. The weather in the season of 1982 was, as in many recent years, very changeable. In the valley it was baking hot, but on the peaks afternoon thunderstorms were keeping everyone off the major climbs. We went up to the Couvercle hut the day before our climb and, although Stephen was small and thin, he had no difficulty in completing the five-hour walk from the Montenvers mountain railway station. The last section up to the hut was full of memories for me. I had been there many times: with Ian Clough who had died so tragically in 1970 at the end of the South Face Annapurna Expedition; with

Dez Hadlum with whom I had shared many great climbing adventures in the 1960s, and who happily is alive and well and living in the Rockies; at one point I had met Gaston Rebuffat and at another Lionel Terray, both great French climbers of the 1950s; and I had also come across Walter Phillip, the Austrian ace from the same era. As we climbed I told my son about these meetings. Like most young people he was singularly unimpressed, and with such a response it is hard to live in the past for long. He was impressed by the scenery, however, and almost walked off into space several times so hard was he staring, entranced by the huge faces and peaks all around him.

Climbing with your offspring in the Alps is both satisfying and frightening, the more so with Stephen because his early years had been difficult. Several times racked with asthma and on two occasions pneumonia, I had been convinced he would die in childhood. He had proved me wrong, and at eight he was accomplished enough to win a place to study music full time at Chetham's School of Music in Manchester. Bolstered by grants and bursaries he had left home at that young age, and was now an independent soul despite his tender years. His health too had improved, and it was no longer a worry.

After a night at the Couvercle hut, and a crossing of the small Moine Glacier, all had gone well with our climb. We had ascended a route that was not in the English guidebook. It was slightly harder and to the west of the normal route up the peak, and took more time, but it offered some entertaining pitches, including one small wall that was like a boulder problem with a nice soft ledge to jump down on to at its base. We sat happily on the summit taking our time, eating some lunch and taking photographs. After a while I noticed with unease clouds brewing away to the south over the Grandes Jorasses, so we started down. The descent off the Moine is easy and I had been down it three times before, so I was confident there would be no problems, but I hadn't anticipated such a rapid change in conditions. Within half an hour of our starting to move again, it was snowing. 'No bother,' I thought. 'Just a passing squall.' Suddenly there was a tremendous flash, followed by a loud explosion and we found ourselves in a storm of some violence. We crouched under a boulder, and put our waterproofs on over our already wet clothes. 'It will soon pass,' I assured Stephen, but it did not. The temperature began to drop and everything was becoming coated with ice.

I heard a voice shouting out in the storm and climbed out from under our sheltering rock to find two Germans, a man and his wife. 'Please, ver is the way down?' he shouted, sounding desperate. I pointed down a crack and chimney system at my feet, now covered in show and verglas, then, worried at what I had seen, climbed back under our boulder to find Stephen shivering with cold.

'We must get down!' I said to Stephen, for I was frightened he might become a victim of exposure. Tying him into the rope again I let him climb down first and then I followed. All went well and Stephen seemed to be doing fine, but in the bad weather we lost the route slightly and found ourselves faced with a difficult crack to descend. We should have roped down, but time was now of the essence; we must get off, and back to the shelter of the hut, for my son was tiring quickly. We were wet to the skin, and the cold was eating into us.

Stephen climbed down the crack, but on reaching the bottom his hands were too cold to hold my rope, which was covered in ice. I started down, and found the crack hard. I realised that if I fell I would take Stephen with me, for he had no belay, and was huddled at the base of the crack obviously shattered. My heart almost stopped at one point, when my feet shot off verglassed holds, but thankfully I had good hand jams which stuck, despite their lack of feeling. With enormous relief I reached the bottom, and from there I could see an easier way round the obstacle. The German couple had watched my struggle from above with obvious fear; I directed them towards the simpler route. The four of us joined up from then on and things improved: we were on to easy ground and, despite the weather, we reached the bergschrund between the rock face and the glacier. Stephen was so exhausted that he could not put on his crampons for himself, and when we got the ice axes out from our rucksacks he just held his apathetically.

The bergschrund was both dangerous and heavily crevassed that year, so I went first and crossed the worst bit, then Stephen followed, held behind by our German friends. Having got him across hesitantly but safely, I cut him a large platform, tied him safely on to a huge ice bollard, then climbed back to help the Germans. Between us we managed to get over these obstacles on to the easier part of the glacier, and after some chocolate we all felt better. We arrived back at the hut just as a rescue team was coming up; a British party had had an accident up on the Cardinal. Thankfully they survived their ordeal.

We never saw the two Germans again, but the chance that brought us together in adversity reinforced again my belief that any kind of nationalism or racism is fundamentally wrong. We are all the same, we have the same strengths and the same weaknesses, and no places teaches us this better than the wilderness and the mountains.

The Alps are now truly charted, and there is little left to do in the way of exploratory mountaineering. Having said that, they can still provide a challenge and much enjoyment, as well as the ultimate in what is still best described as 'Alpinism'. They are of the right scale and I hope that for generations to come fathers and sons, mothers and daughters can go there and revel in the mountain environment and, despite the demands of modern tourism, find there an oasis of peace and tranquillity.

South America

You take the long way home.
Supertramp

For a long time expedition mountaineering has been a source of public interest, and is easily the most publicised and written-about area of the sport. The first book I read about an expedition was *Annapurna* by Maurice Herzog, which described the epic French ascent in 1950. This fired me and my companions and we wanted to travel, to climb and to visit the highest mountains of the world. We reasoned at the time that working class boys and girls simply could not afford to visit the Himalaya or the Andes, and we would have to be content with our homeland hills, but events were conspiring to change our situation. The social revolution which had begun after the Second World War continued unabated, and many more of us entered higher education and subsequently achieved an improved standard of living.

The ascent of Everest in 1953 by John Hunt's party popularised mountaineering in Britain as never before. One of the long-lasting effects of this event was the establishment of the Mount Everest Foundation, a grant-making charity of which many climbers have been grateful beneficiaries. Any group prepared to scrimp and save, who have a worthwhile objective and the necessary climbing credentials, can take part in expedition climbing. You may have to sell your possessions, mortgage your house, give up your job, and travel in great discomfort, but if you are sufficiently motivated then somehow you will get there.

I travelled to Peru in early May 1966 on a 22,000-ton Pacific Steamship Navigation Company cargo boat from Liverpool. The journey was an education in itself, and an extraordinary experience. Out in the South Atlantic we were hit by a Force Nine gale, and the old boat creaked and groaned fit to bust. Shortly afterwards we helped to save a man's life.

One evening, our wireless operator, on loan from the Cable and Wireless Company, was wandering out on deck. He was a young Scot, living in the next cabin to mine, and he and I had been enjoying a few beers (perhaps a few too many) while the boat made its way down the coast of South America. After a few moments he came running back past my door, shouting 'Man overboard! Man overboard!'

A quick count soon revealed that all our crew were still intact on the ship, but the 'Sparks' remained adamant that he had seen a man go past the ship clinging to driftwood. There followed a noisy row between the Captain and his underling.

'You're drunk!'

'No, I swear I saw him. We have to turn the boat around!'

Eventually the Captain, against his better judgement, agreed to turn around and the Scot sent out a general alert to other shipping in the area. To our surprise another ship close by, on the lookout after our message, found a man in the sea clinging to a log! This Peruvian seaman had been in the water for *three* days, having been swept overboard while fishing off Callao. The current had carried him hundreds of miles up the coast. He would not have lasted much longer without fresh water or food, and was almost unconscious when they pulled him in.

Alpamayo, the world's most beautiful mountain, with the north ridge on the left and the south ridge on the right. (Photo: Erwin Schneider)

It took nineteen days to reach Panama, and the crew's only entertainment was to watch the same blue movie every night, projected by a tiny machine on to a white sheet in the galley. After a couple of viewings I had seen enough, but the crew were determined to widen my experience of life, and when we reached Panama, in a break in the unloading of our cargo of Scotch whisky, I was taken to the Zamba Bar. This was less a bar, more a brothel, with some of the most beautiful women I had ever seen, in particular one known to the crew by the title of the White Virgin. I managed to get very drunk on rum and coke, bought for me in a never-ending stream by my shipmates. Still, drunk or not, I was agonisingly embarrassed when the White Virgin decided, no doubt at the crew's instigation, that I should be her next customer and began to smother me with intimate caresses in front of the assembled company!

On arrival in Lima, after 6,000 miles and almost a month at sea, I was surprised to discover how modern and busy a city it was. It enjoyed good communications and there was some impressive Spanish colonial architecture. Everybody spoke Spanish, and it seemed disappointing simply to find a slice of Europe transplanted to the other side of the world. It was a great contrast to India and Nepal, where I had already been on expeditions, which were countries dominated by their own unique culture.

It was not until I had travelled outside Lima, visited the Inca sites of Macchu Pichu and Cuzco, and seen the *barriada* adjacent to the cities, where people live in makeshift accommodation made of cardboard and tin, that I began to know something of the way of South American life. The conditions in which the poor live rival any in Asia in terms of squalor.

I met my climbing companions in Lima: Roy Smith, Dave Bathgate, Terry Burnell, John Amatt and Ned Kelly, our cameraman. They had flown from London to New York, caught a Greyhound bus to Miami, and then a cheap flight to Lima. It was a tortuous way of reaching South America, but at that time it was definitely the most economically viable. I had managed to travel with all the equipment for a very small sum of money, so we were off on the right foot.

Expedition reports make for dull reading, unless there is a great epic story to tell, or a simple matter of life and death is the end result of some disaster. In 1966 our primary objective was to make the first ascent via the north ridge of Alpamayo. This famous mountain in the northern part of the Cordillera Blanca in Peru is known in climbing circles as 'the most beautiful mountain in the world', and the north ridge route had often been tried before, without success. Our secondary aim was to film the climb, which was why Ned Kelly was with us. We were financing this project ourselves, and it was to be Ned's first major mountain film; later he went on to produce such films as *Everest the Hard Way*. The fact that we were successful in both our aims owed much to luck with the weather, and an outstanding lead on the final section of the climb by our Scottish ice climbing expert, Dave Bathgate.

After almost a month of climbing, preparing the route so that we could film to a high standard for television, we were ready for one summit attempt. Alpamayo has an unusual perfect trapezoid shape and in order to achieve a successful ascent from the north side (after overcoming the north ridge) we had to complete the traverse along the crest of the mountain from the north summit to the highest point. The crest is an amazing switchback with massive cornices and extraordinary features and culminates in a final climb up an arrowhead composed only of unstable ice and snow.

On the day of the summit attempt Roy and Dave had set off before dawn, followed by Terry and me as soon as it was light enough for Ned to film our departure. Ned then took off with John along the ridge towards Tayapampa, the mountain immediately to our north, to shoot our ascent in long focus. We tied on the rope and I took a firm belay as Terry stepped out over the first hanging cornice and traversed on to the east face towards the rock band. Out on the cornice the exposure was considerable and to climb off it required a slightly downward movement across clear ice; here the fixed ropes started and I thankfully clasped them and moved up to join Terry. Large steps were cut in the ice and it was child's play, except for the fact that we were on or under the biggest cornices any of us had seen. The altitude began to affect me as I tried to move too quickly. Terry had been at over 18,000 feet for a week but I was fresh to this height; it brought on a cough with a vengeance. One more rope-length and we reached the security of a rock band which was clear of ice and which led upwards for hundreds of feet.

'It made a lot of difference, this rock band,' Terry remarked. 'Pitons into rock are more my idea of safety than ice stakes into bad ice.' Looking upwards, I could appreciate what he was saying; this rock band zig-zagged its way up through the ice, in some places thirty feet across, in others only a foot wide or completely overlaid by snow. We were fortunate that so much of it was bared – over a thousand feet. In another year we might not have been so lucky.

The band was shattered red granite, loose and friable, but the angle was such that most of the way we could put our feet against rock and swarm up the fixed rope, using a prusik clamp for aid. It had been a different story when Dave, Terry and

Roy had first climbed this obstacle, before it was equipped; it had demanded some quite difficult leads. After another hundred feet the rock was overlaid with ice and the route traversed to the west and out on to cornices over the face. I climbed up and landed in an ice cave. Two ice stakes were buried to their hilts into the wall of the cave, for belaying but also to secure a swift descent down the face to reach our tents.

Terry pointed out the finer points of this descent. 'Look out over the face,' he ordered. I hung out on the rope over a huge cornice and drop. 'Can you see the bergschrund?' I could just make it out three or four hundred feet below. 'Well, it's a twenty-foot leap downward to clear it and pretty gripping!'

I peered up to my right and could just discern a faint break in the cornice line; was that where an earlier party of three Swiss had fallen over 600 feet when the snow collapsed and, miraculously, had landed only slightly hurt in the basin where our tents now nestled? Another ice passage and we were back on the rock. The sun was fully on us now and I moved like a man in a dream, drained of all the energy I had possessed earlier that morning. We were climbing fast, although we never caught sight of Roy or Dave, and I had to keep asking Terry for a rest. We were at over 19,000 feet and well on our way to the north summit.

Just before the rock petered out we came upon a second cave. We crawled inside for a breather and Terry showed me where he had found a hammer-axe embedded in the ice; this could only have belonged to the French, who had reached the north summit of the mountain as long ago as 1951, and in the dark had mistakenly thought they had reached the true top. On the way down and in a blizzard, they had been forced to bivouac at this very spot – four people in this tiny ice grotto for a night, a haven discovered by Kogan when things looked at their worst.

Above the cave the rock band ended and we embarked on a traverse leftwards to an ice couloir. I suppose it would have been just too easy if the rock band had been bared to the summit, but as I left the rock I began to feel like a shipwrecked sailor. The traverse turned out to be straightforward and Terry climbed past into the gully, set at fifty degrees and pure ice. After one rope-length it became steeper still, and the next four hundred feet probably had an average angle of sixty degrees. Terry led cheerfully, and used the ropes dangling down with absolute trust. One section had a vertical lip and, even with a rope in place, it was a strenuous pull out and over this projection. I appreciated more and more the French team's performance all those years before, and why our own front men had taken so long to prepare the route for filming.

The ropes made it safe, but near the top of the ridge my heart missed a beat when one of the ice stakes came out as I pulled on to a belay platform to join Terry. 'Don't worry!' he advised. 'The ropes are all joined together in one continuous length, and the Corporal [Roy] has driven a three-foot stake into solid ice at the top. He broke three hammer-axes belting it in, but it would hold you, me and everybody else at once if it had to!' Roy was our strong man; his physique would have done credit to an Olympic weight-lifter.

We decided to have a rest, and I looked back at the route we had followed. The weather was superb, with only some slight cloud away to the north, where lay first Tayapampa then, further north still, Champara, on the Ecuador border. The weather in the Cordillera had been better than we had ever hoped for and, apart from bad weather early on in our climb, we had enjoyed day after day of clear skies and hot sun, although it was very cold at night. Far below now were our tents, and along the ridge northwards was Ned, crouched over a camera, filming our progress.

I saw with alarm that he and John were positioned on a giant cornice; they were both out over a dangerous drop. We shouted ourselves hoarse trying to warn them, but it was no good; they could not hear us and they happily continued with their work.

'Must press on,' I suggested to Terry, and off he led up the last sections of ice which were the steepest of all. Suddenly the slope eased back and we arrived at the top of the north ridge and the end of our fixed rope. An easy traverse, sinking deep in snow affected by the heat of the sun, and we had reached the lower north summit of Alpamayo. We were on the very crest of the mountain, but not quite sure of our altitude. The mountain's map height was given as 20,100 feet but this did not tie in with our own estimates. (Interestingly, revisions made after our visit have downgraded the height of Alpamayo to 19,610 feet.) The north summit is not much lower than the highest point, although between the two are many hundreds of feet of the most horrifying ground you could have the misfortune to have to climb on any mountain — mushrooms of ice, knife-edged and corniced ridges, and those weird formations which seem to be the preserve of the Andes; certainly, I have never seen their like in the Himalaya.

At our feet was a coffin-type trench cut in the snow and inside were Dave's and Roy's rucksacks. Terry and I were to enlarge this into a shelter of some dimensions and leave in it our loads containing food, stove and bivouac equipment, to serve as a dump for future filming operations. Roy and Dave would also use it if they took so long to reach the true summit that they had to spend the night out.

We looked expectantly along the switchback of a ridge. We couldn't see anyone so we moved along a little way to enlarge our view; from there the crest plunged into a crevasse set on the ridge itself. This was followed by an ascending knife-edge which swung to the east into a minor peak of its own, then there was a sizeable drop into a fissure directly under a mushroom of ice. This last looked impossible to get round, with overhung sides and composed of unstable feathery névé. Voices came from the rift under the mushroom; they floated across as if we were out on a fine summer's day in our own homeland hills and not perched on an ice crest at nearly 20,000 feet in the Andes.

Dave emerged from the fissure and attacked the mushroom. This was the most tense part of the whole climb and Terry and I stood frozen in our steps, willing our team-mate round this fearsome obstacle. Balancing on crampon points he gingerly cut away, fashioning a groove in the mushroom itself. Underneath him the ice plunged thousands of feet down the south-west face. Working swiftly with a short axe, he prepared a channel big enough to take his body, then swung boldly on to the side of the bulbous formation. We could only watch and hold our breath. From the rift we heard Roy's voice urging caution; at least Dave knew that if anything did go wrong he was tied to a very strong man. He balanced off the mushroom's side on to a knife-edge of snow, and then he was round and safely off the wierdie. The next section was the crux of the climb. Above Dave's head was the summit edifice, standing proud like a giant arrow; to reach the tip he had to stride a steep ice groove to a col, then he would be out of our sight until the final thirty feet of the summit's tip, obviously the steepest climbing of the whole route.

Roy began to sing a tuneless dirge, interspersed with occasional shouts of encouragement; we could hear him as plainly as if we were sitting right beside him. Dave disappeared and we waited for his reappearance with dry mouths, as tense as if we had been leading ourselves. After a few moments Dave's stetson appeared over the top of the mushroom, and his flailing axe was cutting into the summit tip itself. Eighty-degree snow is not pleasant to climb anywhere in the world, but here, as Dave reported later, he climbed up 'on footholds and handholds that would just have to do'. Roy tied a second rope-length on. Twenty feet only to go, but 'Oops!', Dave slid down three feet as the snow gave way. Fortunately he had his axe buried into the soft whiteness; the Amazon face of a mountain above five thousand feet of space is no place for a fall...

Dave nearly gave up at this point. We willed him on wordlessly, and the next moment it was over – he was balanced on the topmost ice of Alpamayo. A dream had come true, and our expedition had succeeded where so many parties before us had failed.

The summit was so small that Dave had to climb a short way down the opposite side before Roy could try to join him. Dave ran a rope back down the steep summit wall, tied round the tip itself. 'Well, either it will come down for certain, or it's safer than it looks,' I thought, as Roy tested it to its utmost, pulling up the final wall. Rope and summit stayed in position and Roy was able to stand on the tip, a red blotch beside the black dot that was Dave.

We climbed the mountain two more times, and Ned filmed an ascent made by Terry and me. It proved to be every bit as difficult and dangerous as it had looked, and it is no surprise that many parties who have followed after us have finished their climbs at the north summit, not caring to tackle that demanding last section. Ned Kelly climbed past this point and with the help of all the party created an award-winning feature film, *The Magnificent Mountain*. Filming on mountains to achieve a high professional standard is harder and more demanding than simply climbing, and by the time we had completed our task on Alpamayo, most of us were fed up with the effort. We had needed to spend so long preparing the route that we had been left with little or no time to explore and climb any other peaks, although Terry and Dave did make a couple of minor ascents.

On the way off the mountain poor Ned fell into a crevasse. Although I managed to hold him and help him out, he damaged a ligament in his leg and sprained his ankle so badly that he had to ride out on a *burro*. Despite our intention to do other big climbs, it was obvious that our expedition had reached its end.

Climbing expeditions are a unique experience in this day and age for westerners. You live in such close proximity with your fellow climbers that every foible, every quirk of character is mercilessly exposed. Added to this are the physical strains of living at altitude, the necessary load-carrying, the lack of normal food and often an insufficient liquid intake. It takes the character of a saint to remain fresh, cheerful and friendly with colleagues. We were no saints and towards the end of this climb we were running out of food; hunger began to dominate everybody's thinking, pushing friendship, home, family, wives, sex and any other consideration into second place. And so the final days of our descent from the beautiful mountain were marred by petty argument. Too much can be made of these things but I was the leader of the expedition, and I have nobody to blame but myself, for personal example is the key factor in avoiding this kind of ill-feeling.

Once back in the valley we all agreed to go our separate ways: I planned to go to Mexico, then hitch-hike to California, Ned had work to do in the Caribbean, and the rest wanted to see some more of Peru before travelling up to climb in the USA.

We are all still good friends, no permanent harm was done, but we needed to get away from each other's company for a while. In the end the time taken, the effort made, and the masses of equipment we had used for our filming were to be vindicated. One evening in October 1967 the telephone rang at home; on the other end was Ned, speaking from Geneva Airport. He was on his way home from the Trento Film Festival, the leading event of its type in the world for mountain and exploration films. 'Well, old son, we won,' he calmly reported. 'We won the award for mountain films, the Mario Bello Trophy.' Our film, *The Magnificent Mountain*, the film we had all worked so hard to make, was the success we had hoped, and was to be shown on television around the world. At the time I could only choke 'Well done Neddy!' down the phone, but every time I see the film, I am transported back to that arrow's tip in Peru, and recall that fantastic panorama of the mountain world in the Cordillera Blanca – Pucahirca, Huandoy and Huascaran seen from the very top of 'the most beautiful mountain in the world'.

Saying goodbye to my team-mates, I booked a cheap flight from Lima to Mexico City, planning to spend some time there, and then to hitch-hike to California. I was surprised to find the aircraft almost empty, but as soon as we were airborne a steward served me with steak and chips and a bottle of red wine, and I was happy.

'This is living!' I congratulated myself. I gazed out of the window, trying to peer at the Amazon far below, by now into my third glass of wine and quite mellow. I had drunk nothing alcoholic for many weeks, and this intake was having an immediate effect on me. Suddenly, 'Good god, there's smoke coming from the wing! Steward, steward, we're on fire!'

'*Si Senor*, one of the engines is on fire.'

'How many engines have we got?' Being a complete duffer at anything to do with engineering, I tried not to sound too stupid.

'*Dos.*'

'Well, that's a relief,' I said to myself, thinking he had said twelve. Then, '*Dos? Dos?* But that's only two and one of them is on fire! What are we going to do?'

'We are going to try for an emergency landing at Quito in Ecuador,' the steward informed me, 'but first we must get rid of as much fuel as we can. Shall I bring you another bottle of wine?' I promptly accepted the offer.

By the time we were near to Quito I was quite blasé about the whole affair. Glancing out of the window, well into my second bottle, I saw flames as well as smoke coming from the wing. I resigned myself to crashing into the thick jungle below, and wondered idly what our chances of survival might be.

Suddenly our trajectory altered and we seemed to fall right out of the sky. 'Well, this is it. What a bloody way to go!' I mused as our ancient Boeing shuddered and juddered through the air. 'We are going to crash, crash, crash!' The steward had disappeared and, apart from incessant talking over the speaker system in Spanish, which I could not understand, nobody was paying any attention to the passengers.

I braced myself for the impact, but just as it appeared we were going to smash into the trees, a clearing miraculously appeared. Quito! We were on to the runway, and there alongside us I could see out of the window, wildly careering at speed with bodies hanging from all sides, the most ancient of fire engines.

Our plane staggered down the runway, belching flames and smoke, and with a heroic effort the pilot stopped it. The force as he applied the brakes catapulted me forward, and the seat belt nearly cut me in two! I was sore for days afterwards. There were only a few of us on board, but how we cheered!

The ancient fire engine drew up and soon foam, white, soapy and bubbly, was spraying everywhere. Gradually the fire became under control and then was extinguished. We climbed down a ladder and off the plane, to be greeted with wild enthusiasm by the Ecuadorian rescue services. I have never been kissed so often by so many people in my life.

After a brief sojourn in Quito, hot, sticky and humid on the edge of the jungle, I was off first class, courtesy of Varig airlines, to Mexico, the most populous city in the world. I took a room in the *barriada*, the slum quarter of the city. It cost a few pence a day, and the bedding was infested, so I slept in my sleeping bag on my mat on the floor, once I had cleaned the place out.

Over the years I have begun to like travelling on my own more and more, and the seeds of this were sown on my journeys in South America. Alone, you are forced to interact socially with local people, and in Mexico City I soon found friends. At first I met with a frosty reception at my rooming house, because they thought I was from the US – not popular here in South America. Once it emerged I was not a 'gringo', but a plain and simple Yorkshireman, I was swamped with kindness and concern. My new-found friends took me to hear the Mariachis bands, and to the hili game, where, acting on their advice, I bet on a player who was trailing miserably and appeared to have no hope. Suddenly he sparked into life and swamped the opposition, and I won sufficient money to move into a decent hotel.

After a week I said my goodbyes to Juan, Pedro and 'Lita and caught a bus to start my journey to San Francisco. We travelled through the vast urban sprawl, which even then was growing at a rate too fast for the authorities to cope with. People were living in makeshift dwellings of wood, cardboard, and fuel cans. I was fascinated in all that was going on around me, for it seems to me that we depend for our futures on the fate of Latin America, and Africa. Unless the problems there are solved, there can be little hope of peace in the world.

Travelling in Mexico alone in 1966, I never felt either threatened or frightened. Alas, I would not dream of trying to hitch-hike from Mexico City to San Francisco now, because of the dangers involved, especially in the southern US. Still, at that time, ignorance was bliss, and I made my way through Guadalajara, Mazatlan and Nogales, at the US border. I cheated a little and jumped a bus or two, but I had lifts on everything from a donkey cart to a Mercedes motor car.

At Mazatlan on the coast I met some Californians who had come south to surf. I had never tried this sport before but soon, under their enthusiastic instruction, I was lying on a board out in the surf, and I was hooked! The waves off Mexico are monsters, several metres high, powerful and destructive, and surfing was both exciting and dangerous. Before I left Mazatlan I managed to stand up a couple of times and ride the surf, although I spent most of the time in the water. If you can get up on the crest of a wave, balanced on a surfboard, the buzz is extraordinary.

I arrived at the border with the US, after over a week on the road from Mexico City. I was heading for Tucson, the Grand Canyon, the San Fernando Valley, San Francisco and Yosemite Valley to climb, but the impression of the teeming masses in the *Ciuadad* stayed with me. It is a vibrant, dynamic place, but frightening in its implications – by the year AD 2020 it may have as many as 70 million inhabitants.

Eighteen years later I came back to Mexico City, this time as a guest of the Mexican government for an international conference, and staying at the Hilton.

I explained to the organisers that I would like to meet some climbers and have a day out somewhere on the rocks, for I had heard recently that there was outcrop climbing around the city.

'No problem *Senor*! No problem, *manana*.' As this is the classic response to every request in South America, I thought that nothing would come of it, but I was grabbed at breakfast the next morning by Senor Morales, from the Mexican Ministry of Sport. 'One of our best climbers is waiting for you in the lobby. He will take you climbing for the day,' he said. I wandered out into the foyer of the Hilton, expecting to see an obviously tried and tested local hero of the rocks. Instead there was a young boy, about 16 years old, carrying an ancient old nylon hawser laid rope, standing self-consciously by the enquiry desk.

I ambled over to introduce myself, and found out he was known by the nickname 'Apego', which means 'stick like glue!' I was soon to find out why.

We set off by public transport on what seemed like a Cook's tour of Mexico City; a bus, the underground, another bus, and then a lift in a minibus and we were there. Mexico City's premier outcrop turned out to be like Ilkley or Millstone Quarries, but set in the middle of a large housing estate. The rock was volcanic, and the climbs hard, but young Apego moved up them like an automaton. He obviously had the moves wired, but even so, if you have climbed a lot yourself, you can soon tell how good someone else is by their technique and the way they move. Apego was brilliant. He was lithe and dark, very strong, particularly in the fingers, and had a flashing smile. There was no bravado about him, and he was very modest. The climbs became harder and harder, and I ended up hanging off his old rope – far more frightening than climbing the rock, but I just could not stay in contact.

For someone so young, Apego knew a lot about climbing. Although he hadn't a good rope, he had reasonable footgear (he was wearing EBs) and a rack of ancient nuts, by which he protected the climbs, all of which he led. His ambition was to visit Yosemite Valley. 'There are many young climbers here in Mexico City, but we cannot afford to travel. It is hard to get a visa to the US, and we must do military service before we are allowed to go abroad in any case,' Apego explained wistfully. Soon we had to start our long journey back across the city. I had a reception that night, and insisted that Apego came with me.

The reception was in one of the best restaurants in Mexico City, and Apego and I arrived back late from our climbing to present ourselves at the door still wearing sweaters, jeans and trainers. Mexicans are fabulous hosts, and nobody blinked an eyelid as the Minister of Sport came over and asked if we had had a good day on the rocks.

I could not leave Mexico without visiting Popocatepetl, first climbed by the *conquistadores* in the sixteenth century, situated to the south of the city, and an extinct volcano over 17,000 feet in height. I had no equipment with me, but Apego turned up with some old boots, crampons and an even more ancient ice axe. With Apego was his sister, Dolores, who was much older than him. I was surprised to find that there are quite a few women mountaineers in Latin America, and it was she who had started him climbing. The ascent of Popocatepetl is not very interesting, rather like large, extinct volcanoes everywhere and at over 17,000 feet it is a slog without any technical difficulties. But the view from the summit is breathtaking. We had spent the night below in a hut, and as we climbed the easy slopes we could see distant mountain ranges, and the beast that it is the city.

I had swiftly to return to that city to catch the plane to New York, but not before a tearful goodbye from Apego. I have not heard from him since that day. I enquired of him from Mexican mountaineers I met on Broad Peak in 1989, but they did not know of his whereabouts, not surprisingly considering the population and size of Mexico. If ever he does read this I would wish him to know that, for me, in the words of Neruda, 'Your memory is of light, of smoke, of a still pool. Deep in your eyes the twilights burned. The dry leaves of autumn whirled in your soul.'

The Himalaya

*The more one sees of the Himalaya, the more one wants
to see.*

Sir Francis Younghusband

The Himalayan chain swings in a fifteen-hundred-mile arc through Asia, a geo-graphic freak containing the highest mountains of the world, and the ultimate possibility in mountain experience by man on this planet. The Himalaya are made up of dozens of ranges with thousands of peaks, many of which have still never been attempted, and some of which have even yet not been approached. Every type of challenge for mountaineers and rock climbers is to be found there, but these mountains are not solely for the extreme climber nor the professional explorer; there are unfrequented valleys, untrodden passes, easy but worthy unclimbed peaks, besides the most demanding technical challenges to be found on high mountains anywhere. Every mountain lover should make it their ambition to visit the Himalaya, but be warned that to travel there is no idyll, for you are subjected to extremes of climate, and exposed to serious health hazards and to dangers un-matched in other mountains. To get the most out of any visit to the Himalaya you need to have wide interests; it is there that four of the world's great religions meet, and the difference between life in Islamic Pakistan and Buddhist Tibet, for example, is acute. Much time is usually spent in reaching an objective, for there are long approaches, and often at the journey's end there is little in the way of high standard technical climbing. Mountaineers only interested in such matters are better off elsewhere, but for those who are keen to travel, have a sense of wonder, and are open to new experiences and willing to adapt to different standards and conditions, a visit to the Himalaya will be unforgettable. A journey to any other mountains in any other part of the world may not equal it.

I have now been fortunate enough to visit the Himalaya several times, and on some occasions travelling to and from our destination has been a saga in itself. I have travelled to India twice by sea, and once journeyed to Kathmandu from England by road. In 1968 I was a Churchill Fellow to India, and after leading the Mukar Beh expedition travelled throughout the country from north to south on a study tour. In 1989, in between leading treks and climbs in the Karakoram range, I travelled widely in Pakistan. The impressions gained on such journeys remain, and can never be forgotten. You quickly realise that the life of the western nations is untypical of mankind generally, the majority of whom are still without enough food, adequate clothing, shelter or health care.

My first opportunity to visit the Himalaya came in 1961. At that time I was living in Derby, and working in fine art printing. A group of local climbers, mainly members of the Oread Club, were forming an expedition to visit the Kulu Hima-laya in India and they invited me to join their party. This was the first time any of us were visiting a range outside Europe. Fortunately, we were being advised by people with previous expedition experience; unfortunately, our advisers favoured the large expedition pattern. We must have been one of the largest and weightiest parties ever to arrive among the lesser Himalayan peaks.

Many of the books about Himalayan expeditions have been dull, predictable, and badly written, yet the mountains remain wonderful. Kulu is typical. Although it contains within its boundaries no really high summits – the maximum altitude of the range is just under 22,000 feet – precipitation in the area is greater than in other Himalayan ranges, and therefore the permanent snow-line is around 12,000 feet, and the scale is grand. 'Kulu' is the name of a town and a valley, and is loosely applied to a group of mountain regions. Through the valley rushes the Beas, one of the great rivers of the Punjab (Land of Five Rivers) and of the Himalaya. Above all else, these watercourses have shaped man's destiny in these regions. They are frightening to behold in all their power, sweeping along huge boulders when in flood, and they are the main cause of the most serious erosion problems in the world. The difference in the physical geography of the different regions of the Himalaya is extraordinary. The Karakoram, without doubt the grandest and most impressive of all the ranges, is really a vertical desert, with little or no rainfall in its valleys. In contrast, an area like Kulu is thickly wooded in its lower regions, lush and green and almost reminiscent of the European Alps – but Alps on a unique scale.

In 1961 we travelled to India by first-class passenger ship, Liverpool to Bombay, and life at sea was a revelation to me: a round of parties, games by day and night, drinking and ceaseless feeding. The luxury intensified the horror of what awaited us in Bombay, and the impact of India on that first visit remains with me to this day. I was appalled by the degree of poverty spread so openly before us; in other parts of the world there is human degradation and squalor, but nowhere is it so manifest, so paraded, as in India. I wandered in the streets of Bombay and was shocked to find human beings starving and destitute. Here was the India of all the reports, with its rigid caste system, its sacred cows, its filth and its poverty. A typical young inhabitant of the rich western world, I was outraged by what I saw but it was really only when we journeyed north from Bombay, travelling slowly by train, that I began to appreciate the vast scale of it all. Every station had its kaleidoscope of Indian life: the homeless living on the stations, the rich boarding their first-class air-conditioned carriages, the perpetual travellers, the beggars, the filthy urchins and the fantastic, naked, wandering sadhus. I gazed in awe through the windows of the train at this seething mass of humanity.

We made every possible mistake during this expedition, and typical of this was the fact that we had brought from England almost all the food we would eat. Most of it had been donated, and our largest single food stock turned out to be Christmas pudding! To munch our way through the hundreds we possessed we had to be highly inventive with our cooking, and we found that they made a fine breakfast fried in butter. We engaged six Ladakhi high-altitude porters, of whom four were very raw indeed and nearly useless as mountaineers. Fortunately, of the other two, Sonam Wangyal became a close friend and was the best porter I have been with in the mountains. We got into a few scrapes on this trip, mostly due to our inexperience, but it was an exciting journey which remains significant in my memory. I even think I saw the fabled yeti!

I was sitting on a steep grass spur overlooking the Malana glacier, resting before descending down on to its snout a good distance below. Across and to the left of me were high cliffs and suddenly on these I saw something move. 'Yes!', it was a large animal traversing the rock face, and as I focused in on it, I was genuinely surprised to see in such terrain what I took to be a brown bear. It moved rapidly along the precipice until it reached a point well above the snout of the glacier, from where it descended down steep ground to gain the easier upper reaches of the ice. Standing upright, it ascended at speed, and I could see that it was covered with brown hair and as large as a fully grown bear. When I mentioned what I had seen to my incredulous companions on my return to camp, their reaction was predictable: 'Bloody seeing things! Hallucinating!'

By this time the bottom end of the Malana glacier had become quite difficult – the first few hundred feet were a mass of crevasses, rotting ice and falling rocks. A few days after my 'sighting' one of our party, Steve Read, fell into a crevasse when the ice gave way. Fortunately he was unhurt, although cut and bruised, but I was now able to persuade my companions to investigate the route with me to see if there was another way to get on to the glacier, avoiding the dangerous lower parts. I wanted to find out how the animal I had seen had managed to cross the cliff faces.

A feature of Himalayan climbing is the load-carrying, and with that large party in 1961 we were having to do a lot. The next time we were ferrying loads, instead of going down the normal way a few of us climbed up the grass spur to investigate the animal's route across the awesome cliffs. We found a rough but definite track, and began to follow it across the rock barrier. It was hundreds of feet long, and spectacularly exposed, and we thought at the time that it must have been used by the local shepherds to cross from one valley to another to find grazing for their animals. On reflection, this could not have been the case, for it would have been impossible to drive goats and sheep along here. All the same, we did not think of the yeti mystery.

Some years later I went to a lecture by Charles Allen called 'The Yeti Legend' which really made me think. I became more interested in the possibility of such an

The author in the Kulu Himalaya. (Photo: Derrick Burgess)

animal existing, and thought back to the Malana Nullah in 1961. The beast I had seen had been upright, so it is unlikely it was a bear. The fact that it was going up the glacier seems to indicate that it was crossing from one deep, thickly wooded valley to another; perhaps this is its preferred habitat, not the higher, more remote areas where yeti-hunters normally look?

Since our visit many other parties have been to the Malana Valley, and some have even used the path we discovered, but none of them have seen any signs of the animal. The people of the valley will have little or nothing to do with outsiders, but they do apparently believe firmly in the existence of the yeti, and so did our Ladakhi porters. The story is found all the way from the Indian to the Nepalese Himalaya, but not in the Karakoram, perhaps because there are no dense forests in the lower reaches of the region, and therefore no suitable habitat. Like the Loch Ness Monster, the yeti keeps us all guessing, but if it does not exist who was responsible for the route high above the glacier we climbed across in 1961? Frankly, if I had not seen some sort of animal up there, we would never have dreamt of trying to climb across those cliff faces. If it was the yeti, it must have good route-finding ability, balance, and an amazing sense of direction. It would be an asset as a member of any Himalayan expedition, and could earn a good living in this day and age safely guiding trekkers over the high passes of the Himalaya!

Himalayan climbing is far more dangerous than any other form of mountaineering. Several of my friends have died in these regions, and each trip I have been on has had its share of what are best termed 'narrow squeaks'. Sometimes it is not the expected hazards of avalanches or storms which pose the most serious threat. In 1961 my closest shave was in dealing, in my role as 'Doctor Sahib', with a porter who became mentally ill. It began with his being nauseous with severe head pains at a high camp on a difficult mountain, Indrasan (20,410 feet). The camp was situated on a plateau under the final ridges of the mountain, and reached from below by a long and arduous climb up De Graaff's couloir, a 2,000-foot long channel, the upper sections of which were steep and dangerous due to avalanche possibilities. Derrick Burgess and I were attempting to climb Indrasan, and other members of our team were making for an easy summit nearby, Deo Tibba (19,687 feet). We were all forced to retreat back down the couloir, to our Camp 11, where we joined up with Sonam Wangyal who was nursing Chosfel, the sick man. They had descended earlier than us, but Chosfel had moved so slowly down the couloir that he and Wangyal had been forced to bivouac in the open, and had only reached the camp late on their second day.

Wangyal had been doing his best to nurse the invalid, but nobody had any idea what his illness was. I took charge, and as Chosfel was shivering we moved him to a large tent and put him inside two sleeping bags. Although his temperature was almost normal, he trembled violently and his pulse was irregular, so Wangyal and I lit two Primus stoves and placed them in the tent. While I was in my own tent getting some medical supplies, I heard blood-curdling screams, then Wangyal shouting for help. I dashed back and found Wangyal struggling with Chosfel, who had crawled out of the sleeping bags and stuck his feet in the flames of the stoves. He was screaming and writhing in pain, lashing out in all directions with his fists. Only then did I realise his illness was not physical but mental.

It was impossible for me to talk with him, for he only spoke Ladakhi, a form of ancient Tibetan, but with Wangyal's help I covered his feet in burn dressings and got him back into the sleeping bags, where he lay in a stupor. I stayed with him until supper-time, when he was apparently sound asleep. As I was eating my meal, another shout from Wangyal brought me rushing back to their tent. Chosfel had got hold of a small glass bottle, broken its top off and with the jagged edge had slashed his own neck. I nearly fainted as blood gushed from the wound, and working to staunch the flow I was sick (too much Christmas puding!). Eventually the bleeding stopped and the ever-reliable Wangyal moved into the tent to watch over the patient through the night. We managed to give Chosfel a strong sedative and the hours passed without further trouble.

Next morning everyone was awake early and after breakfast every scrap of equipment and food that could be carried was made up into loads. The Ladakhis must have been carrying about ninety pounds each, whilst we had seventy or more. Chosfel seemed better and capable of descending, despite his injuries, so we started down, with Wangyal, Chosfel and me roped up in the rear of the column. Wangyal was leading, ready to help Chosfel, and I was well back as anchor man.

At one point we had to traverse diagonally down an ice-cliff from a platform at its top; the passage was marked with red flags, and we were moving down it together. Suddenly, with a piercing scream, Chosfel ran straight towards the edge of the drop, obviously intending to jump over it. Taken by surprise, I was almost dragged after him, but I rammed my axe into the snow and his rope whipped round it as he reached the edge. The rope came taut as he leaped, the axe held, and Chosfel was stopped in mid-air like a jack-in-the-box, shooting backwards and landing at the platform's edge. I held him tight on the lip like a hooked fish until Wangyal had climbed back and we could drag him inch by inch away from the edge. He lay whimpering on the snow while Wangyal – the only time I saw him lose his temper – threatened and scolded him as a parent might an erring child. This appeared to calm him down, but we were taking no chances. I abandoned my pack in order to be able to watch better and hold him and after a breather we set off once more, Wangyal on a long lead rope, with Chosfel and myself tied barely fifteen feet apart.

The others had disappeared, unaware of our troubles. As we caught up with them, Chosfel, in full view of an amazed audience, gave another piercing scream and tried to jump over a small barrier cliff between us and the party below. This time I was ready and yanked him back to terra firma on which he landed with a crack, snarling and spitting. He leapt to his feet and, yelling like an animal, came straight at me, wielding his ice axe. 'Wangyal, Wangyal, for Christ's sake help me!', but it was too late for Wangyal to do anything and so, with the desperation of terror, I rugby-tackled Chosfel at the last possible moment, diving and clutching his knees together, bringing him down, winded, to earth. We rolled over and over amidst the crevasses, fighting for possession of his axe. Chosfel got on top of me, a knee in my throat, and the axe was slowly being wrenched out of my grasp. I was choking. Suddenly he was snatched off me like a baby and I heard a resounding crunch as Wangyal hit him in the throat with his fist. He crumpled sobbing in the snow as I lay gasping. Wangyal came over and helped me grimly to my feet. Then without a word he walked back, kicked the unfortunate Chosfel to his feet, and frog-marched him down the last steep slopes to the flat glacier bed.

Chosfel made one final weak attempt to do himself an injury by trying to jump into an open crevasse, but Wangyal and I were too quick for him. The rest of the party were struck dumb by the performance; our cameraman, Ray Handley,

Chosfel – the axeman cometh! (Photo: Bob Pettigrew)

was so amazed that he failed to film any of what would have made a sensational sequence ...

I had to go back up for my pack and my day was crowned when I fell into a crevasse, wedged into its head, hanging from my pack frame. I do not know if Chosfel's example was contagious, but hanging there from my shoulders, unroped, feet kicking clear, I swore and giggled to myself alternatively; this really was the limit! And I was laughing out loud by the time Bob Pettigrew and Steve Read, who had waited for me, climbed back up and lifted me out.

Our psychotic Ladakhi was in the porter's tent when I got down to base, having gone ahead with Wangyal. He was lying peacefully on a sleeping bag, then suddenly he began to scream again. I made him take two sleeping tablets, which had no effect, then another two, still nothing and later in desperation, two more – three times the normal dose. Ten minutes after, he passed out and slept for thirty hours, waking calm but weak and sick. As soon as he had recovered sufficiently, we dispatched him to the valley, pensioned off from our enterprise. According to the local secretary of the Himalayan Club, he had never been on an expedition before and enquiries revealed that he was known throughout Kulu as an unstable character ...

Our base camp in the Malana Valley was dominated by superb rock peaks to its south, the Manikaran Spires and Ali Ratni Tibba, and for the whole of our expedition in 1961 I was keen to climb them. The problem was that, typical of many groups with limited experience, we had set ourselves so many objectives (not least the survey and mapping of a huge area of mountains to the east of our position), that there was little time left for climbing what are, despite their imposing profiles, really lesser peaks. Towards the end of our stay, we split into two parties, one to continue exploring and mapping, the other (made up of Ray Handley and myself) to attempt the Spires. We knew we had very little time left, for every day the signs of the monsoon's arrival became more obvious; it was due in mid-July.

We took Wangyal with us, for by then I had become personally attached to the dark-skinned, toothy little man. He appeared slight but his looks belied his strength; he was the best load-carrier, and about the only porter I have met in the Himalaya who seemed to climb because he liked it. He had fire in his soul, and his flashing smile plus his enthusiasm and climbing enterprise made him a boon to any party. We also took Zangbo, the youngest of the Ladakhis, whom Wangyal was training as his apprentice and to whom he delegated all the menial tasks like washing up and lighting stoves.

The four of us left Base late in the afternoon to follow a branch of the Malana glacier into a vast cwm behind Ali Ratni Tibba. Here we pitched camp on hard snow at around 14,000 feet, directly below a small but steep ice-fall which we guessed would lead us directly to our objectives. This was an impressive site, reminiscent of the Mer de Glace above Chamonix. The peaks all around were granite spires, and would have merited the description of *Aiguilles*. Next morning Ray and I set out to attempt the passage of the ice-fall which, although short, looked dangerous and difficult. As we moved up to its base we were conscious of being watched; nervously eyeing us from above the ice-fall were some chamois. While we stood pondering on our route, the chamois suddenly took flight and bolted across the snow slopes out of sight, to reappear in a rushing mass down the side of a rock spur, traverse below us on the glacier, and race past our tents. Their swift reappearance meant that there must be an easier way than the route we were contemplating, hidden from view on the other side of the spur. All we had to do was to pick up the chamois tracks and follow them up easy snow slopes to the saddle, level with the top of the ice-fall. From there more easy slopes led to the faces of Ali Ratni Tibba and the Manikaran Spires. The highest of the spires attracted us, but it looked a difficult climb and, as we had already wasted several hours of daylight, we decided to return on the next day for a serious attempt. Closer at hand was another pinnacle of the Manikaran group and, after we had kicked steps methodically up a wide couloir, a rock scramble up perfect granite led us to its summit at 17,391 feet.

The descent was pure joy; once off the rock it was possible to glissade every foot of the way back to camp. Standing and sitting, we whooped our way down the slopes, evidently surprising Wangyal and Zangbo by getting back before they expected us – we found them perched on a boulder in the middle of the glacier, singing merrily. My first suspicion took me to the bottle of whisky carried in the medical supplies for illness or celebration. But no! On opening the medical chest, to Wangyal's hilarious delight, I found a full bottle, corked, of what appeared to be whisky. It was several days before I discovered that I was carefully keeping a bottle of cold tea, and when this happened Sonam Wangyal was nowhere to be found.

At dawn next morning we and the Ladakhis left our camp to make straight for the highest of the Manikaran Spires. The weather at this time was fine in the mornings but by noon thick cloud usually developed and, soon after, snow was almost guaranteed. The monsoon could not be far away, so we hastened to make sure of at least one major first ascent. We gained height rapidly and at 7.30 a.m. reached a deep snow groove which led upwards for several hundred feet to the final steep wall of the Spire, from this angle very much like the Aiguille du Géant.

We roped up; Wangyal insisted on coming too and Zangbo had little choice but to follow his master who was cheerfully preparing to lead a second rope. We front-pointed with our crampons up the groove, axe spikes plunged up to the adze at each step. This was enjoyable after all our recent slow progress climbing which is the norm in the Himalaya. This peak was the right size and altitude to climb in a single day, Alpine fashion. Up and up we climbed; laughingly, Wangyal tried to overtake us but his rope-mate slowed him down. We reached rock and scrambled up easy granite to the final steep head wall. The rock was grey here but, just like the red granite we had found on Indrasan, as firm as could be wished. Shortly before midday we got to a platform about eighty feet below the summit; here we changed to a single rope of four. Barring our way was a slightly impending wall. Belayed by Ray, I traversed across the foot of this to reach a bounding chimney on the Malana side which I climbed for several feet until it narrowed to a crack and forced me on to the wall itself. The last part was severe and exposed but well protected by running belays, and the final move was a mantelshelf on to the summit.

This was as fine a balcony as you could wish for; an almost knife-edged ridge sporting an obelisk or tooth which had shown prominently from the base of the Spire. This was the true summit, on which I now balanced and to which the others came up one by one as I took in their ropes. We sat with our feet dangling over the edge, as happy as four climbers will be anywhere in the world after climbing a virgin peak. Our height was 17,696 feet. We watched the clouds rolling towards us from the south, and looking down between our feet we could see, thousands of feet below, the green of the Manikaran Valley. Away to our north was the huge bulk of Indrasan. Wangyal was pleased with himself; he had led well and could have made the ascent without our aid. Zangbo was raw, and he needed assistance from the rope to get up, but it was evident he had complete trust in his senior partner.

Ray and I decided it was best to rope down to the platform eighty feet below, and draping the rope round the summit and down the face we quickly regained the shelf. There we stood waiting for the Ladakhis who were hesitating and talking excitedly. 'Perhaps they don't know how to abseil,' Ray suggested. This turned out to be the case. We were about to climb back up again, when Wangyal launched himself into space, hanging by his arms on the rope, and proceeded to descend hand over hand, singing and laughing at the Sahib monkey antics. Zangbo was less enthusiastic and we stood by anxiously, ready to field him as he wearily grappled his way down to our stance.

This was to be the last climb of that expedition, for the very next morning the monsoon rains arrived, forcing us to retreat to our base camp in a heavy downpour. Twenty-five years after our ascent of the Manikaran Spires, a young friend, Stephen Hunter, was in Manikaran village. Pointing up at their summits, the local Lambo-dar or head man informed him, 'No one will ever climb the Manikaran Spires. The gods would never allow it!'

This, my first major journey outside Europe, awakened me to many things: to an interest in travel, in geography, and in other cultures and religions, to an awareness of the wider social and economic problems facing the world, and to a degree of self-knowledge that was not always comfortable. I had been very frightened on many occasions during this expedition, often more so in the face of imaginary dangers than when I had encountered the real thing. I had behaved badly at times, particularly on the outward boat journey in a relationship with a girl who I had just used, without any real depth of feeling on my part. I also had to accept that my immature characteristic of placing affection on, and wanting it returned from, close male climbing friends remained with me. Perhaps it was too late to change now, but travelling had unsettled me and I found it almost impossible to concentrate on my work once I returned home. I sat dreaming of travelling, climbing and expeditions, despite doing work which had once been of great interest to me. I remember at this time being responsible for a limited edition gravure reproduction of Salavador Dali's 'Christ of St John', one of the most brilliant paintings of this century. Once this challenge would have made me happy and satisfied, but now I could not be content. I wanted to travel, to explore the world and myself.

It is no use sitting around expecting to be invited on other people's trips – unless you're very famous or rich this just does not happen in the climbing world. With friends in the Rock and Ice Club, I began to plan a major climbing expedition, and the idea to try to climb Gauri Sankar, where we eventually ended up in the Autumn of 1964, was solely my own. How six of us reached Nepal and our Base Camp at 7,800 feet, the lowest in Himalayan history, set in the Rong Shar Gorge, ten minutes' walk from the Nepal/Tibet/China border, is an epic in itself. It involved a year of frustrating preparations, lack of funds, an overland drive from Britain which took more than six weeks, and several weeks of marching across Nepal in the monsoon rains, our bodies covered with and debilitated by blood-sucking leeches.

Nepal is a mountain kingdom and in 1964, once outside the Kathmandu Valley, there were no roads to speak of. The country is not as stark, nor the mountains as impressive, as in the area around K2 in the Karakoram Himalaya, but the terrain is incredible. Our walk to Gauri Sankar started just north of Kathmandu and traversed some of the major valleys of the range such as the Sun Kosi and Bhote Kosi. There were no maps at that date, and no one had been to the west side of the mountain that we were attempting.

For each person who takes part in an expedition the story is different. It would be easy for me to dwell on the problems of sheltering the porters each night on the march in the pouring rains, or ferrying loads through the Rong Shar gorge over such dangerous ground that the porters refused to do it, but over twenty years on my keenest memories are different. Despite the brilliant performance of my companions in nearly climbing the mountain, a feat which at that time would have been decades ahead of what had been achieved technically in the Himalaya, a more personal event has stayed with me – a nightmare of nearly drowning that I will never forget.

During the walk-in our party split into two, with Don Whillans, Ian Clough, Terry Burnell and Dez Hadlum travelling light in the lead, and Ian Howell and myself bringing up the rear with the porters carrying the food and equipment.

The monsoon that year was the heaviest in living memory, and after we had turned north up the Bhote Kosi valley, the crossing of side streams, swollen by rain into rivers in some cases, was becoming more and more difficult. Near Jogat, Ian and I with all our porters had spent a terrible night in the open, huddled under a giant tarpaulin we had brought for this purpose and suffering the worse onslaught of leeches I have known. During the night, I had woken and shone my torch around under the tarpaulin. I was appalled at the sight. Ian was lying opposite me on a pile of kit bags, and his face was covered with the creatures. I woke him and we spent some time burning them off with a cigarette; it was a delicate operation, and when we had finished he looked as though he had suffered an attack by a knifeman.

Dennis Gray and Ang Namgyal helping porters to cross a river on the way
to Gauri Sankar in 1964. Making a later crossing the author almost
drowned. (Photo: Dennis Gray Collection)

A little later I had to perform an even more delicate operation on myself when I found two of the smaller leeches on my testicles! Leeches can be a real problem at times. Once you have burned them off with a smouldering cigarette the wound continues to bleed, for they inject an anti-coagulant as they feed. A dozen feeding simultaneously on an ankle is no record, and if you pull them off by force, the head usually remains beneath the skin and the wound can fester.

We set out early the next morning, and almost immediately we found our way barred by a rushing torrent. Debilitated by loss of blood, the wet and the cold, I was not feeling either fresh or rested as I stood facing this river. As if in a dream, I watched Ian tie a rope around himself. Using a porter's stick, and taking with him two of the strongest of the porters for mutual support, he waded diagonally across the water to the other side, where he tied the rope securely to the tree as a hand-line for us to use in following him. Such crossings marching into the mountains with heavy loads take a long time, and organising 80 porters, and getting their loads across a river can take several hours. Once we had the bulk of our column across Ian decided to move on. If you are not careful, most of a day will be used up, as porters in the Himalaya will quite cheerfully wait around until it is too late, thus earning themselves an extra day's pay. And who can blame them?

I was to be the last to cross the river, and just before me was Ang Namgyal a Sherpa boy, to whom we had all become very attached, and who had been given the nickname of 'Yum Yum'. Despite the leeches and the rain, his good humour and earthy sense of fun had kept us laughing. He started out and, as he was small, the force of the water was affecting him more than his older companions. All Himalayan rivers are very cold and your body soon becomes chilled; though Yum Yum clung to the line stretched across the water, his hands soon became dead. In my experience all the peoples in these regions are frightened by water, and I was soon to find out why!

I shouted from the bank to Ang Namgyal, 'Go for it. Stop pissing about!', but he was getting weaker. Suddenly I realised he was not going to make it, and then to my horror he let go of the rope and with a shout was gone, carried away by the current. I am not a strong swimmer, and courage I believe has nothing to do with your reactions in such situations, but I ran down and jumped in after him.

Amazingly I found I had hold of him – the current had moved him back into the middle of the watercourse – but as soon as I grabbed him, he lashed out and hit me, and although I managed to hang on we both sank under the surface. My lungs filled with water and I panicked as never before, sure I was going to die. I thrashed about and changed my grip on the equally panic-stricken Yum Yum. I grabbed him round the neck and we were back on the surface, being carried along like straws by the water. It was bitterly cold, and my struggles were getting weaker. We went under once more, and this time I let go of Ang Namgyal. My lungs filled again, and I was suffocating. Suddenly, where the stream joined the main Bhote Kosi river, it widened and became shallow, and we were both thrown up to the surface again. I stood up in the shallow water and there a few feet away was Yum Yum. I wallowed over to him, grabbed hold, and we jointly staggered to the river bank, where I lay, bringing up green and yellow bile. Ang Namgyal quickly recovered, and within minutes was on his feet and grinning, shrugging off the incident – like other mountain peoples, Sherpas are fatalistic. I, on the other hand, have never been able to forget it. I never told my companions about it, but it left me so frightened of river crossings where you actually have to get into the water and wade or swim, that I will only do it if there is really no other possible way to get across.

It took a long while for Ang Namgyal and me to catch up with Ian Howell and our porters striding out for Lamobagar, our night's destination and the last village on our route. 'Where the hell have you been?' he demanded. 'Swimming!' I replied lamely.

Gauri Sankar, at 23,442 feet, is one of the most famous peaks in the Himalaya. For many years it was thought to be the highest summit in the world, and it is a holy mountain to Hindu and Buddhist alike; Gauri is another name for Parbati, the goddess of love, and Sankar is her consort or Siva the destroyer. The mountain is visible from just outside Kathmandu and is worshipped as the dwelling-place of these two immortals. Thirty-six miles west of Everest, Gauri Sankar spreads over the Nepal–Tibet border like a giant umbrella, a twin-summited peak with a north

The north face of Gauri Sankar (left) whose summit Don Whillans and Ian Clough almost reached in 1964; the second summit (right) was reached by Peter Boardman's party in 1979. (Photo: Erwin Schneider)

(highest) and south summit. It is guarded on all sides by steep ridges and precipices, deep gorges and rock barriers. Several reconnaissances had been made before our own attempt, all concentrating on an approach from the north which apparently offered the only chink in the peak's armour; none had gained a real footing on the mountain, and each party declared it impossible to climb.

Due to a recent border agreement between Nepal, Tibet and China we had been able to get permission to attempt the mountain from the west side, which was totally virgin ground. A real possibility in 1964 was an attack on our Base by Khamba tribesmen, a marauding group of Tibetans who had continued to fight the Chinese and lived mainly by plunder. In 1959 a Japanese party had suffered this fate whilst reconnoitring the mountain's north side, and we were warned before leaving Kathmandu not to go into Tibet on any account. The border was sited at a bridge on the Tibetan side of the Rong Shar gorge. We knew we had somehow to find and force a route up the west face of the mountain.

After weeks of continuous route-finding problems, including cutting a trail through the bamboo forest lower down, and the hardest technical climbing on rock, snow and ice then accomplished in the Himalaya, our lead men, Don Whillans and Ian Clough, backed up by the Sherpa Girmee Dorje and Dez Hadlum were high on the north face of the mountain. (Incidentally, it is sad to note that of those four only Dez has survived. Ian and Girmee perished on later expeditions, and Don died of a heart attack in 1985.) The face was actually in Tibet but, as we were high on the mountain, we judged that no one would really worry. We were spread out over miles of ground, and Ian Howell and I were in a camp on the north ridge keeping the others supplied with food and equipment. Communication was difficult and, apart from Girmee, the other Sherpas had found the climbing too difficult to accompany us safely, so we were having to do all our own load-carrying.

At last, up on the face, our attempt was reaching its climax. Don and Ian (who was also known as 'Kludge', the word for a Scottish WC) planned to prepare the last section up to the easy ground below the summit from a tent we had placed in an ice grotto. The face was huge and complex, but the climbing was mainly on ice, rather like one of the major ice routes in the Mont Blanc range, perhaps the North Face of the Droites. Once this had been achieved Dez and Girmee were to join them with another tent and help them to place a camp on the very summit slopes for use in case of emergency, or indeed if the final slopes should prove more difficult than they appeared. After several days of working on the upper part of the face the way was almost open and the moment to try for the summit arrived at last. Dez and Girmee, carrying the tent and other supplies, left the ice caves of Camp IV. They climbed up to a grotto, which we had called Camp V, and on past this haven to join Don and Kludge, who were on the difficult section up to the north ridge junction but only a short distance from achieving their aim.

They came up with the leaders just as Don was traversing into a gully which exited on the ridge – barely three hundred feet to go. 'Hell! It's pure bloody ice,' he observed, as he stared at a seventy-degree green wall which barred the way. There was no hurrying over this and Don had to resign himself to several more hours of laborious work. 'You'd better drop the loads and go down,' he advised Dez, 'whilst we finish the job off.' Dez hesitated, but there was little to be gained waiting around in the perishing cold of the north face, so he and Girmee began to descend.

Don and Kludge stuck grimly to their task. Progress was desperately slow and they used the last possible rope for fixing, a 150-foot climbing rope, on the first part of the gully. Apart from the rope they were climbing on, the rest of the expedition was having to move around solo, relying completely on the prepared route. Chip, *gasp*, chip, *gasp*; Whillans cut his way up, but time flew by and the increasing cold became unbearable. We had been on the mountain for so many weeks, our autumn attempt was running into winter and it was now late November. A couple of hundred feet to go then Don made his decision. 'Better to come back tomorrow and finish it. We'll dump the tent as soon as we reach easy ground, then pick it up again as we try for the summit. If necessary we can spend the night in it on the ridge before climbing down. Let's go back!' His voice rasped in the rarefied air of over 22,000 feet. Suddenly, without warning, the whole slope shuddered and seemed to collapse. Above their heads, from the side of the gully in which they were standing in steps, ice broke away, to come hurtling down in an avalanche of large proportions. Telling us about it afterwards, Don said his immediate thought was, 'This is it . . . the bloody end!' It happened so swiftly that neither he nor Kludge had time to react. Luckily the ice runnel they were in sheltered them from the worst of the avalanche, although it buried and battered them with its debris, almost choking Don and knocking Kludge off the slope where he hung from his belay.

They were shaken by this narrow squeak and surprised to find themselves still alive. They feared for Dez and Girmee. The carefully prepared route, the labour of days, had been swept away in a matter of seconds. 'Oh God! It must have taken them with it!' Once more fortune smiled on us, for a few minutes before the avalanche fell Dez and Girmee had reached Camp IV and climbed into the ice cave to make a brew. They heard a sound like thunder and the ice around them reverberated, but the avalanche roared harmlessly overhead, showing the worth of such shelter. Don and Kludge breathed again when Dez reappeared in answer to their anxious shouts. Getting down the steeply angled ice where the route had been damaged was no joke: Don had lost his axe, and Kludge his hammer, and it was late in the evening before they reached safety.

What a disappointment! At one point, against all the odds, success had seemed a certainty; at the next, all was in jeopardy and luck and skill had just got them down alive. With no prepared route or ice equipment, and only one climbing rope, they had little option but to retreat and the next day found the whole party safely back at Camp III on the north ridge.

Ian Howell and I had spent many days in this position, but for the others who now spent some time resting at this site, it was a chance to savour the incredible views of Cho Oyo, Everest and, most impressive of all, Menlungste, our near neighbour. The party was unwilling to pack in completely with success so nearly in its grasp. We sat watching the north face for signs of more avalanches but nothing fell and we decided that the one that had occurred must be a freak. How could we give up with the summit so near? Why not one last attempt? To gain Camp III we had climbed a huge, steep face of rock and ice which we had called the 'Little Eiger'; if we stripped the rope in place on this we could have one last shot.

In retrospect another attempt was against all good sense: our food was almost finished and we were carrying up potatoes to live on at Camp III; everyone was tired after more than eight weeks of climbing; as the days slipped into December it was becoming increasingly windy and cold. However, a good carry of the remaining food and equipment by Ian, Terry and Dez (Girmee refused to go back up, and I was ill by this time) got Don and Kludge back into position in the ice grotto of Camp V. As they moved back up they repaired the route and placed rope removed from other parts of the climb. Don was going flat out this time, climbing, we all agreed, the strongest any of us had ever seen anyone do on a high mountain. He chopped and cut his way to the grotto and beyond – this was before the introduction of curved picks, when steep ice was climbed by laboriously cutting steps – backed up as ever by Ian Clough. Up and up they climbed until they were once again at their high point, in striking distance of the summit.

The cold was intense. 'My feet are fucked, Don,' Kludge gasped. 'I've got frost-bite.'

'Hang on just a bit longer, we're almost there,' our hard man replied.

Then, *crack*! 'What was that?' Don paused in his endless cutting to listen. Nothing. The axe began to swing again. Then another cracking sound and the whole slope began to tremble. 'Christ, it's going to avalanche again! Down, as fast as you can! It's unstable after the other fall.'

In spite of numbed feet Kludge needed no urging, and down they both fled.

Ian, Dez and Terry waiting at Camp IV could not understand the panic, until they heard Don shouting at them to 'get the hell out of it!' The tone of his voice told them he was scared and that was enough – the whole party belted off the north face at the double. Providence had been with us yet again. As they sat resting at Camp III on the ridge, a roar and a tell-tale white stream pouring down the north face confirmed for them how close they had come to disaster.

'What a mountain!' Don said later, when he told me the story. 'It's a lady! A red light came on as if to say "come one more step up and you're bloody dead!" We took heed and she let us off her chopping-block.'

Thus ended our attempt on Gauri Sankar in 1964, a terrible disappointment. I could take some personal consolation from the fact that the organisation, taking into account our lack of funding and support, and a budget a little under £3,500, had been as good as most expeditions had so far managed. When I finally did arrive home (I had to travel across India with the equipment, then journey back by boat to Britain, and didn't get back until the early part of 1965), Whillans demanded 'What do you think we should bleeding well try next?'

'A face climb ... the South Face of Annapurna,' I replied. I had spent hours in Kathmandu before leaving discussing this possibility with Jimmy Roberts, an ex-Gurkha officer with an unparalleled knowledge of Nepal. I immediately put in an application to the Nepalese government, but the country closed its doors to climbers at that time, and it was not until 1970 that it became possible to try the face. When the chance came I could not go, but Chris Bonington led and organised the attempt and Don was there at the end with Dougal Haston to complete the first major face climb in Himalayan history.

The Annapurna climb was marred by the loss of Ian Clough in an avalanche. I had known Ian since he was a boy and a cub reporter on Bradford's *Telegraph and Argus* newspaper. Like me, he had begun his climbing at Ilkley's Cow and Calf Rocks, but his forte was mountaineering and particularly winter climbing, which had drawn him to live and then work as a guide in Scotland. He and his wife Nikki lived for the mountains, and loved the simple life in their croft in Glencoe. I used to stay with them when I worked in Scotland in the mid-sixties, and their loving relationship was a joy to see. Both their lives were to be tragically short, with Ian's death on Annapurna in 1970 and Nikki's some years later, a victim of cancer. Our high point on Gauri Sankar's north face in 1964 was due in no small part to Ian's tremendous drive, for he was always willing to carry the heaviest loads, and to do the menial tasks such as cooking. He was the perfect foil for Don Whillans, who tended to leave such mundane chores to others! When Menlungste's West Peak was reached by Andy Fanshawe and Alan Hinkes in 1988, they could see Gauri Sankar's north face and could not believe how far Don and Ian had climbed almost 25 years before. I count myself lucky to have been in Nepal with them.

I never lost my interest in Gauri Sankar, but it was put out of bounds by the Nepalese government. In 1978, they finally agreed to accept applications to climb the mountain by joint parties, made up of foreign climbers and their nationals. Peter Boardman and I immediately put in an application for the mountain for 1979. An American group led by Al Read received permission to attempt the peak in the spring season, and we were given the autumn. With John Roskelly in the lead, the Americans carried out one of the most audacious climbs in recent mountaineering history when they succeeded, after following our route on the mountain low down, in climbing directly up the south-west face. And so the mountain had been climbed, but its south summit could still be attempted and this also would be a major challenge.

Peter and I decided to try this with only four climbers from Britain, and we invited John Barry, then the Director of Plas y Brenin, and Tim Leach. Tim was almost my next-door neighbour in Guiseley and had done much of his early climbing with me. Although still only twenty, he was a brilliant Alpinist and had soloed routes like the Droites north face and the Super Couloir in the Mont Blanc range. My family was still young, and my work at the BMC very tying, but I was determined to try to get away. Then disaster struck at home, and my wife was taken into hospital with suspected cancer. I had to drop out of the Gauri Sankar trip, and Peter brought in a Swiss colleague, Guy Neithdart, a guide from the International School of Mountaineering.

My wife underwent major surgery, then, thankfully, we were told that she would recover. I continued working at the BMC and, in between, ironed, washed and cooked for our children. It was a grim time, especially for poor Leni ill in hospital, but we were cheered when news came through of Peter's party's success on the South Peak of Gauri Sankar on 8 November 1979. I was delighted that young Tim, who I had helped to teach to climb, had been with Peter, Guy and Sherpa Pemba Lama to the summit; unluckily John Barry had missed out due to a fall in which he had fractured his wrist, but he was otherwise OK. Peter added to his success by writing a best-selling book, *Sacred Summits*, about the climb. Thus ended my own association with this challenging mountain and, for the time being, with what Peter described in his book as 'this half-dread, half-thrill prospect of Himalayan climbing'.

In 1968 I received a Churchill Travelling Fellowship to lead an expedition in the Kangra Himalaya of India, and then afterwards to carry out a study tour of the country investigating cultural and social problems. The mountain we wanted to climb was Mukar Beh, a 19,910-feet peak situated north of the Kulu Valley in the Solang group. The area is outstandingly beautiful and we walked in at the end of May to a Base Camp at Beas Kund through rhododendron forests in bloom, and out on to green alps (although we were surprised to find the snow line down below 10,000 feet). Our party was a small one – John Ashburner, Liam Carver, Sonam Wangyal and me – and the challenge great for, despite the apparent lowliness of the mountain by ultimate Himalayan standards, it could only be reached by first

The equipment found at Geoff Hill's camp on Mukar Beh.
(Photo: Dennis Gray)

climbing two lesser summits. Ladakhi Peak (17,525 feet), Manali Peak (18,600 feet) and Mukar Beh were all joined together in sequence along a continuous ridge. The year before our climb the mountain had seen almost feverish activity by Himalayan standards, with attempts made by an Indian party, then by an American and finally, in the late autumn, by a group led by the Australian, Geoff Hill. One feature of this area is the precipitation – I have never seen it snow anywhere else the way it does in the Kulu and Kangra Himalaya. In 1961 Derrick Burgess, Wangyal and myself had been trapped for five days in a storm under Indrasan, and if we had not had the indefatigable Wangyal to dig us out every hour I am sure we would have been buried alive. This may sound like wild exaggeration, but it is precisely what had happened to Geoff Hill's party in October 1967.

After many difficulties our small group finally climbed Mukar Beh in 1968. We were retreating in good order off Ladakhi Peak down easy snow slopes, carrying immense loads made up of all our equipment – at that time of year the possible onset of the monsoon meant that we needed to reach Base Camp as quickly as possible – when we made a grisly discovery. Near our Camp 1, sited on a slope

The author (left) showing the King of Nepal around the British exhibition in Kathmandu, 1982.
(Photo: Mike Cheyney)

above a ridge, we found a tent-pole sticking out of the snow. It had become exposed from its previous winter's covering of snow and ice by the thawing of the summer sun. It was about a hundred feet lower than our own tent, and must have been marking Geoff Hill's camp! We dug and dug and soon unearthed rucksacks, clothes, ice axes and crampons; they had been well equipped, but they had made the mistake of placing their camp on a narrow ridge. The last entry in Geoff Hill's diary read as follows:

Day XIII. Thursday 25th October. Foul weather. Only 2″ of each end of Pemba's tent showing above the fresh snow which must be 2–3 feet deep. Climbing now out of the question. The problem is to get out as soon as possible, but not safe today. Food and fuel are abundant, so will sit here until conditions are more favourable and hope that we don't get 10 feet of fresh snow!

Unfortunately for Geoff and his two companions, Suresh Kumar from Bombay and Sherpa Pemba, it probably did snow as much as ten feet on that October day in 1967, and they were literally buried alive the same night by a cornice forming over their tent on the ridge. They had been caught in that exposed position by one of those rare but major Himalayan storms which defy all previous experience. When we dug up their tents we were astonished to find a large bag of apples, fruit from the prolific orchards of the Kulu Valley; despite the passage of time, the apples were still fresh.

My fourteen-week study tour of India which followed was a marathon, carried out first in great heat, then during monsoon floods. Travelling alone in India is exhausting, because of the heat, the flies and the impact of human misery, which tends to be greater than if you are travelling in a group. By the time I flew home from Sri Lanka, I felt I had learned a lot. I had stayed everywhere: at India's grandest hotel, the Taj Mahal in Bombay, with a Swami near Jaipur in his humble abode, in a colony of untouchables near Madras, and at a Buddhist monastery near Kandi. By then I had seen and experienced enough for one trip and I was glad to come home, my thirst for travel temporarily sated. Soon after arriving back in Britain I began to make plans to get married, with every intention of settling down and becoming a model husband and father. However, as Robert Service so wisely observed, there are 'a race of men who don't fit in', and I later had reluctantly to admit that I am one of their number.

Many years passed before I could return to the Himalaya, but in 1982 I was back in Nepal, representing the BMC at the UIAA 50th General Assembly in Kathmandu. The Nepalese government made a grand affair of the event, and there were exhibitions, a film festival, a gathering of prominent mountaineers from around the world, and a conference on 'The Future of the Himalaya'. Lord Hunt spoke about the conservation problems facing the region, and I was asked to deal with 'The Future of Mountaineering in the Himalaya'. In order to write the paper I carried out extensive research and some of this revealed frightening implications for those regions. The effects of mountaineers visiting the Himalaya are limited, except that they are the explorers, the example which others wish to follow. The impact of trekkers who are motivated by the mountaineering ethic is more acute, and an important trekking industry has grown up in countries like Nepal in a little over two decades. More areas need to be opened up, and many more peaks made available, to stop overcrowding in any one area by providing more objectives for climbers. Everything should be carried out from the mountains, including all rubbish, all cooking should be by kerosene to stop the felling of trees, and all trekking companies in countries like Britain should be registered. After I had delivered my paper I was a little awed when I was invited to show the King of Nepal around the British pavilion at the mountaineering exhibition. This turned out to be a relaxed and informal visit, and in the spirit of the occasion I wandered around our exhibits with him, wearing jeans and trainers. Luckily, a shirt and tie had been contributed at the very last moment by Jimmy Roberts.

Kathmandu had changed out of all recognition from my last visit. We stayed in a Sheraton Hotel, we arrived by jet (in 1964 we had driven in from India by Land Rover), and there were so many tourists in motor cars that the whole valley seemed about to grind to a halt in one colossal traffic jam. The Tibetan refugees were no longer camping down to the south of the town, but were in the bazaar running many businesses and the restaurants. Nevertheless, the magic of the valley was still there, and on one cold, starlight night we journeyed out of town in a jeep to listen to some Thamangs playing their drums. It was impossible not to react to the powerful rhythms, and I was up dancing till the early hours with my hosts, intoxicated by both the music and the *chang*.

After the meetings were over I had just twelve days left, and with a close Japanese friend, Takao Kurosawa, and a couple of the delegates from the UIAA meetings, headed up into the Ganesh Himal. Takao and I wanted to climb a rock spire called The Fang, but we realised as we moved swiftly up into the area, via the Trisuli Valley, that there was little chance of it. The weather was inclement, and became worse and worse until, sitting under our objective in a small mountain tent, we were in a snowstorm. Takao was becoming increasingly ill. We suspected

Leila Peak in the Karakoram. (Photo: Dennis Gray)

pulmonary oedema, and there was nothing for it but to retreat back down into the valley. At the lower altitude Takao quickly recovered, and we then had an enjoyable few days trekking out via a high col and Gatlang village across towards the Langtang area, before we headed back into Trisuli Valley. A few nights before our intended return to Kathmandu, I was camping in a remote spot when my tent door was opened in the night. An English voice demanded out of the dark, 'Is Dennis Gray here?'

I stammered out a 'Yes', wondering what major sin I had committed.

'A message for you from Mike Cheyney.' A letter was passed in, and by torchlight I read the sad news: Alex MacIntyre had been killed on the South Face of Annapurna, and Mike, joint head of a trekking and mountaineering agency, was trying to co-ordinate attempts to recover his body from the foot of the face. Would I return to Kathmandu immediately?

I left by first light and was back in Kathmandu that night, having run the length of the valley to Trisuli Bazaar and cadged a lift back to the capital in a jeep. Attempts to recover Alex's body failed – it was impossible to get a helicopter to fly to that altitude – so in the end we had to agree to leave the body at the foot of the wall, where it would quickly be covered by avalanches and the winter snows. Situations such as these prompt deep personal questioning. I had worked with Alex for over three years, known him since he had arrived at Leeds University as a fresher, and followed his subsequent mountaineering career with both disbelief and admiration, for it encompassed everything from bold new face routes in the Himalaya, to the North Face of the Eiger Direct in winter, and new routes on the North Face of the Grandes Jorasses. Now he was dead, killed by a stonefall whilst descending from a two-man attempt on a projected new route on the South Face of Annapurna. Alex, who saw things so clearly with his razor-sharp mind, who looked like a rock star, a doppelganger for Marc Bolan, who might have been so many things, was dead

Non-climbers may be forgiven for believing that we mountaineers are not only crazy, impelled by some kind of death wish, but also uncaring about our loved ones at home and the effects that such events and losses have upon them. In my experience this is not true: we *are* obsessed with our climbing, and with the mountains, but when we stop and think we are just as feeling and caring as other groups in society. We have our ways of dealing with such grief and hurt, both formal and informal, and on this occasion a group of Alex's friends held a wake at the Tibetan Inn in Kathmandu to remember him and pay tribute to him. It was an international gathering, with climbers there like Peter Hillary from New Zealand, Fred Fromm from Australia, René Ghilini from France and the Burgess twins from Canada. There was nothing organised, it just happened, and looking round the room that night I was, despite our sorrow at the loss of our friend, glad to be of that company.

Himalayan climbing and travel is changing fast, and areas that were once so remote they required weeks even to reach the Base Camp can now be gained in a matter of days. Such an area is the Hushe in the Karakoram where, in September 1989, I led a trekking group – we reached our final camp, from where our party climbed to an easy summit Gondo Goro (around 19,000 feet), only four days after leaving the valley. This has been made possible by the opening up of many of the high valleys, connecting up the villages by jeep roads.

It is incredible what jeeps (and their drivers) can do and I have never witnessed a better performance than when we travelled from Skardu to Dassu in July 1989, *en route* to the K2 Base Camp. I had dreamt of visiting the Baltoro Glacier, Concordia and the K2 area all my climbing life. I was aware that this was the most impressive of all Himalayan regions for the sheer number of its challenges, with every mountain revealed on this route from Paiju, the Biafo, the Ogre, Trango Towers, the Lobsang Spires, the Mustagh Tower, Masherbrum, the Gasherbrums, Chogolisa, K2 itself and many more. It all adds up to the greatest concentration of climbing potential in the world, and when I was invited to lead a group to this area I agreed without hesitation.

Several weeks later, after delays due to the heaviest rains for years which closed the Gilgit–Skardu road for weeks, and washed away our jeep road from Skardu to Dassu, I began for the first time to realise the magnitude of the task. Leading a commercial trek is a lottery and the K2 trek was a baptism of fire! I had seriously underestimated the difficulties and from the first day it proved to be challenging and dangerous work, beginning with the traverse through the infamous Braldu Gorge. This was followed by a river crossing where I was forced to stay put in mid-stream, absolutely petrified and almost a hypothermia victim, to help across one of our party. (He had the beginnings of an illness which turned out to be so serious we had to leave him behind a few days later at the Paiju Camp.) However, if I am giving the impression that the whole venture was overly serious, that is misleading. We had a lot of fun, and our Balti porters were as honest and as humorous a bunch of people as I have been with in the mountains. Some of them were Shia Muslims and each evening above our camps, they sang and lamented for their Iman, Hussain, killed many centuries before in conflict with Sunni Muslims over the succession after Mohammed's death. At this time, Muhareem, they indulge in self-flagellation, and the rhythmic beating of fists on chests, rather like tom-toms, is an unforgettable noise.

Our group of trekkers was a large one, but they all respected the mountain environment, and each had their own personal reason for wanting to reach the K2 Base Camp. For some it was the ambition of a lifetime, and this made me aware of how we, who have been mountaineering for years, take our knowledge and familiarity with the mountains almost for granted. Not all trekkers are so careful, however, and some of the campsites in this, the greatest mountaineering arena in the world, had been left in an appalling state. Litter and rubbish were everywhere, with human faeces liberally in evidence, causing plagues of flies.

We left Askole, the last village on the route, and after crossing the Biafo glacier stopped for lunch by a stream. Donald Hawksworth, the trekker who was ill, was being sick, and I decided to remain behind with him and send the rest of the party off with our Hunza Sirdar. Two of our kitchen staff, both Hunzas, remained behind to help me, and after resting for a while Donald declared he was well enough to carry on. Donald was a classical musician, an organist, interesting to talk with, and, though in advanced middle age, still active in the mountains and out regularly Munro-bagging in Scotland from his base in Aberdeen. Unluckily, he had contracted dysentery at the beginning of our trip in Rawalpindi, and was now feeling very debilitated, his weakness exacerbated by the heat, for that day the sun was shining out of a cloudless sky. We reached a huge boulder called Korophon, and then after resting set out for one of the most challenging sections of the route to Concordia, the traverse of the cliff faces to reach Bardumal campsite. After crossing the faces it is necessary to cross a river, sitting in a 'bucket' across a cable bridge, to gain the campsite. Donald became more and more ill, and our position suddenly began to look serious. I was dressed in a T-shirt and shorts, with trainers on my feet; in my rucksack I had first-aid equipment, a jersey, some emergency food, and a Gore-tex anorak, but nothing really suitable for an emergency bivouac at this altitude with a sick man. We *had* to reach the camp so I decided, not realising the true nature of the cliff faces we had to traverse, that we could carry Donald across.

Just as we set out I met a party of Austrian climbers returning from an unsuccessful attempt on K2 in foul weather. They were disconsolate, for they had lost one of their party, killed by an avalanche. They looked at Donald and advised us to stay put; they too were travelling light, their equipment being several days behind them and they had to reach Askole to seek shelter. They could not help us, so nonchalantly I declared 'We'll be OK!' The crossing of the cliffs which followed was one of the most dangerous sections of the whole route to K2, and a slip anywhere could have been fatal. I decided that the only way to make progress was for one Hunza to go in front, with Donald resting on his shoulders, and for one to come behind him holding him from the rear, whilst I climbed just below him on the worst sections holding him to the rock face. Somehow this worked, and the two Hunzas were magnificent. After hours of struggling we finally reached the river bed and half-supporting, half-carrying our invalid we walked the mile or so to the bridge. Two of our Balti porters had come out to meet us, carrying food, sleeping bags, and warm clothing. The only thing they had not brought was what we craved most – something to drink. The water in that region is now so polluted that it is not safe to drink without treatment; despite our parched throats we did not dare drink from the streams, although our Hunzas did quite freely.

We crossed the river in the inky blackness of night, and it was an eerie experience sitting in a bucket suspended in space, unable to see but hearing the mighty river rushing below. We reached the opposite bank and staggered on, with the Hunzas still carrying Donald, whilst I carried his rucksack. When we finally arrived at the campsite the rest of our party could hardly credit our arrival, staggering in out of the Himalayan night. The Hunzas had done a great job, but they paid for it dearly over the next few days when both of them were taken ill, their resistance shattered by the physical efforts they had made. Fortunately we had a doctor with us and the latest and most comprehensive of medical supplies. Donald remained behind at our next campsite at Paiju to rest and recover, and he was able to rejoin our trek several days later.

Leading trekking parties is normally straightforward, but the K2 trek is special. It is the most demanding and perhaps most dangerous route of its type in the Himalaya. When we finally reached Concordia, all of the group confessed that they were happy to be there, but that it had been so demanding they would never attempt it again!

I now look forward to leading treks to other Himalayan peaks, and to other regions of the world. I cannot forget the friendships forged, the laughter, the challenge, the singing and dancing of the porters when they are happy. I have perhaps dwelt overmuch on the dangers, but the experience is so memorable that we can only know ourselves and life more fully as a result. The Himalaya is above all else a place where you can do this: 'Om Mani Padme Hum Hri.'

The Lakes and Kenya

O Dawn
What language do you use
To instruct the birds to sing
Their early songs
And insects to sound
The rhythm of an African heartbeat?
Susan Lwanga

The Lake District, where I spent so many weekends in my youth, remains a favourite climbing area, so when the chance came to live there as the warden of a centre, I eagerly accepted without giving too much thought to any kind of long-term career plan. I finished at Leeds University in 1969, then helped for a short time at a Home Office special unit dealing with young psychotic boys – that yielded a rich slice of life! While I was part-time lecturing in Further Education to HM Forces in the south-west on behalf of Exeter University, the job in Coniston came up. So with my young wife, who took on the position of Domestic Bursar, and our frail son, I moved to live at Brantwood, Coniston in March 1970.

Brantwood, the former home of John Ruskin. (Photo: Dennis Gray)

Brantwood had been the home of that 'eminent Victorian' John Ruskin, and was being used at that time as a centre for liberal studies and the arts. We discovered all too soon the reality of trying to run a large estate with only limited funds. We had to look after 260 acres of lowland fields, shoreline, woods and open fell, while also organising a wide variety of courses and activities, and being responsible for all the domestic arrangements of the studio and house with its art treasures, a wine cellar and a bar for which I held the licence. Usually our courses were aimed at those in Higher Education, and ranged from a week's lectures on, and reading and analysis of, the works, life and times of the Lakes poets to three days of outdoor pursuits for art students who would then produce a piece of creative work reflecting their experiences whilst canoeing, sailing, rock climbing or hill walking.

We lived in a Lakeland stone house on the edge of Coniston Lake, surrounded by woods and banks of rhododendron and azaleas. The whole area, the house and the surrounding glorious countryside, was pervaded by the persona of John Ruskin and we could not help but become experts on his life and works. Brantwood had a long history before the author of *Modern Painters* moved there and built it up. For instance, it had once been the headquarters of the Republican movement in the eighteenth century, and a clandestine newspaper was printed there calling for the abolition of the monarchy. I would give guided tours around the house to visitors, many of them students from the United States writing theses on Ruskin's life and work. A man of many interests, he even lent a hand in the development of mountaineering. He had no time for the technical side of the sport, dismissing our antics as 'monkeys up greased poles', but he did play a major role through his writings in the nineteenth-century popularisation of the Alps and in the new appreciation of the beauty of mountain scenery. His range of interests is reflected in over 80 books that he wrote, and his place in the history of art, literature and architecture is secure. Brantwood was, in his lifetime, home to one of the finest private collections of art the world has ever seen and included, amongst many other works, literally dozens of Turners hung in almost every conceivable nook and cranny of the building.

By the time we arrived at Brantwood the estate had lost most of these treasures, but the walls and fifteen bedrooms in the house were still covered with over 100 paintings by lesser-known artists such as Prout, Godwin and Collingwood. The whole estate was run by a trust who were also responsible for Bembridge public school on the Isle of Wight, and a picture gallery. There was also the Ruskin museum in Coniston and sundry houses around the town belonging to the estate. In one of these lived 90-year-old Mrs Parsons. She was one of the trustees, and a daughter of Walter Parsons the painter. All over the house she had paintings by Stubbs, Bonington, and her father – her collection would be worth a fortune today.

We soon became part of the life of the community and every Tuesday night after closing time we used to assemble to meet other locals in the bar of the Sun Inn, where we talked and sang until late into the night. We learned about the form of the local hunt and their songs, the difficulties of sheep farming, and the life of the quarrymen high on Coniston's Old Man who cut green slate for export to Canada. One of our neighbours on the east shore of Coniston was Bill Grant, the Chief Forester of Grizedale Forest. He and his wife Elsie were Scots and we soon became firm friends. Bill had ambitious plans to develop the area for recreation and sport and, like me, had been a Churchill Fellow. These were early days in the shift from using the area solely for economic forestry to developing other beneficial activities for the community. Bill's most ambitious plan was to develop the old buildings in the Grizedale Valley, including the hall and its outbuildings, into a theatre and recreation complex – quite a contrast to its use as a prisoner-of-war camp during the last war. At Easter 1970 I gave one of the first performances in this theatre-to-be, a lecture on mountaineering to a packed house, mostly seated on bales of hay. The proceeds of that evening helped to pay for building a proper stage, and anyone visiting the modern Grizedale theatre today might find it difficult to envisage those humble beginnings.

My wife and I found our work at the centre very demanding. She had all the chores to organise, like the cleaning, the laundry and general domestic arrangements, while I had to deal with the chef. He held the highest possible *Cordon Bleu* qualifications and could, when he wished, turn out incredible meals but if the wind was in the wrong direction and he just could not be bothered then we got fast food, long before the fast food era. He was emotional and unstable, and I had many confrontations with him. Once I was walking up the drive one morning to the centre to start work when he came bolting out of the kitchen door, screaming abuse and holding in his hand a large meat cleaver. I did not wait to stop and argue, but turned tail and ran back the way I had come, pursued by the chef aiming swipes with his knife at my back! The sight must have afforded great entertainment to the students looking out of Brantwood's arched stone dining-room window. It transpired that our self-righteous chef was upset because he had caught one of our two kitchen girls in bed with a course member. Why he had been sneaking round the house I never found out, but clearly, to placate him, I would have to do something.

The offending man in the case was called Black, and, as it was a Sunday and the first morning of the course, I was not sure who this was. However, to my amazement, there, at the top of my list of students, was the name of the lecturer in charge – Mr Black. Clearly he was the guilty one so I sent for him to come to my office and, feeling very self-conscious and embarrassed, began: 'I think you could have shown a little more of a sense of responsibility. I mean, what you do in your private life is your own affair, but to be caught like this when you're in a position of trust is a bit off! ... It puts me in a very difficult position.'

The students that week were from Liverpool and their lecturer was a native with a Scouse accent and a fine turn of phrase. He looked at me as if I too had become a candidate for immediate treatment. 'What the bloody hell are you talking about?' he demanded.

'You were caught in bed by our chef with Margaret, one of our kitchen staff, I understand?' I stammered.

'You're bleeding crazy,' he countered.

'But ...' I faltered. Then a thought struck me and I looked further down the course list on my desk. 'Oh Jesus! Wouldn't you know it!' One of the students listed half-way down the page was also named Black; of course it must have been him that the chef had caught *in flagrante*. 'I am terribly sorry,' I started to apologise, but Bill Black, realising immediately what had happened, began to roar with laughter. I began to laugh too and we almost ended in hysterics supporting each other upright. Bill and I were both later elected to the British Association of National Coaches (Bill as Mr Volleyball), and at the annual dinner we rarely failed to rib each other about the incident.

At about this time my first book, *Rope Boy*, was published. To my astonishment it received rave reviews in both the national and climbing press, and the only sour note was sounded by Ken Wilson, then the editor of *Mountain* magazine, who personally reviewed the book and gave it a mixed reception. Fair enough, but he also accused me of 'living in a world he doesn't understand'. I was a bit disgruntled, but kept my peace. I was heartened when, a little later, Rob Wood, a former contributor to *Mountain*, and Alastair McKeith wrote a response to Ken Wilson's review, totally of their own accord and without my connivance. Jim Perrin, writing about the history of the magazine in its 100th anniversary issue many years later, described this article as 'one of the weightiest raps on the knuckles that any editor can ever have received'. Such knockabout controversy is rife in certain sectors of the climbing fraternity, and non-climbers are often bored to distraction by the pettiness and childishness of it all. My hands are not entirely clean, so I won't indulge in further comment and just be thankful that this small set-to did not appear to affect the popularity of *Rope Boy*, which sold out its first printing, and came third in the *Yorkshire Post*'s choice for the Book of the Year in 1970. This was more successful than I could ever have dared to hope.

I continued to climb although it was difficult to find the time. At weekends it was impossible to get away from the centre; as one course left on a Saturday morning after breakfast, another arrived that same day in time for the evening meal. The house and bar had to be cleaned, equipment had to be examined, course arrange-ments finalised and bedrooms made ready. Most of my climbing was either with course students or solo midweek. I did manage several new routes, including a short vicious crack in the Duddon Valley, on a small cliff down by the river. It was an off-width and I was stuck in it for ages, until I managed to turn round through 180 degrees, ripping my trousers in the process, but now able to reach a 'Thank God' hold set high above my right hand facing upstream.

I also pioneered a route on Cam Spout in the Scafell group with Dave Musgrove, The Spout, and some climbs with Tom Green on the sandstone sea cliffs at St Bees Head. One of the cliff climbs was very loose, one of the hardest climbs I have ever managed, with first a difficult wall section, then another crack which was steep and overhanging, rather like Botterill's Crack at Ilkley. Climbing at St Bees was much in vogue when I lived in the Lakes, with new climbs regularly being discovered. Because it is dirty, dangerous and loose, modern climbers have tended to ignore its possibilities, and it is now neglected. This is a pity, for its big plus is acres of unclimbed rock with lots of adenturous potential.

Every weekend the Lake District is swamped by 'off-comers' but midweek, especially in the winter months, it is still possible to walk long distances on the hills without meeting another person. Winter lingered late in 1970, and one of my most exciting days was on Dow Crag, the Coniston region's major climbing ground. In early April I soloed 'A' Gully. I took a difficult exit at the top of the climb by mistake, and was suddenly struck by the thought that if I had an accident no one would know for hours – the whole of the mountain was deserted. My crampons slithered and grated on the loose rock and I could not find good hand holds on the buttress I had climbed to avoid an ice smear on my right. Finally, with a feeling of utter relief at arriving at the top of the rock rib, I stepped off on to a bank of steep snow, hard as concrete. Soon my short axe had fashioned a ladder of steps to a cornice that I took almost by a Fosbury Flop, vaulting over my axe.

There was not a soul around as I stood on the summit that April day, and I could see the whole of the High Fell country to my north and, out to the west, Barrow and the sea. It was as clear a day as I remember in the Lakes. Suddenly I noticed in the sky to the north a green object, hovering but stationary. It was a long way away, over Langdale or thereabouts, and I watched it, fascinated, for some minutes. Suddenly it stopped hovering, and accelerated away to the west at incredible speed, disappearing out of sight so quickly I had to keep reminding myself it had been there. If was the classic saucer shape and, though until then I had never given the UFO case any credence, as I scrambled down through the snow to the Walna Scar road I was no longer such a sceptic.

In the cellars at Brantwood was an intriguing problem: a strong room with a thick metal door that no one in living memory had been able to open, for the keys had long since been lost. Stories were common amongst old folk in Coniston that in there was Ruskin's fortune in gold, reputed to have been made by his family's business as sherry importers. With my deputy, Ken Smith, I resolved that we would find out the truth by getting into the room. We worked at it for days, oiling the hinges and lock system, and then one Saturday, in between courses, and armed with crowbars which had been gathered from diverse sources, we started prising at the door. Albert our handyman, Tom Green, a young climber, and anybody else we could muster were there to give a hand. After tremendous efforts we managed to open the door an inch or two, then three, then four and slowly, after hours of toil, we had opened it sufficiently to squeeze inside. By the light of a head-torch we could see that the large strong room was empty, except for a dusty bundle of something wrapped in brown paper in a corner. What did it contain? Money, shares, deeds? Our excitement by this time was intense, but our hopes were soon dashed when the bundle turned out to be only paintings! Only paintings … At that time works by lesser-known artists, which these were, did not fetch much at auction. Today our find of over twenty paintings would make a fortune, for we had unearthed works by Collingwood, Godwin, and even several of Ruskin's own drawings!

My wife and I were happy living in Coniston, but if we were realistic we had to admit that the amount of work at Brantwood was almost overwhelming. We had been too generous in the conditions we had accepted on appointment, and we had neither the back-up staff nor the resources needed to run such a complex and demanding operation. Our most serious worry, however, was the health of Stephen, our baby. He had been born with a lung damaged and was constantly ill, suffering with asthma and twice developing pneumonia at Coniston. The local doctor was increasingly concerned about him and advised us to seek a drier climate. The Lake District may be a beautiful spot, but what helps to make it so is the abundance of water – it is fine in the lakes, the tarns and the river, but it also comes tumbling out of the sky in vast quantities. At Brantwood that year we registered over 80 inches of rainfall, whilst down in West Yorkshire 30 inches fell! We had to move. After a stormy meeting with the Secretary of the Trustees we decided to give notice, and moved back south to the Leeds area, buying a house in Guiseley, near to the open countryside which includes Ilkley Moor.

I began work in the printing industry again, and then heard about a job that was on offer in Nairobi. This seemed like the answer to our problems. Nairobi, despite its altitude of over 5,000 feet, has the kind of climate that Stephen needed. Even in the drier air of Guiseley he was constantly ill, and on one occasion I had had to run in the middle of the night with him in my arms to get a doctor; he had almost choked to death with asthma, and needed a life-saving injection. I was offered the job, and early in 1971 we flew out to Kenya, leaving behind our weaver's cottage in Guiseley as a base to come back to. My task was to train up a local to do the work under the Kenyan government's Africanisation scheme, a plan with which I fully sympathised. Our anticipation was intense, and we looked forward to climbs on Mount Kenya and Kilimanjaro, and visiting the plains of Amboseli, the game parks like Tsavo, and the beaches around Mombasa and Malindi.

The realities of Nairobi didn't quite live up to our expectations. Although we had subsidised housing, it was still phenomenally expensive and a small bungalow cost as much to rent as if it was in Central London or Paris. We lived in a cosseted suburb of the city, Hurlingham, and all around us were expatriates working on contract for various commercial enterprises in Kenya. The nearest most of them ever got to an African was in ordering their servants around. Our next-door neighbours, a couple from Engelberg in Switzerland, were an exception. They were experts in hotel management, working with an African company 'up country', and had taken the trouble to learn Swahili. I soon took to my job, as a manager in a large printing and publishing concern in Nairobi, with both a litho and gravure plant, producing everything from leaflets to cartons, from books to the largest newspaper in the country, *The Nation*. It was a revelation to me to see how well the Africans and Asians we employed had taken to a technical industry like printing; the machines often had a higher output than their British equivalents. Sometimes the quality was not so good, but this was often due to climatic problems and understandable, as the operators had usually only undergone a crash course of training.

I quickly learned about the problems facing modern Africa: its soaring birth rate, the drift to the towns, tribalism, the massive unemployment and the corruption. We employed over 600 people, most of whom were Africans, and had Kikuyu, Luo, Kipsigis and Kisii in our factory. Many of the white-collar jobs were done by Asians, and all the accounting and bookkeeping by Ismailis. We had a modern factory right in the heart of Nairobi and most of our equipment was as good as money could then buy – the company was owned by the Aga Khan, whose businesses were a model in East Africa. Some of the British executives had been resident in Kenya from before independence and, although publicly they made profession to being altruistic and supportive of Africanisation, they were in private prejudiced racists who held views that appalled us. They seemed genuinely surprised that we did not share these views, that we did not think South Africa was the white man's Utopia and all blacks inferior.

Our first weekend in Kenya was memorable. We had arrived at the end of a week and had not been able to make any contact with other climbers. Ian Howell, by now the leading climber in East Africa, was away in the Himalaya, but he had sent me some details of where the climbing areas were, and told me that the Mountain Club could be contacted every Wednesday night at their headquarters, an impressive log cabin on the perimeter of Wilson Airport in Nairobi. Apparently the nearest climbing to Nairobi was down the road towards Mombasa, on a cliff called Lukenya. On our first Sunday in Nairobi, after taking Stephen to see the game park on the outskirts of the city, we headed down the road looking for the cliffs.

After driving for about an hour we saw on the hillside to our left crags spread out over a large area of ground. We pulled the car off the surfaced road (then the only one in the country), parked and decided to walk up through the Bundu to investigate. I was in shorts with Stephen on my back in a papoose, and in the lead I quickly learned my first lesson about the African bush: you do not set off willy-nilly to walk through it, for every tree is covered with thorns as sharp as razors. We had also underestimated the heat and the distance to the rocks. It took us an hour to reach the first, by which time we were cut, bleeding and thirsty.

I was keen to climb, however, and we wandered about the base of the cliffs, scrambling from buttress to buttress. We had no rope with us, and I looked for something that I could climb solo, whilst my wife stayed at its base with our son. There were several buttresses, of varying heights, up to about 300 feet. I picked a crag that was about 80 feet high, and up its centre was what I took to be the line of a very classic climb, for it was highly polished. 'Funny,' I mused to myself, 'there are no climbers here today, and yet this route looks like it has had hundreds of ascents. There must be a lot more climbers in Kenya than I had imagined!'

I set forth, climbing up the superb granite, and all went well until about half-way up. I was just reaching across to make a Severe move to my right when a rock smashed into the face just above my head, and ricocheted off into space! 'Bloody hell! Where did that come from? Must be a sheep or goat wandering about up there!' was my reaction. The next moment, I had made the move right on to even more polished rock, when another boulder came bouncing down the cliff and whistled just past my head. In terror I screamed out, and looking up saw what I took to be climbers at the top peering over the edge of the precipice.

'Watch what you're bloody doing!' I yelled, but *whoosh*, another rock came whistling down, passing as close as the second. Shaking, I peered upwards again, and then I realised that they were not climbers wearing white crash helmets above me, but baboons! I must have been on one of their runs, which explained why the rock was so polished! I climbed down a few feet, then traversed left across the cliff face at a speed I had not achieved before. All caution was thrown away and I made some dramatic dynamic lurches leftwards; anything to get away from the mad monkeys! I climbed down to rejoin Leni and Stephen. 'We had better get down,' I decided, cowardly. Being a rookie, I was not sure if the baboons would attack us or not; we subsequently learned they will generally leave you alone as long as you do not go near to them or their runs.

Below us was a wide dirt track which we followed to the main Mombasa road. Hot and tired, we hiked back to our car, feeling very much in need of a drink. At the side of the road was an African hotel and club called 'The Small World'; we went inside and were met with a warm welcome. The place was full of charming, beautiful young African women who took it in turns to cuddle Stephen, dancing round the room with him, and then made us a wonderful meal of Irio, a Kikuyu dish. We stayed a long time, drinking beer, and ended our visit with a kind of sing-along, with Leni playing a guitar and all the girls joining in. The bill for all this hospitality was ridiculously small. As we went out into a starlit African night, a few men started arriving, obviously customers, but surprisingly we saw no women with them. When Ian Howell arrived back from Kathmandu a short while later I was telling him about this super cheap bar we had found at the base of the local cliffs. He chuckled, then laughed out loud: 'That, man, is the local brothel!'

Soon we had made contact with the members of the Mountain Club, but I found it difficult to find climbing partners until Ian returned from abroad. I met and climbed with the American Phil Snyder, then a novice, and leading a swashbuckling type of existence, travelling, living rough and ekeing out a living selling jewellery which he and his girlfriend made whilst sunbathing on Malindi Beach. Phil was later to go on to great things, making the first ascent of Mount Kenya's Diamond Couloir, now the most famous route on the mountain, and later becoming warden of the Mount Kenya National Park. Another American climber, Denis Burkhart, who was in East Africa as an aid worker, shared with me what was then a great adventure, a first ascent at Kenya's premier rock climbing site, Hell's Gate.

Hell's Gate is now a reserve, a magnificent gorge with huge cliffs up to 500 feet in height on both sides. It is renowned throughout Africa for its wildlife; in 1971 you would often see lions. The rock is volcanic, cracked vertically to give unique columnar sections and it varies in quality, with narrow rotten bands sandwiched in between the columns. The gorge is situated above Lake Naivasha, about two hours by car north of Nairobi, and it is possible to drive up and into it. In the car I had then I could almost drive to the foot of the rock face, for it was specially prepared for riding through the Bundu, with heavy-duty springs and a reinforced chassis.

At the entrance to Hell's Gate is a rock pinnacle, Fischer's Tower. Ian Howell once soloed up this, only to find, on trying to descend, a rhino waiting at the bottom. He traversed round the spire trying to get off, but the animal simply followed him round. He was up there for hours before the beast finally lumbered off! There are many unique problems to be dealt with when climbing in Africa.

Once you are through the first part of the gorge, the famous Main Wall on the northern side, it opens out into a kind of plateau with small hillocks out of which some fine cliffs stand proud. The best of these is probably the Spring's Wall, which has the only waterhole in the gorge at its base and the animals come there to slake their thirst.

Leaving Leni and Stephen at the waterhole with Bob Chambers, then the presiding spirit of Kenyan climbing, and other friends picnicking by the side of our car, Denis, Joe (another American) and I set out one July Sunday to attempt to climb the oft-tried central section of the Spring's Wall. Although there were few climbers in Kenya at that time, and even fewer visiting areas like Hell's Gate from abroad, this was a very sought-after first ascent, and I was determined to do it. Looking up at the cliff face I could see that it was seamed with cracks and bounded on its left by a broken gully, which would be an obvious descent route if we could get to the top. In the centre of the wall was a crack which bent from left to right, and it was cut at two-thirds height by a prominent roof. It was in overcoming this, which would be the crux, that success would lie.

The first sections of the climb proved to be easy; we climbed a groove, traversed along a grassy ledge leftwards, to a tree and then followed a more difficult hanging crack behind this, which led on into a sharp cut groove giving access to a good ledge below the real difficulties. Here was the slanting crack and there, above our heads, the large roof. By this date nuts for protection were common and Hell's Gate, with its many fissures, affords good placements. I set off up the crack looking like a Christmas tree – I had brought from Britain many such objects, and Denis and Joe had also pressed on to me their supplies, which included the early Chouinard hexentrics. These proved invaluable. At that date we were still climbing on hawser laid nylon rope and, with Denis belaying it round his waist, I climbed the crack bridging and jamming as I went. It became harder and harder until I reached the roof high above my companions' heads, and there I stuck trying to find a way round the barrier. I carefully placed a nut in the crack below, pulled hard on the sling attached to it noting with relief that it was well jammed, clipped my rope through it and then tried to climb directly over the roof. I almost succeeded, but not quite!

I had a good hold in one hand, but nothing for my feet, and being about ten feet above my protection I panicked. I had to get down, but I was hanging in space.

'Shit!' Over the roof there was nothing. I struggled and swore and, just as my right hand was about to open and come off the hold, my feet regained contact with the rock under the roof, and I managed to get my left hand back into the crack underneath this and slither down on to a good hand jam. 'That was bloody close!' Then I noticed a few feet down from the roof itself some small holds leading rightwards to what appeared a good ledge. I decided to try this alternative.

'Watch my rope, I nearly fell off that time. I'll try to turn the roof on the right,' I shouted down to Denis and Joe as I set forth. The rock was dirty and I had to clean the holds as I went with a piece of wire. I reached to just below the good ledge without too much difficulty, then, surprise, surprise, saw that the good ledge turned out to be sloping. Here was the crux: getting on to the bloody thing. I tried to get a knee on to it, but I was wearing shorts and only succeeded in grazing my kneecap. Rock climbing in Africa in summer is a thirsty and hot business and the heat that day was intense; the sweat poured off me and my wet hands were slipping off the holds. I realised I must move or fall. Putting both hands on the sloping ledge I swung into a mantelshelf. Although I almost skidded off, I got my left foot on to it and I was up. We had cracked it! Nothing would stop us now, and I called down to Denis anxiously waiting below. I reached easier ground, but could only get a belay by untying and extending my rope with slings. The pitch had turned out to be 155 feet in length. Denis followed in his usual immaculate style and, as the crux traverse and mantelshelf were delicate and technical climbing, his forte, he soon joined me. Joe, who had the physique of an American footballer wearing all his padding, had no such easy time. He managed up to the roof, removed the last protection and then announced that he was stuck! I clung on to his rope from my waist belay, and Denis clung to me. I peered down and saw with alarm that the other climbers at the base of the cliff were leaving; it was getting dark, and Leni and Stephen were now on their own. I comforted myself with the thought that they would be OK sitting in the car, safe from any prowling animals. I could hear them faintly calling out but couldn't think there was any problem.

Joe was now tiring fast. 'I'm falling,' he kept telling us, then suddenly he lost contact and was flying through the air like a trapeze artist. The arch was acute but he managed to grab the rope with both hands and almost do a runner as he came whipping across the cliff face. When he came on to me, the strain was great, but I had learned from my accident in the 1960s always to carry a leather belaying glove for my right braking hand. I managed to field him, but he hung down the rock face unable to reach our ledge. Denis and I could not pull him and he stayed suspended in space. Meanwhile it was getting dark; in Kenya there is only a short period at dusk before the inky blackness of an African night descends. We had to get off and quick.

We eventually solved the problem by sending a tied-off fixed rope down to Joe which he climbed whilst Denis and I pulled with all our might. This worked and Joe arrived breathless and exhausted on our ledge. I was becoming more and more concerned about my family below, and as soon as we had sorted out the ropes and coiled them we solo climbed in the gathering gloom to the summit. We then climbed carefully down the gully; all the time I could hear Stephen's mournful little voice crying out.

We reached the valley floor and I ran over to the car. Leni and Stephen had not been able to get inside after all, because they had lost the keys. To add to their misery, Stephen had been playing round a fire they had lit and had fallen, put a hand on to the embers and burnt his fingers. Thoroughly frightened, knowing that all around there were wild animals, they were in a sorry state and I was full of remorse. Fortunately I had spare car keys and Denis, as usual calm and organised, produced some burn ointment and dressings from his rucksack to treat Stephen's hand. I was so concerned at these events as we drove back to Nairobi that I never gave our ascent a second thought, but the following Wednesday at the Mountain Club meeting, at the American's insistence, I wrote it up in the New Climbs book. I decided to call the route 'The Springer', and it is now, I understand, regarded as one of the classic climbs of the Gorge.

Life in Kenya as an expatriate was a honeyed existence; I was paid much above British salary levels, and our standard of living was high. I had to work on some weekends, and midweek I was in my office before seven most days, but I was usually home in time to go out for a run before sitting on the porch of our bungalow with my 'sundowner', the first drink of the evening, as the sun set. We tried to see as much of the country as we could. We visited a Masai enkand to the south, and Mombasa and Likoni on the coast. We camped on the plain at Amboseli, where I had to keep fires going all night to keep the animals away, and travelled through the Tsavo game park, which covers an area as big as Wales. We visited Thika, with its tea estates and coffee plantations, the Rift Valley and the Aberdares, and of course Mount Kenya. The Mount Kenya trip could be done in a weekend from Nairobi, as long as you could get away on the Friday early enough to get through the park gates before they closed for the night. We loved the travelling, the country, and its peoples, but we found that many of our fellow expatriates did not share our enthusiasm. Worst of all seemed to be many of my work colleagues, with their constant criticisms of everything, from the poor African's lack of education to the quality of the beer. They never ventured out of Nairobi, and spent most evenings entertaining each other while all the donkey work – the preparing of the meals, the serving of drinks and the washing up afterwards – was done by the self-same Africans they so despised. I found this extremely depressing, and after one or two unpleasant experiences I avoided their company socially.

Shortly after our arrival Ian Howell returned from Nepal where he had been a member of an international Himalayan expedition to Mount Everest. Ian's work at that time meant that he often had to take off to the USA, but in between he packed in a non-stop round of climbing, work and socialising. He is the legend of Kenyan climbing, and has now lived for 21 years in that country. No one knows Mount Kenya or the cliffs of East Africa as well as Ian does, and he has pioneered something like 300 new routes on them. He has climbed to the high summits of Mount Kenya, Nelion or Batian, over 60 times, built a hut on the top of the former and has put out eleven new routes to the summits of that peak. Some of those routes are amongst the hardest mountaineering challenges in Africa. Coincidentally, Ian started his climbing career at one of my own local outcrops, Almscliff. Funnily enough, his companion on his first climb was a schoolfriend of mine, Brian Evans – they were at the same training unit doing their National Service. I met Ian when he was starting out at Brimham Rocks, and we seem to have been friends from that first encounter. I soon gave him the nickname by which he is known to everyone – 'Pin'. Tall, dark, loose-limbed and handsome, Ian was unmarried when we lived in Kenya, and enjoyed the life-style of a well-heeled bachelor, cruising around in a smart Saab car. (He is one of the best drivers I know, and once drove me to an

Ian Howell, the Kenyan bundu basher, back in 1964. (Photo: Dennis Gray)

appointment through London traffic at speeds touching on 100 miles an hour, weaving in and out like a Grand Prix racer. Somehow we never appeared to be in any danger, and we even made the meeting on time. Now a family man with a daughter, he drives a little more sedately.)

We were soon out climbing together in Kenya, where Ian's knowledge of the local terrain, the climbs and the pitfalls was invaluable. He warned me about the dangers posed on the cliffs by the snakes, particularly the puff adder, but I dismissed this, saying that snakes had never bothered me. They hadn't ... that is, until I met one of these. I was climbing up a crack on Ndaya in the Rift Valley and pulling out on to a ledge when a puff adder slithered across in front of me. 'Bloody hell!' I had never seen anything quite as terrifying in my life. I had seen cobras in India, but this monster was incredible. Its head was bigger than a fist, its body as thick as a man's leg, and it was about eight feet long. Shaking with fear, I clung to the cliff for a long time before I dared move again.

Ndaya is a beautiful cliff situated in a remote area of the Rift Valley and to get there we had to go by jeep, provided by Denis Burkhart, courtesy of Uncle Sam. One Sunday Ian, Denis and I drove out there, riding through classic thatch-roofed villages, with waving children and singing women out working in their shambas. It was fine and sunny. Even during the rainy season in Kenya it seems to be fine for much of the day, and rains mostly at night. For the rest of the year it is usually dry and sunny, with only the occasional thunderstorm to worry you.

We arrived at the base of the cliff in the open jeep. Denis, who was recovering from the effects of over-indulgence at a party the night before, decided he would take a nap sitting in the driver's seat, so Ian and I roped up and set off up a climb in the centre of the steepest part of the cliff. This route was called The Party Grooves, and had the reputation at the time of being the hardest rock climb in Kenya. It was typical of much of the rock climbing in Kenya, which is superb, having been pioneered by climbers with a grounding in the sport in Britain. Most of it is bold and adventurous, without resorting to aid. Ndaya is about 200 feet high, the rock is firm and clean and, rather like the Hell's Gate cliffs, it is seamed with cracks; The Party Grooves proved to be a succession of these.

That Sunday, I was leading. I had managed to overcome the first difficult pitch, and was high on the second when I heard a peculiar buzzing sound. It became louder and louder. 'What the hell is that?' I shouted down to Ian.

He cocked an ear, then suddenly. 'It's bees, *killer* bees!' The second part of the sentence was said with feeling and emphasis and I sensed that Ian wasn't kidding.

In front of my face was a pocket, a two-finger hole. This was the famous crux move that, on the first ascent (led by Martin Harris in March 1966) had held up the party for a long time.

'Bloody hell!' The noise came nearer and nearer. Three weeks earlier in Zambia a swarm of these bees had killed three climbers; the situation was getting desperate. I almost fell off, I was shaking so much but, pushing the middle fingers of my right hand into the pocket, pulling as hard as I could and then walking up the wall with my feet, I almost leapt up into the air, grabbed a ledge and was up. I climbed the next thirty feet to the top as if the hounds of hell were after me and, without belaying, simply ran as fast as I could holding the rope until it came tight. Ian needed no instructions from me; as soon as the rope was taut, he started to climb, and I just kept moving away from the cliff as he ascended. Until the bee threat we had been finding the climbing quite hard and it had been taking us a long time, but now Ian raced up the cliff like an orang-utan. He was with me in seconds.

'Run,' he shouted. 'For Christ's sake, *run!*' The sky was black with bees and I needed no more urging. We ran away across the top of the cliffs, then down the easy hillside on the edge and were relieved to see the bees being carried away on a slight breeze over the top. I had only been stung a couple of times, but it hurt like hell. Ian grinned with relief and told me the horrific story of how he had been attacked on the Main Wall at Hell's Gate, and how once again only fast movement upwards had saved his and a friend's life.

Climbing in East Africa is certainly never dull, and it can even have its moments when you think you're safe on the ground. We arrived back at the jeep to find Denis sitting mute, wide-eyed and motionless in the driver's seat. 'What's bloody wrong with you, Yankee boy?' I demanded.

Denis, always quiet, always gentle, suddenly shouted out, 'It was a fucking leopard, a full-grown leopard man!'

It transpired that after we had left he had fallen asleep. Cramped and uncomfortable, he had woken after a short while to see staring at him, through the windscreen, sitting on the bonnet of the open jeep, a huge leopard! These cats are dangerous and will attack people. During all the time we had been climbing the animal had sat and stared at Denis, and all he could do was sit still, utterly terrified

The author leading The Party Grooves, Ndaya. (Photo: Ian Howell)

and totally unarmed, staring back. He had been stuck like that for ages, and the leopard had only run off when we had come walking up through the bush from behind. 'Let's get out of here!' I pleaded. 'Killer bees, leopards, what next?'

'Elephants,' laughed Ian, as he revved the engine, swung the jeep round, and handed us each a bottle of Tusker beer.

Lukenya, the outcrop near to Nairobi, is a beautiful spot, and we used to camp there at weekends up on the summit of the hill. On Saturday nights we would hold barbecues, drink beer, and talk climbing with our friends, many of whom were visiting from Europe or the USA. We would build bonfires and sing into the African night, where the stars and constellations wink and glitter as in no other place on earth. Around the Kenyan climbing scene there were many characters; they were not so active on the cliffs, but they were old and wise in the ways of Africa. They knew Swahili and some could sing Kikuyu songs. They had a thousand tales to tell and lived the sort of life of which most Westerners can only dream. One such was Bill Woodley, an authority on elephants, and Warden of the Mount Kenya National Park. An unforgettable personality, he used to fly down to our meetings in his own light plane from his base up on the mountain.

One night we were camping out there, when the unforgiveable happened – we ran out of beer! Ian and I volunteered to drive down through the night and get some from the Small World. On the way back up with our precious cargo we were met with an exciting and memorable sight as I drove my car right into the middle of a herd of Thompson's gazelles. They were the finest creatures I have ever seen, and as we drove along one of them actually leapt over my car, a remarkable feat. How anyone could kill one is beyond me.

I was always looking for new route possibilities in Kenya, and on the track below the summit of Lukenya was a huge boulder, about 70 feet high, split by a vertical corner crack. I persuaded Ian that this was worth trying, but on arriving at its foot one Sunday morning we found that the first section from the ground was less than easy. I tried and failed to get up the short but vertical wall with its tiny holds. Ian then took over and, although between us we had the first few feet strewn with protection devices, he couldn't make any progress either. I decided to try again and throw caution to the winds. With a move sequence like a gritstone boulder problem I managed to climb it but in my keenness to get to grips found I was up in the crack without any equipment. Fortunately there was a chockstone and using the rope I tied myself to it and brought Ian up. I am pleased to report that Pin for once had a real struggle to climb up to me, and typically was full of praise for my eforts. 'Bloody hard, bloody hard,' he kept saying. Then he pressed on and climbed the corner above our heads in immaculate fashion which I found equally 'bloody hard' in trying to follow him. We called the climb KL, which stood for the company I worked for in Nairobi and not, as some have thought, a secret African charm.

This climb sadly turned out to be my swan song. My sister rang from Britain the following week to tell us that my father had developed lung cancer and was seriously ill. My mother was long dead, so he was on his own. The situation worsened and we heard later the same week that he was to go into hospital for major surgery that weekend. We dropped everything and flew back to Britain, hoping all the time that we might be able to return to Kenya, but we never did. My father emerged from his operation minus a lung, but carried on cheerfully singing, playing the piano and entertaining others until shortly before his death a year later.

Kenya is one of the best countries for any climber to live in or visit. It has outstanding high-altitude mountaineering on Mount Kenya and Kilimanjaro, and superb crag climbing in remote areas set amongst wonderful scenery. I remember the latter more keenly than the former, and share Ian Howell's enjoyment 'in exploring these cliffs out in the bush, where the access is as much fun as the climbing which in some cases is dirty, vegetated or loose and invested with killer bees, snakes and scorpions!' Some day I will go back to Kenya, and I hope to be able to climb once again above the Bundu on some remote crag, whilst in the distance we might hear an African talking drum beating out its story. *Jambo!*

The BMC

The lunatic, the lover and the poet, are of imagination all compact.

A Midsummer Night's Dream

I arrived back from Kenya in autumn 1971, and a chance meeting at a climbing club dinner led to my involvement with the BMC, the national body of mountaineering in Britain. The BMC had been founded, after ten years of debate, in 1944 by the singular efforts of Geoffrey Winthrop Young, then the President of the Alpine Club. Initially it was a gathering of the 'Ivy League' of British mountaineering, mainly made up of the old established clubs – the Scottish Mountaineering Club, the Climbers' Club, the Fell and Rock and so forth – each with their own fiefdom, and each with a strong vested interest. The growth of the sport outstripped any of their expectations, and in almost every town over the next forty years new organisations and clubs were established to cater for the ever-increasing numbers of people taking up mountaineering. This fact, plus the government's burgeoning interest in sport and recreation, the quickly evolving technical nature of the activity, and the explosion of interest in other leisure pursuits out on the hills, once solely the preserve of the climber, has forced the BMC to successively reorganise at an accelerating pace.

Before my appointment at the end of 1971 as the first ever Professional Officer of the Council, two events occurred which were to be significant in the future of climbing. The first was the report of the Wolfenden Commission which had made a recommendation that government should become directly involved in the funding of sport in Britain. This led to the setting up of the Sports Council in 1972. The second was the Cairngorm tragedy when five children and a student teacher perished whilst taking part in an expedition organised by the Edinburgh Education Authorities in November 1971. This alerted many in the climbing world to the serious nature of some of these organised programmes and the need for mountaineers to have more input into their planning and control. The result was a massive confrontation between those involved professionally in educational activities in the mountains and the BMC, the dispute that was to dominate my early years of working for the Council.

It was evident that, by 1971, the volunteer staff at the BMC simply could not cope with the growing amount of work – the liaison with statutory agencies such as the Forestry Commission, the National Parks, the Water Authorities and the Nature Conservancy Council, the effects of the developing interest in mountain activities by the Education Authorities, and the demands of advising and looking after the needs generated from within the sport itself. The advent of the Sports Councils meant that grants were now available to fund professional help, and the BMC management quickly completed the formalities and obtained funding to appoint a National Officer. A small office had been acquired before this event, and when I arrived at the beginning of 1972 it was functioning in the plush surroundings of Park Row, in the Regent's Park area of London. Besides the mountaineers there were many other sports administrations housed there. These were to be the offices of the new Sports Council, the body being set up with responsibility for funding English and British sport (there are separate bodies for Wales, Scotland and Northern Ireland), and our landlords were the Crown.

Sport in Britain is traditionally run and, despite protestations to the contrary, is a hive of political intrigue. Each activity is represented by a national body, and there are literally dozens of them, supporting everything from athletics, football and golf to hovercraft sailing and metal detecting. All the national bodies are members of the CCPR – the Central Council of Physical Recreation – which acts as their forum and does its best to represent the needs of sport to government, provide services such as parliamentary and taxation advice for its members, and generally act as a lobbying and representative organisation.

I knew nothing of all this before January 1972, and it was a revelation to me. Thus I started out from an office barely big enough to turn round in, and with a young typist, into what were then uncharted waters both for myself and for mountaineering. I was in two minds about this challenge: on the one hand I held (with my peers) that climbing and climbers were not interested in either organisation, rules or national bodies, and that a part of the sport's essential appeal was its sense of freedom and anarchy; on the other I could understand the need for some support, some planning, and protection if mountaineering were in the long run to preserve its integrity.

I had made it plain on appointment I would not move to live in London, and I used to travel down for two or three days each week and work around the clock to keep up with the developing workload. One of my first tasks was to complete the BMC's plans to take over the administration of the Mountain Leadership Training Board. It had been developed jointly between the CCPR and the Council since its inception in 1964 and had thrived under the leadership of its Chairman, and former BMC President, Jack Longland. It was already by then one of the biggest training schemes in British sport. At the setting up of the Sports Council, administration of such schemes was handed over to the national bodies concerned, which meant that the BMC would need more staff and a bigger office. During those early months I was bewildered by the complexity and bureaucracy of sport administration. I was astounded at the strength of feeling about certain issues, and it was obvious that the Cairngorm tragedy would loom large in debate as the formal enquiry as to what went wrong got under way.

I embarked on a series of 'whistle-stop' tours around Britain to speak to member clubs and groups about what we would be doing for the sport in the immediate future. Our aims were to combat threats to the mountain environment more vigorously than hitherto, increase our role in the mountain training field, improve services and so forth. In short, we needed more money, and more members to carry out the tasks we were now planning. It was obvious that unless we took action the sport would begin to suffer adversely. My first visit was to Birmingham, a packed open meeting organised by the Midland Association of Mountaineers. Accompanying me was the Hon. Secretary of the BMC, Peter Ledeboer, a diminutive figure and a good soul. With nothing but the best of intentions he began the evening with a rather over-long introduction of me, which included reference to the fact that I was working on a plan to take over the administration of the mountain leader scheme. At this a member of the audience sprang to his feet, ran down the outer aisle, leapt on to the stage and began to attack poor Peter, screaming 'Murderers, molesters!'. Sitting on the platform alone with Peter, I should have moved to his aid, but I was transfixed. Luckily, others in the audience jumped up to help restrain the apparent madman and Peter was unscathed. We realised later that this outburst had been inspired by the climber's firm conviction that such schemes as mountain leader training were directly responsible for the Cairngorm tragedy. He felt that by providing such certificates the mountaineering world was encouraging those in authority to have a false sense of security, and that without such training schemes the Edinburgh school party would never have been allowed on to Cairngorm on the weekend in question. It was a controversial viewpoint, but the incident illustrates the depth of feeling and why the mountain training dispute later reached such highs and lows of both argument and ill feeling.

My first year in office passed quickly. Our second child Robin was born – unlike Stephen, he was robust and healthy – and I was beginning to find life a strain. I was on call day and night, with meetings the length and breadth of Britain, and being Mr Mountaineering meant I was under tremendous pressure from the media whenever there was a serious climbing accident or a major climb under way. It became obvious that the Council in its present state was just not up to achieving the standards that mountaineers now expected of it. Almost every weekend I was faced with demands for action from climbers I met on the crags or in pubs. Mostly they wanted more effort to help expeditions, more work to solve access problems, more services, more technical information and the independent testing of equipment, but it was the BMC's role in the mountain training field that created the most unease. It mattered not one whit that some of these critics were old friends, or that we were already working to the limit of our ability within the available resources. I began to be unhappy about the fact that we did not have our policies clearly defined. We were spending too much effort on peripheral ideas such as a proposal for a feature film on mountain safety, and not enough on core activities to do with access, conservation work, equipment standards, and so on. I was spending so much time tearing around that I could not think the thing through; I recognised the weaknesses in what we were doing, but had neither the experience nor background of such organisations to suggest alternative methods. Inevitably these problems led to conflict and both the President and the Hon. Secretary resigned. The morale of the BMC had hit rock bottom, and I was extremely worried, about it, about my young family, and about my uncertain future.

Waiting in the wings, however, was Alan Blackshaw, the person best qualified to set about the task of reorganising, redirecting and galvanising the organisation into the kind of national body that mountaineering needed. Alan was then an under secretary in the Department of Energy, and author of the classic Penguin handbook *Mountaineering*. He took over the BMC Presidency in the summer of 1974 and, with the support of our colleagues, the late Dave Partridge as Hon. Secretary, Bob Pettigrew, who knew the mountain training field as well as anyone, and Mike Baker, the secretary of the Alpine Club whose legal brain helped to sort out constitutional niceties, we set about the task in hand. First we had to sort out an agreed set of policies and aims for the BMC to follow. A broad-based group of climbers was recruited, and meetings were held under Alan's chairmanship throughout Britain. Many changes were suggested and implemented, and as a result the committee structure was enlarged, and a new constitution made the Council more representative and led on to individual members and trade firms being able to join as well as clubs and organisations. We decided to move the BMC to Manchester in order to be geographically more in the centre of our activity, and

Peter Boardman. (Photo: Dennis Gray)

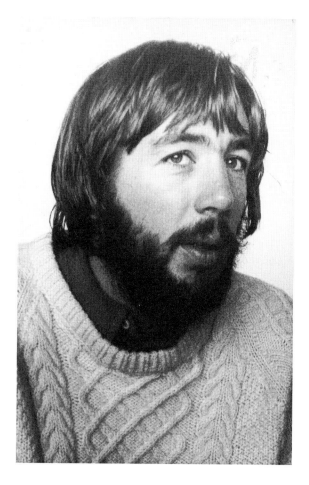

to change the professional cadre and recruit a General Secretary. The pace of change and activity was breathtaking.

Alan Blackshaw's stamina was impressive throughout his three years as President, for he also had professionally to deal with the effects of the energy crisis, and later to administer a large government department in Glasgow. Decisions had to be hammered out in many of the policy areas, and the meetings were often a riot, taking place in pubs, with all those present well lubricated by the local brew. I well remember an argument over mountain training policies between Ken Wilson, the BMC's tame Rottweiler, and Tom Price, a small, quiet-spoken, man of great erudition and authority, and then the Dean of a teacher training college. Tom was subjected to the most verbose of attacks at full volume by his fellow committee member, and the strange logic of this argument was that 'climbing is about dying; if you do not want your pupils to die then you should not take them climbing!'. This was easily turned around by Tom: 'If climbing is about death how come you haven't done us all a favour by doing some?', providing the rest of us with mirth and a little light relief during one of those hectic gatherings. However, that argument went much deeper. The BMC's future role in mountain training was the one area on which we could not agree. The topic was so complex it needed a separate group to look at it, with someone of the highest eminence to chair the investigation, and we invited Lord Hunt to help us out. He agreed to take the project on, and I was made Secretary of the committee.

The BMC moved to Manchester at the end of 1974, and I was appointed to be the first ever General Secretary. We then needed to recruit a new National Officer, and from the galaxy of talent who applied for the post selected Peter Boardman. Although he was then only in his early twenties, with the physique and looks of a lumberjack, Pete possessed a thoughtful maturity which struck all who knew him. He was an English graduate, with a love for and deep knowledge of classical literature, and he and I would engage in wordy debates (usually shouted across the BMC offices) about the merits of our favourite poets, with me defending the moderns. Peter already had an impressive climbing record when he arrived at the BMC, with many hard Alpine climbs behind him and successful expeditions to Alaska and the Himalaya. The events of 1975 were to catapult him to fame as one of those who reached the summit of Mount Everest by the South-West Face route in the autumn, and as the last person to see Mick Burke before his disappearance on his fateful summit bid. Over the next three and a half years we were to become close friends, and his death on Mount Everest in 1982 left a painful void. It was always fun to climb and debate with Peter; although later he became street wise, in his early days at the BMC he was at times capable of a wide-eyed innocence that always caused amusement. He was a great fan of A. A. Milne, and young crag rats would go glassy-eyed in amazement at the quiet-spoken BMC National Officer, who had completed such demanding climbs, making his point and illustrating it by quoting from *Winnie the Pooh*!

We located the BMC in the new Manchester University precinct centre, and by the early part of 1975 had completed the move from London, turning the concrete box we were renting into a functional office. We recruited support staff, including a dynamic Office Manager, Rita Hallam, an old friend of my Derby days – we had worked together in productions of the infamous 'Cyclists, climbers and runners pantomime'. We finished all our work on hammering out the BMC policy guidelines, and we waited for the Hunt Committee to report which it shortly did. Its recommendations were unequivocal, stating that the BMC should have overall responsibility for policy-making in the mountain training field and that low-level certification should be discontinued and replaced by a simple report system. It was agreed unanimously by Hunt's group that such qualifications as the Mountain Leadership Certificate, with its basic demands in technical performance, were open to misuse and that the level of competence that it confirmed upon the holder was capable of being misinterpreted.

The recommendations of such an eminent committee should have been accepted, and a reasonable compromise reached, but this does not take into account the personalities involved, the strength of feeling from the mountaineers and the educationalists, and the vested interests that had been built up and there is nothing like tinkering with other people's livelihoods to encourage ill will. This was to be the beginning of the greatest confrontation in the history of British climbing.

The BMC published the *Hunt Report on Mountain Training* in July 1975. By this act we made available to interested parties a copy of the report, several thousand of which were distributed, and we invited all and sundry to write to me with their views and comments. It was clear from the response that the climbing fraternity were fully behind the Hunt recommendations, but that the outdoor centres, local education authorities, schools and youth organisations were less enthusiastic. And so the battle lines were drawn and the debate became more and more heated. Bob Pettigrew, himself an educational adviser, had taken over the BMC Presidency, and Jack Longland (as Chairman of the Training Board, against the reforms), rallied his troops on the other side, including such influential groups as the wardens of mountain centres.

In order to break this deadlock the BMC Management Committee, elected from the whole climbing world, decided to adopt the Hunt Report as its policy on mountain training, and ordered its officers to take the necessary action to implement its wishes. The Mountain Leadership Training Board refused to accept this action and so the fateful step of axing its existing membership and forming a new group was decided upon by the Council. The constitutional legitimacy of this action is still a matter for debate, and even the BMC's own legal advisers were split on whether the Council had the right to do it; still, we did it, and then all hell broke loose! The Sports Council intervened and stopped that part of our grant which could be identified as earmarked for training. Jack Longland continued to hold meetings of the rival board while we held meetings of a new forum, and the whole affair become daily more bitter. Both Lord Hunt and Jack Longland, each a former President, resigned their BMC membership, objecting to the 'style' we had adopted in trying to bring about the reforms. Whilst I could understand Jack's attitude, John Hunt's left me dismayed. He had been one of the main instigators of the form of the report's final recommendations, and could have used his influence to help us bring them about without so much ill will. Instead, as soon as the report was finalised, he refused to take any further part in its implementation.

The media became interested at this point, and whilst we had lost the battle for support from the mandarins in government departments, we certainly managed to get public opinion right behind us. We had learned quite a lot by this time of how to get a lobby going, and we inserted an appeal in our official magazine *Climber* for every mountaineer in the land to contact his or her MP. Hundreds did this, on the basis that the Sports Council had acted *ultra vires* against a national body of sport, and against the wishes of its members and elected representatives, and had illegally stopped a grant!

Times were now getting hard at BMC headquarters; we had lost a large part of our grant and we could not meet our ongoing expenses. To add to this we were having one of our perennial disputes with the Inland Revenue, and by the end of 1975 our position was desperate. Encamped in my office in Manchester were a Tax Inspector and a Bailiff, with the former threatening both poor Brian Monk the treasurer and me with a jail term unless their demands were met soon. The one good aspect of the dispute is that our credibility with our own constituents rose ever higher, for they saw that the officers of the BMC would take whatever action was necessary to protect the sport. Even in those dark days there were moments of light relief. Although it was against Peter Boardman's nature to confront anyone, and he was at times critical of the strident style adopted by some of our spokesmen, he was convinced of the soundness of the Hunt recommendations. He and Doug Scott decided to chain themselves to the railings at the Houses of Parliament to draw attention to the action of the Sports Council, and to demand that our grant be reinstated. Rita Hallam and I had great difficulty dissuading them from this course of action. 'You'll die of boredom Peter,' was our advice. 'No one will take a blind bit of notice!'

At this juncture Denis Howell, Minister of Sport, sent for me, and we took a three-mile walk together to discuss the situation. 'For God's sake stop your people contacting their MPs. I've never known anything like it. You bloody climbers are all mad!' he remonstrated. Denis and I were old combatants by that time, and he was a man I respected. He was a bit like a climber himself and loved a singsong in the pub (especially Welsh hymns) and a verbal punch-up. 'You need to get talking to the opposition!' was his advice. 'Get hold of Jack Longland and sort the thing out over a drink!'

'It's not that simple . . .' I assured him, 'but we will call off our MP-baters!'

Whilst all this was going on Leni had given birth in that summer of 1975 to our third child, Helen. It seems to me now that she was almost a saint putting up with the next few months at home; whenever I was there, the phone never stopped ringing with calls from the media, BMC personnel and members, and supporters to our cause.

In the middle of this unpleasant stalemate Jack Longland rang me out of the blue, and we arranged to meet secretly in a pub in Buxton at Christmas 1975. I had known Jack from boyhood, a larger-than-life character playing a wide range of roles, from Everest climber and athlete to classical scholar, lecturer, Director of Education and broadcaster. It was hard not to be envious of his gifts, and the more the dispute had developed the more he had grown in my own estimation. He had used all his considerable influence to stop us, for he believed he was right, but there was no rancour at our meeting and we laughed long and loud at the dirty tricks we had both employed to blacken each other's case. We agreed that we had to find some way out. The solution emerged shortly after in a rather typically mysterious way, when the Alpine Club offered both sides in the dispute an independent arbitration process. Both parties quickly and gratefully accepted, especially the BMC as a condition of agreement to this was the restoration of our grant. With money in the bank we would be able to pay off our debtors.

The subsequent arbitration hearings must be unique in climbing history, for they took place in a proper court format at the Lands Tribunal. Our case was presented by Dr Will Butler, a Vice President and top cancer specialist, whilst the opposition's case was presented by Roger Putnam, a member of the Warden's Association. Witnesses were called, depositions made, and in the end the arbitrator's report was accepted by all sides. Low-level certificates were to go and reports came in; the Training Board is now independent in policy-making, but the BMC has the largest number of seats within its membership and administers it activities; and the Instructors' qualification is in the purview of the Council, overseen by its own training committee. The name of the scheme was changed to the Mountainwalking Leader Training Scheme, and everyone has subsequently been so happy about it that we wonder now what the dispute was all about.

Once the training dispute had been settled we could turn our attention to BMC activities in other areas, and over the next few years we developed a range of services for our members, including insurance schemes, cheap travel and reciprocal rights in the European Alpine club huts. The latter came about through our membership of the world body of mountaineering, the Union Internationale des Associations d'Alpinisme, and I was by this date the Council's representative on that forum, where we represented British mountaineers and were a member of the executive committee. Our own committee structure had continually to be expanded, although not without much soul-searching. New area committees were set up to represent districts where rapid climbing developments were taking place, and further specialist groups were recruited to cover developing areas such as climbing walls, international relations and access work. They needed to be looked at by experts in isolation from other Council activities.

One of the features of mountaineering is that we seem to have a range of experts upon whom we can call in times of need. For example, if you want an eminent botanist, there is almost sure to be one in the climbing world, likewise a neurosurgeon, a publisher, or even a libel lawyer! It amazed me how almost everyone we approached readily agreed to give us help for nothing; if we had had to pay for the advice we got on the basis of normal professional fees, the cost to us would have been astronomical. The same situation seems to exist throughout British sport. I was struck, however, by one sad fact: it is very difficult to interest the younger and more active climbers in the work of the Council and this means that much of the committee work is carried out by the older, less active members. This can cause problems, for in the climbing world, just as in every other walk of life, there are a few, a very small few, who prosecute their views as if they were involved in mainstream politics. They plot, scheme, lobby and waste much time and resources. Significantly, the few such people involved in the BMC are more active in committee rooms than on the mountains. My hope for the future is that active climbers will come forward in increasing numbers on to the committees; against such forces the time-wasters will soon be exposed for what they are. . . .

Peter Boardman teamed up in 1976 with Joe Tasker (who for a period almost lived at the BMC office), to plan a great climb of the West Wall of Changabang. To train for this they would spend evenings after work hanging in harnesses off meat hooks in the Manchester Cold Storage. They used to go down there late in the evening to be locked in a giant meat safe with all the carcasses of beef until the morning; once inside there was no way out for the door was on a time lock. Peter's most desperate experience of the Changabang climb was their final night in that safe before their departure, when we had all been out celebrating in the pub. Peter confessed he had thought his bladder might burst, hanging all night from a meat hook with no place to go! The climb was significant in the history of British climbing, and Peter's outstanding book about it, *The Shining Mountain*, won a literary prize and opened up new vistas. It became obvious that the BMC would soon lose his services for he wanted to spend more time in the mountains, to climb, write and travel. When Dougal Haston died, Peter was appointed to be his successor as Director of the International School of Mountaineering in Leysin, and left the BMC in 1977.

The BMC grew and grew over the next decade. When I started work for the Council there were a little over 100 clubs in membership, including the Scottish ones, but by 1988 the figure had grown to 267 in England and Wales, with a further 73 in membership of the Mountaineering Council of Scotland. There was also by that time 6,690 individual members and 74 trade firms (categories which had not existed previously), plus 236 organisations. This growth and development was the result of the work of many hands too numerous to mention here, but I do wish to acknowledge their contribution. Some, like John Bradley and John Cunningham, are now dead, whilst others, old friends like Nat Allen and Dave Gregory, are still keenly involved. The number of outside bodies with which we had to deal also grew apace; government agencies proliferated during this period and more and more of their legislation impinged on our sport. The new popularity of nature conservation and bird protection also meant that we had to spend more and more of our time in these directions. A real problem was the re-establishment on the crags of the peregrine falcon, so we developed a system of voluntary agreements where birds were protected in the important nesting season.

New rock climbing districts were developed in the 1970s and 1980s, including the Pembroke sea cliffs, the Llanberis slate quarries, and the limestone free climbing in Derbyshire and Yorkshire. Many of these sites were of the highest interest in conservation terms, and designated by government decree as 'Sites of Special Scientific Interest', thus the BMC's role in negotiating access to these regions became acute. We recognised that climbers would respect better if put on trust, and we persuaded the authorities to try a system of voluntary agreements instead of using their statutory powers. So far this has worked excellently, with only a few minor infringements.

We recognised that it would be difficult to replace Peter Boardman, but once again when we advertised the post of National Officer an outstanding group of young mountaineers applied. We selected Alex MacIntyre, a 24-year-old law graduate from Leeds University. Like Peter, he had already clocked up an impressive record of climbs in the Alps before joining the BMC, including two new routes on the North Face of the Gandes Jorasses, and the North Face of the Eiger, via the Direct in winter. He had also visited the Hindu Kush and specialised in Scottish winter climbing (even though, although his name made him sound like a Scot, he was a Yorkshireman, born near Hull). In other ways, Alex was as unlike Peter as it was possible to be. He looked as though he could have been a rock star, with a crown of black curly hair, and the good looks of a teenage Marc Bolan. He was impetuous, extremely intelligent and combative in debate, with a mind like a razor, but charmed all who knew him by being contrite if he had overstepped the mark, and by always being ready to party and join in. I had known him from university

Alex MacIntyre – a mind like a razor. (Photo: Terry Tullis)

days, when we had called him 'Dirty Alex' – he had once taken a bet that he would wear the same clothes day and night throughout a whole term!

My relationship with Alex was different from my relationship with Peter, for he was more 'up-front', more vociferous and argumentative, qualities which served him well in selling the BMC's policies to young climbers who tend to be anarchistic. He was not the world's leading rock climber, and preferred the challenge set by the high mountains and in 1978, as a member of a joint British and Polish expedition to Changabang, ascended its South Buttress in 11 days, climbing Alpine style. Alex was on Changabang instead of wielding a pen at his desk in the BMC office because I believed (and still do) that leading young climbers must be allowed the time to keep up their own activities otherwise they soon lose touch with the main stream of their sport. Still, there has to be a balance, and it was two years before Alex could participate in another major climb, when he ascended the East Face of Dhaulagiri, again with Polish climbers.

Alex's legal mind often helped us to sort out policy options, and during his time at the BMC we had a second confrontation – in which he acted very much as a peacemaker – this time concerning the future of Plas y Brenin, one of the Sports Council's network of national centres which had been designated the National Centre for Mountain Activities. Few people in the active climbing world could see a real role for the centre, and it was using up massive amounts of taxpayers' money which many thought could be better spent on core activities such as access, conservation, equipment testing, safety counselling and expeditions.

This period was not exclusively concerned with serious discussion; far from it. It was during Alex's involvement that the events behind one of the classic stories of the Council occurred. In 1974 I had conceived the idea of a biennial national conference, to bring together as many British climbers as possible and to focus on the development and history of our sport. For this event we chose the spa town of Buxton, with its Victorian opera house, Octagon Theatre, bars and exhibition complex, and the weekend soon became an institution to which we brought the biggest names in current and historical climbing terms. Bonatti, Heckmair, Lowe, John Gill, Randy Leavitt, Diemberger, Alex Kunaver, Warren Harding and Messner all gave lectures, and there were films, talks and debates, and in later years a light-hearted cabaret. Initially the conferences were introduced by Ian MacNaught-Davies, who then gave way to climbing television presenter Alistair Macdonald.

We would take over a hotel for the weekend as the conference nerve centre, put up all the speakers and officers there, and use it as a place for entertaining any VIPs such as the Minister of Sport, who on two occasions opened the event. In 1978 at the end of the conference I had retired to bed in the early hours. Bob Pettigrew, then the President and my room-mate, and I were fast asleep when a tearful Rita Hallam burst into the room.

'You must do something. Do something!' she insisted. 'They're flooding out the hotel.'

I simply rolled over, but Bob the dutiful President crawled out of his warm bed, and disappeared down the corridor with Rita. I was asleep again in a trice, but was soon roused by a returning Bob.

'Get up Gray,' he commanded. 'We need you. I've never seen anything like it.'

It was my turn to be frogmarched down the corridor to stop outside one of the bathrooms, where Bob hesitatingly opened the door. The sight that greeted me was staggering. There in the bath was one of our overseas guests, with two well-known climbers, plus a good-looking blonde woman . . . all very naked. The taps were full on, and water was flowing everywhere, mostly down through the ceiling on to the room below!

'Bloody hell chaps,' I began.

The biggest of the bathers stood up in all his nakedness, and stopped me in my stride. 'It's OK,' he said, 'I'm a plumber!'

It took some strong words from Bob to persuade the miscreants out of their bath, and back into a bedroom. During all this an American climber, also naked, took advantage of the chaos and climbed out of the window of the bedroom and on to the front of the neon-lit hotel, egged on by the hordes (most of whom had gatecrashed and should never have been there in the first place!). I ran over to the window and hung perilously out, almost in tears by this time for fear of the police, the scandal and the hotel management's disfavour, to plead with the climber in question to come back in. Fortunately, it was a typical March night, with a howling gale and driving sleet, and our Yankee boy soon got fed up of being out there freezing his bum off!

Order was finally restored and we extracted firm promises from the occupants of the room, who included Mo Anthoine, John Porter and Al Rouse (both of whom, for some inexplicable reason, were in drag), Peter Minks, Brian Hall and Henry Barber, to behave themselves and go quietly to sleep. As we crept back down the corridor to our own bedroom, Bob remarked that he had been relieved to see that Alex was not involved in these disgraceful scenes. I didn't want to disillusion him, so I didn't tell him that I had spied a curly head peeping out from under one of the beds. Alex obviously didn't want to risk provoking Bob's wrath!

Alex left the BMC at the end of 1980 to pursue a full-time career in mountaineering as an equipment adviser and lecturer. He wanted to continue to explore his own abilities and limitations on the big faces of the Himalaya, and with Roger Baxter-Jones and Doug Scott he enjoyed a great success on the South-west Face of Gosainthan, one of the 8,000-metre peaks. A short while later, in autumn 1982, we were all stunned to hear that he had met an untimely death on Annapurna.

I had watched his departure from the BMC with a mixture of envy and fear. Envy, because I was left behind trapped in a daily round of meetings, minutes, phone calls, car journeys and debate, and fear, because I recognised that his yen to climb the big faces of the Himalayan peaks in Alpine fashion was so futuristic that he would need great good fortune besides his brilliant mountaineering ability if he were to survive into old age. The deaths of Peter Boardman and Alex in the same year represented a horribly low point in my years of working at the BMC, and were the saddest events of the whole period. Their friends were determined that their memory would remain with British climbers, so we set up two memorials. The one to Alex is a memorial hut at Onich in Scotland, and the other, for Peter and for Joe Tasker who perished with him on Mount Everest, is a literary prize, now established as the leading award for mountaineering writing in Britain. I was happy to play a part in setting up these tributes to two great friends.

Although I was so tied one advantage of working at the BMC was the opportunity it gave me to meet many climbers from many countries; our home was often their stopping-off place. Similarly, in my position as our UIAA delegate I was able to travel quite widely. We had a succession of very supportive Presidents and Vice Presidents, including Bob Pettigrew, Tom Price, Dr David Roberts, Don Whillans, Bill Peascod, Paul Nunn, Al Rouse and John Neill, who did their best to take some of the workload from me, but like Topsy it just grew and grew and this meant that I was working more and more hours and my family commitments suffered. My eldest son Stephen had shown great promise as a musician and had been awarded a grant to study music, but inevitably we had to pay a contribution to make up his school fees. The BMC was not rich, and it was hard to make ends meet, but something always happened to make me stay at my desk. And so the years rolled by. Presidents and other elected officers and employees came and went, but I stayed on, becoming more and more immersed in sports politics and a member of so many committees that if challenged I could not have named them all. I was everything from Vice Chairman of the Outdoor Pursuits Division of the CCPR and a member of that body's executive, to a member of the board of the National Coaching Foundation and of Plas y Brenin.

Each period at the BMC was enlivened by new developments and debates, and as the 1980s progressed we had once again to review our range of activities. We produced our first ever corporate plan, to satisfy government's demand for an increased financial accountability, and created a new post – Access Officer – to help the BMC become even more active in this crucial area of its work. And once again we found ourselves involved in a major row, this time over the development of rock climbing competitions.

I was and still am dead against competitions taking place in the natural environment of our sport – the cliffs, outcrops and even quarries on which we climb. The potential damage of such an event, with spectators, route preparation, litter and disturbance to other climbers, was unacceptable. Fortunately, it quickly became obvious that the only really meaningful competition for rock climbers would be on specially prepared routes on artifical walls. Using an existing cliff would not only give local climbers an unfair advantage, but would also probably cause enough damage to the rock face to ensure bitter conflict between conservationists and the perpetrators.

These were difficult times for me. I was being forced to recognise that climbing had changed irreversibly from the days of my youth, and that, while there were still those who were attracted to the hills by the magic, poetry and beauty of them, there were also many young people who were coming into the sport just for the physical activity of problem-solving and technical mastery. The majority seemed to have very little real feel for the mountain environment. As the debate developed the BMC became more and more isolated internationally, until by 1987 we were the only member of the UIAA to oppose organised climbing competitions. Many young British climbers were travelling to the competitions abroad, performing well, and returning full of enthusiasm for the activity. It was becoming obvious to me that unless the BMC acted we would be faced with a schism and another separate body might be formed to look after the competition side. This would post a real threat to the well-being of mainstream climbing for it meant that one area of the sport would be outside the control of the fraternity. I could see what was happening in other sports like tennis, where the agents and promoters and not the participants call the tune, and I feared for climbing. We had to act.

In 1987 Chris Bonington was elected President of the BMC to succeed John Neill. He and I were old friends. I have always had reservations about his approach

Jerry Moffatt in action at the Leeds International, UIAA World Series, 1989. (Photo: Dennis Gray)

to climbing – too much emphasis on material gain? – but he is an outstanding figure, progressive and active and he recognised that the issue of climbing competitions must be resolved. We organised a debate and invited the climbing media, and pro and anti views to take part. Opinion began slowly to shift within the BMC Management Committee, and this was reflected in the columns of both the domestic mainstream climbing magazines, *High* (by then the official magazine) and *Climber*. Discussions were then held by all BMC areas and in the Mountaineering Council of Scotland, and in the end the overwhelming view was that we had no choice. We changed our policy to a support of climbing competitions on artificial structures only, with an assurance that we would continue to oppose any attempts to organise such activities in the natural environment.

The first organised UK competitions on specially constructed artificial walls were held in Leeds in 1989, with first a local event at the University and then a full international at the Queens Hall in May on behalf of the UIAA. This latter was a tremendous undertaking. A suitable artificial wall took almost a month to prepare; it was prefabricated in Grenoble and then transported to England. The whole event was mainly the work of a trade member of the BMC, DMM International Ltd, and two of their directors, Richard Cuthbertson and Paul Simkiss. I was responsible for finding a suitable location for a competition and for the liaison with the UIAA. The British climbed superbly in the event, and in the Super Final Jerry Moffatt electrified all who saw him by a climb unlike any which had been witnessed before. With a series of dynamic moves, he powered his way to the top of the wall to become the clear and decisive winner. Unhappily, in the women's section, the British were outclassed by the French, who were dominant at Leeds. Climbing is still a male-dominated sport in Britain, with sexist attitudes prevailing and macho images uppermost in the climbing press and the media. As a result, British rock climbing does not attract the kind of participation among women that is now common on the Continent.

No one knows where climbing competitions will lead, but they are surely here to stay. They will be responsible for another rise in rock climbing standards, and an ever more scientific approach to preparation and training. Unfortunately, in Britain the organisational problems and a lack of funding make many people reluctant to get involved in the administrative side, even though it was a British climber, Simon Nadin, who was declared the world's first-ever rock climbing champion in 1989. Perhaps competitions will settle down to being an important sideshow in the mainstream development of the sport, unless of course a way of packaging the events for television can be found. If the problem of the boring preliminaries can be overcome, and sponsorship found, then climbing competitions might well take their place alongside bowls, snooker and darts as compulsive television viewing!

In my last years at the BMC we had the best all-round cadre of professional staff we had ever enjoyed, with Chris Dodd as our Training Administrator, Lesley Smithson as our Office Manager, Scotsman Bill Wright as Access Officer and Andy Fanshawe as our National Officer. Very much in the Peter Boardman and Alex MacIntyre mould, Andy was in the front rank of young British mountaineers, and came to the BMC with a great climbing record behind him, including a first traverse of Chogolisa (25,148 feet). I was by then recently divorced and living on my own in a small house in Leeds 6, and working once again around the clock to counteract the inevitable loneliness I felt at no longer having my family around me. My children were growing up fast and needed me less, so I spent my spare hours either working for the Council or writing articles for the climbing media. Then there was one of those accidents which can change your life. It happened at the UIAA executive meeting in May 1988 at Oviedo in Spain.

Oviedo is a small town in the Basque region of Spain on the edge of the Picos Europa mountain range, where the Spanish Federation hosted the UIAA meetings. Traditionally on the final evening these ended with a banquet in one of the famous restaurants of the town. I had just taken delivery of a hire car, for I had to drive to Santiago the next morning to catch a plane back to England, and I went on to the meal with all the car papers, cash, travellers cheques, bank card and cheque book, and my passport on me.

After the meal I stopped off on the way back to my hotel for a drink with Robin Walker (a British climber who lives in the area) and the Czech climber Jiri Novak, and I well remember going up to the counter and ordering and paying for the beer. Events became a bit hazy after this; somehow I became separated from my two companions and set off to walk back alone. I was crossing a small square with palm trees and a grass lawn, when two men came up to me and said *Buenas noches*. I felt no alarm for everyone in Spain had been very friendly and, somewhat merry, I returned their greeting. Suddenly they grabbed at me, and sandwiched me between them. I began to struggle, then three other figures appeared, giving me no chance. I wrestled as hard as I could, until *Wham!*, a club came down on the back of my head, and my knees began to buckle. I felt hands going into my jacket pocket, and I lashed out again, until a second blow to the head finished me and I began to laugh as I lapsed into unconsciousness. I was laughing at my stupidity; I should have known better than to have been carrying all my papers late at night, out on my own.

When I came to I was lying face upwards looking at the stars. It took me ages to find my hotel doorway, for I was badly concussed, and eventually the police arrived and took me off to their headquarters. What followed was a farce. I could not make them understand what had happened – they thought I was noisily drunk – and it was even harder to make them see that all my papers, money and so forth had been stolen. Perhaps a crime like that was most unusual in that sleepy town. After what seemed like hours a doctor appeared to examine me; again he spoke no English. I kept being sick and going dizzy, and whilst they were taking a statement from me, I fell off my chair. All I could think about was catching my plane the next day at Santiago, and eventually I agreed to contact the British consul there as soon as I arrived to sort out the problems over my papers and my money. Then they simply took me back to my hotel in a police car with a wailing siren which must have woken up all the other delegates!

After a couple of hours' sleep, and borrowing some money from Bill Putnam, I set off on the long drive to Santiago. I had to head south towards Leon, then pick up the motorway system leading west to Santiago. For the first part of the journey I gave a lift to a hitch-hiker, dropped him out in the country near Leon which I by-passed, and drove on to the modern road system beyond. I kept feeling dizzy and was anxious, for the top of my head was split and aching. I had worked it out that I had to drive fast in order to catch my plane, and I was racing along at about 80 mph when a sweeping bend loomed up in the motorway. Then I blacked out momentarily. I ran off the motorway and tore through a boulder field. I became conscious of a drop on my right, so I made a split-second decision and swung the car round. The offside tyre exploded and the car careered into the fence on the edge of the motorway; I had come off the road at a point further down that was not so protected. I was a tennis ball hitting the net as the fence enveloped itself around the car.

As I was crawling out of the wreckage a Spanish driver, most concerned and very helpful, who had witnessed everything, came running down off the motorway. The motorway police arrived, similarly concerned, but then the *Guardia* turned up. I was an Englishman in the middle of Spain with no papers and no means of identity, driving a Spanish-registered car. I think they took me for a terrorist. I was forcibly spread-eagled across the bonnet of their car, with a gun at my chest and some very difficult explaining to do! The resultant epic took several days to sort out. The car was a write-off, the British consul proved to be worse than useless and I missed my plane home. I had to talk a local hotelier into letting me stay at his place until I could get some money and another air ticket organised, and the whole thing had to be co-ordinated via long telephone calls with my secretary Lesley Smithson who proved to be my saviour.

Several weeks later I was to find that the result of this débâcle was damage to the sacro-iliac nerves at the base of my spine, due to the whiplash forces imposed on smashing the car into the fence. Luckily I had been wearing a seat belt; I have no doubt that being catapulted through the windscreen and hitting a steel chain fence with such momentum would have spoilt my rosy complexion! It had all been a shock, and I had to start to think about my future. For a while driving was agony, and my back gave me much pain; I was forced to admit to myself that I was not as young as I had been. Carrying out my tasks as General Secretary with the necessary vigour was for a time nearly impossible. After late-night meetings in winter, I would arrive home and only with difficulty be able to get out of my car. I began to think that the time had come to retire from the BMC and do other things with my life. I felt the Council needed someone younger to lead the professional staff, and my mind was made up to leave when I fell victim to a well-meant spoof that went wildly wrong.

A young climbing acquaintance resident in Brazil, Tom Curtis, sent a joke letter inviting me to visit his country to run some climbing courses for their clubs and federation. Tommy is a madly eccentric, kind and generous personality, and an expert at practical jokes, and he had made the letter look convincingly official, signed by some Portuguese-sounding person I had never heard of. At the time when the letter arrived, in the summer of 1988, all the national bodies of sport were being encouraged by the Sports Council to widen and improve their range of inter-national contacts. I relished the thought of visiting and climbing in Brazil and meeting with climbers there, so I sent the invitation to the Sports Council after discussing its contents with Bob Pettigrew, Chairman of the BMC Training Com-mittee. Nothing happened for weeks, then one morning I received a 'Personal, private' registered letter from the Sports Council. They had passed on the invitation with my agreement to the British Council with a request for funding, and the latter had checked with their officials in Brazil only to discover that it was a hoax! They felt that I had some explaining to do! I realised that this looked bad for me, and that it could be thought that Tom Curtis and I were in cahoots.

I immediately copied the Sports Council's letter to the BMC President, with an explanation of my own part and the background to the story. It was the kind of joke that I had played on other people when I was young and the sort of wheeze that the Bradford Lads, the Rock and Ice and many other groups of that era would have appreciated, but the reaction of Chris Bonington and others of the BMC Executive took me completely by surprise. They decided to hold a Committee of Enquiry and Chris advised me to seek legal advice!

To say that I was upset about this is an understatement. I could appreciate their concern, but all previous Executives would have been happy to support my view of events. The Committee of Enquiry made tongues start to wag, which could only be damaging to the BMC, as well as to my own reputation. I suddenly realised that my position *vis-à-vis* this Executive was as an employee and not as a friend, as had been the case in the past. In an organisation like the BMC there are many different ways of running the show, and I did not want this to be my reason for leaving, but the thing was allowed to drag on. The enquiry went ahead, they found that I was blameless, and informed the Sports Council, but one of the self-appointed guardi-ans of the British way of climbing, Ken Wilson, seemed determined to make as much of the affair as possible. I did not want to bow out on a sour note, but I was now convinced that there were other things to do in life; I had made my contri-bution and my time had come. I gave in my notice.

Thus ended the extraordinary experience of working for almost 18 years for the sport that I love so much. I came away with happy memories, especially of the many friends I had made over the years, and keen to support the Council and its work in the future. It is true to say that if the BMC did not exist it would be necessary to invent it, for there is a demand for its work and services, and climbers desperately need to be represented so that their sport may be protected.

On the Fringe

Je m'en vais chercher un grand peut-être.
Rabelais

During the 1960s and 1970s there was a quickening of interest in free climbing throughout Europe. New areas were developed, new methods adopted, and new groups came to the fore. They often caused the old established Alpine federations much consternation, and the new practitioners were dubbed as mere 'sport climbers'. When the late Jean Juge, a great climber who ascended the Eigerwand at 65 and President of the UIAA, saw a film about modern free climbing in the USA, his comment to me afterwards was that it was OK, but it was 'not real Alpinism'. 'Why not?' I asked. 'Because they are not wearing breeches and boots,' was his reply. The movement, however, was unstoppable and as new areas were opened up I became keen to visit them, to meet the local climbers and to sample first hand the developments.

One activity that gave me the chance to be involved was lecturing. I had started this in the early 1960s, speaking to climbing clubs, free of charge, about my travels and climbs. I am a member of five such clubs (typically for someone who has been climbing for some time – you tend to join in different regions, and keep up your membership when you move away), so giving a talk at club evenings became a fairly common occurrence. I began to build up my expertise and connections and in the winter of 1968/9 I gave over seventy lectures the length and breadth of Britain. I have enjoyed some exciting and amusing experiences, from the projector and hall catching fire at a Nottingham Climbers' Club event in the 1970s, to speaking to 2,000 people in the Preston Guildhall, as well as lecture tours abroad, in Poland, Sweden, South Africa, Holland, Belgium and Ireland. My proudest lecturing moment came at the end of the 1970s when I was invited to address the Cork Literary and Philosophical Society, the oldest learned society in Europe with origins going back to the eighteenth century. I cannot accurately recall my subject – 'Men, Myth and Mountains', I believe – but I do remember turning up in jeans and an open-necked shirt to find myself in front of the most glittering of assemblies. The men were in evening dress, and the women in gowns, bedecked with diamonds and pearls. I mumbled my apologies for being late, and for the state of my dress, but declared I was a Dillon (well, my mother was!). This seemed to suffice. When I signed the lecturers' book I was humbled to read the names of some of the previous speakers: Charles Darwin, Charles Dickens, George Bernard Shaw and W. B. Years! But back to climbing...

I had always been aware that there was some outstanding climbing to be had on the fringe of the Alps, and visited areas like the Wilder Kaiser and Wetterstein ranges in Germany as early as 1954, when I had been over there to run, but it was not until many years later that I started to visit the crags of Western Europe. They were then being developed just as fast as my homeland cliffs. My first stopping-off place was the Belgian Ardennes, and more precisely Marche les Dames, Freyr and Darve, where a climbing meet was organised by the Belgian Alpine Club. These crags were to become a favourite climbing area.

Like all the cliffs in the area, Freyr is limestone, and really a series of large buttresses set above the river. The highest of these is over 400 feet, and the rock is compact and firm, with much of the protection on the climbs being gained from *in situ* pitons. Originally many of the climbs were ascended artifically but now they are mainly climbed free. It was here that I had one of my narrowest escapes. I was climbing with Tim Leech, and we were descending the cliffs in the dark. We still had to gather up our equipment, but were supposed to be back in the hotel already for dinner with our Belgian hosts. It is very difficult to move around the Ardennes hillsides in the dark, so we decided to rappel back down the way we had climbed up. Tim was descending first, and as I came down, he was setting up the next position. Our final descent to the ground was from off a tiny stance, and I decided to go first. Tim had set up the abseil, and placed (as he thought) the double rope through a sling, threaded into the eye of a large piton. I gingerly lowered myself off the ledge, and suddenly the rope had come off the belay, and I was shooting through space!

As I gathered momentum, my left hand by sheer good fortune coiled round a large flake of rock, and there I stopped, hanging in the dark a hundred feet off the ground by just one hand. 'Help!' I gasped. Tim tried to reach me and I had to heave myself up before I could grab his outstretched hand; luckily, he had kept himself tied to the rock face. 'What the hell happened?' I demanded. When we looked at the piton where the sling had been, we could just see that in the dark Tim had in fact threaded the rope through only one side of the sling and therefore it had simply pulled through.

'Sorry,' he mumbled. I was angry but I realised how contrite he was; he knew he had endangered my life, and he did not exactly make a habit of such mistakes. We set up the abseil again, made a joke of the whole affair, and lowered ourselves into the night, to arrive with many apologies a long time later at the hotel. Jean-Pierre Gailly met us anxiously at the door. '*Ça va?*' he asked. 'Bleeding *ça va!*' I replied ruefully.

At Christmas 1969 I was contacted by a company looking for someone to go to southern Spain to check out the potential for developing rock climbing in the district during the winter months. Years ahead of their time, they wanted to fill up some of their charter flights with climbers seeking warm dry rock in November and December. I had only ever heard of rock climbing in the north of the country, but I agreed to investigate the possibilities.

From Benidorm I could see some quite high mountains, but the local people suggested I look first at Calpe, a short distance up the coast. There, they assured me, was a large rock! First I needed a partner. The Spanish Federation in Madrid gave me the name and address of the only climber they knew of in the area, and on Christmas Eve 1969 I located his house in Alicante and knocked on the door. He answered the summons, but spoke no English; I had little Spanish and at first he seemed to think that I was trying to sell him something! Finally, with my foot in his doorway, I made him realise that I did not want to part with the battered baby Fiat at his gate, but was inviting him to go into the mountains with me.

When he turned up the next morning he looked like a fugitive from the film *The Glass Mountain*, in corduroy trousers and jacket, and heavy boots. We set off for Calpe, then a small, sleepy fishing village, and as we approached I became more and more excited. Dominating the whole area was a feature similar in size and shape to the Rock of Gibraltar, whose seaward face seen in profile looked steep and spectacular. 'Has anyone ever climbed the faces, Pedro?' '*Nadie!*' my Spanish guide replied.

We arrived at the rock's base and then drove around it, for its oceanic side had a kind of marine promenade which went right under the rock face. We stopped, and as I looked up the wall I had to admit that with the equipment I had brought, and Pedro in his big boots as my companion, I had not a hope in hell of climbing it. But it looked good. It must have been 1,000 feet high, of good limestone, and the heat from the sun that Christmas Day was such that you could have climbed there in shorts and a T-shirt. 'What a find, what a find,' I thought, 'but not for today.'

We went on to the Benidorm side of the rock, which boasted some slabs, and after picking out an easy-looking line and roping up on Pedro's old hawser laid rope I set off, wearing my EBs. I soon discovered that the slabs were thin from the word 'go'. They must have been Very Severe by British standards, and finding belays at each pitch end was difficult. We had a hammer and some pitons, but found the rock so compact that placing them was difficult. My companion was much fitter and stronger than he looked, and followed successfully where I led, though he found some difficulty climbing in boots. A rope-length from the top we came to a crux section. Try as I might, I could not get up, and scared myself when my foot skidded off a small incut – my companion's rope work was a bit old-fashioned, and if I had fallen he probably would have been strangled. It was a bit like solo climbing. In the end I solved the crux by the devious method of lassoing a spike above my head with a long sling!

The ascent was pure joy, and after five rope-lengths we reached easy ground to complete, I believe, the first climb at Calpe. I was surprised to find extensive buildings at the top of the rock; apparently this had been one of the strongholds of the Moors in Spain. The descent which followed was equally surprising – a simple walk down a steep path inside a tunnel hewn from the rock itself which brought us sweaty and breathless in only a few minutes back to the car.

We had a magical time over the next two weeks exploring rock faces that had never been climbed upon, like Ponoch and the Torre de Emmedio, and visiting the mountain ranges to the north, where Pedro came into his own. There, ten years earlier, he had climbed extensively on Puig Campana and Aitana. We also found time to celebrate both Christmas and New Year, and it became obvious to me that if British climbers of that era started coming out to Calpe, they might have great difficulty catching the plane back home – at that time you could buy four bottles of reasonable wine for a pound!

I returned to Britain and reported that the area had potential, but shortly afterwards the holiday company that had been so far-sighted went bankrupt. Calpe was to be developed by some Spanish climbing friends from Barcelona, led by Jose Anglada, and is now one of the most popular winter rock climbing venues in the world. In 1985 I met a young hot 'rock jock' who was enthusing about some climbing he had done in Spain over the Christmas period, at a place called Penon de Ifach. It was a while before I realised that he was talking about Calpe Rock. Feeling superior, I told him, 'I've climbed at Calpe too. I was there at Christmas 1969.' He looked at me in a kindly way and said, 'Oh yeah? Was it on a Saga package?'

In the early 1970s I visited Scandinavia several times, and made close friends with a Swedish climber called Olaf Ohgren. In 1974 my family and I made the trip to

Sweden, and as we rolled off the ferry Olaf was there to greet us. We climbed at Gothenberg (reminiscent of rock climbing at Tremadog in North Wales), Haggsta just outside Stockholm, and then drove north to climb on cliffs almost within the Arctic Circle, big, lonely crags with something mournful and oppressive about them. The Swedish climbers organised a party in my honour at a refuge. I have never seen so many people get so drunk so quickly – it seems that the Swedes, like their Finnish neighbours, drink with just one aim – and by nine in the evening the event was over. Olaf and I, teetotaller and 'family man', were the only two left on our feet and had to keep going out into the blinding night light to look for collapsed climbers who were in real danger of freezing to death.

In early March 1977 I returned to give lectures at Lulea University, just south of the Arctic Circle, Stockholm, and Umea, where Olaf lives. I was surprised by how cold it was, and impressed with the way the local people cope with this extreme environment. Their houses were so well insulated that you could sit around in your shirt-sleeves. During the day we went cross country skiing or ice-climbing, and at night downhill skiing on a floodlit slope outside the town. It was light for about four and a half hours in the middle of the day, and even more mournful than in summer. At that time Sweden had the highest suicide rate in the world, appreciable when you consider that they have 24 hours of daylight in one season and almost complete darkness in the other, and that every time you step outside in winter you need to be clothed as if you were climbing in the Himalaya. I never went anywhere without full down suit, hood, gloves and double boots.

Calpe Rock. The author pioneered a route here up slabs on the left-hand side of the picture. (Photo: Dennis Gray)

A highlight of this visit was an ice-climb I made with Olaf and two Norwegians, probably the toughest characters I have ever met climbing. They lived in a small town inside the Arctic Circle, the only climbers in that area, and had climbed every weekend for the last eighteen months in either northern Sweden or Norway. They camped out every night, sleeping on reindeer skins, and eating raw fish and pemmican. We set out on the journey to reach this climb, north of Umea, on cross country skis; by that time I was just about used to the 10-mile bashes which they considered a short trip. We reached our cliff in the early afternoon, and left our skis at its base before struggling up a gully deep in powder snow. As we climbed I had to envy my companions their physiques; Olaf was tall, lithe and blond, and the Norwegians like giant trolls. They steamed up the snow, leaving me, a midget by comparison, sinking in up to my thighs. We reached the cliff and gazed up at the rocks draped with ice and snow. It was getting dark, but my companions had head-torches permanently fixed on their helmets – I suppose if you climb regularly in such an area much of your climbing is done in the dark!

Despite living in isolation, without other climbers around them, the Norwegians were remarkably technically proficient. (Perhaps climbing, like walking and running, is instinctive for human beings, who must always have had to do it in their primitive past.) The biggest of the Norwegians set off in the lead like an automaton up the ice curtain which draped itself down the rock face. At times the ice was thick, at others his crampons scraped through to the rock underneath, but his speed was impressive, and he had climbed a rope-length, belayed and begun to bring up his companion before Olaf and I had sorted out our tangled ropes. Olaf set off. This was the first time I had ever seen him ice-climbing, so I watched with keen interest as he moved confidently upwards. He was as good on ice as he was on rock, on skis, in a canoe or orienteering, and soon he too was up the ice pitch and bringing me up. By now it was dark, and the cold was intense; I was thankful to be kitted out from head to toe in down. I set off to lead the next pitch, and stuck about thirty feet above Olaf. My head-torch was not working and I was worried that an ice bulge above my head might be the crux, although the Norwegians were already up and over it. I was in trouble; the cold and the dark were getting at me, and I had no protection between me and Olaf. 'Oh God,' I moaned. 'I can't bloody well do it. I can't see!'

I could hear Olaf swearing away in Swedish below me, obviously getting impatient at this English climber who was such a coward, then a light appeared just above my head. It was Christian, one of the Norwegians. 'Do you need a rope?' he demanded. Hanging from the picks of my ice-axes, in the dark, my feet almost marking time on ice-glazed rock, I needed no further excuse.

'Yes, yes please!' I pleaded apologetically, and soon the deed was done. In retrospect it was a good job they had waited for me, for without a light I needed a pull to get over the ice bulge. I joined them on a large ledge, and Olaf soon climbed up to join us. The rest of the climb was easy, up snowy gullies frozen hard with névé into which our crampons bit with a fierce crunch. I had to take my gloves off for just a moment to relieve myself, and nearly got frostbite at both ends!

We reached the summit of the rock buttress just as the full moon came up. By its light we could see out on to the hillsides around and our way down the steep snow slopes at the side of the rock, and after a short rest my companions were off again, with me floundering in their wake. Just before we reached the base of the gully to regain our skis, I was carried down several feet and almost buried by a snow slide. It took me back to the time in the Cairngorms in 1965 when I was covered, and I had to be dug out by a rescue dog; I have had a more than healthy respect for avalanches ever since.

Our route back to Umea lay across the surface of a large frozen lake. In the middle was a lamplight, and under it, in the Arctic night, a Lapp fishing through a hole he had bored with a huge metal corkscrew. He had a kind of fabricated cover for some protection from the biting wind coming across the lake, and I marvelled at his ability to sit it out in such a place, all alone and so cold. I could see from the hole that the ice was only about a foot thick. 'What will we do if it gives way?' I anxiously asked Olaf; I am not accustomed to being out on a frozen lake in the middle of the night. Olaf thought for a moment.

'Do? We'll drown of course!'

'Bloody hell!' was all I could think of to say. Perhaps it was appropriate that my lecture at Lulea University was to be on 'Why man takes risks'!

Over the next few years I visited many fringe climbing areas. In Greece I climbed on the beautiful limestone which has been developed north of Athens at Varybopi, when I attended the Olympic Games at Munich I visited the Frankenjura for the first time, and more recently in Yugoslavia I climbed at Paklenica, where we experienced exceptionally bad weather, with freezing cold and snow high up in the mountains. But, although the free limestone climbing in Yugoslavia is on a par with most that has been developed around Europe in the last twenty years, and I have never climbed on rougher rock anywhere (including the gabbro on the Isle of Skye), perhaps the best fringe climbing for both enjoyment and accessibility is to be found in France. From bouldering at Fontainebleau outside Paris, to limestone outcrop climbing at centres like Saussois, Saleve, Cormot, Buis, Boux and the Calanques, I have enjoyed many days of moving up firm French rock. Many British climbers believe that French climbing is simply a case of moving from *in situ* bolt to bolts, but an ascent of, say, the Arc-en-Ciel at Saleve would quickly change their mind. The French climbing ethic *is* different from the British, but it is no less admirable. French climbing is about overcoming technical difficulty in a reasonably safe environment, while British climbing is about adventure and a climber can be badly injured if he makes a mistake.

Besides the limestone outcrops, there is also 'European big wall climbing' in France, at the Verdon Gorge, at Presles and in the Vercors, a limestone mountain range near to Grenoble. In 1975 I enjoyed a climb at Vercors with a young friend that was to be significant for him as the start of a dazzling but short career at the forefront of British climbing.

I met Tim Leech one night in 1974 at Caley Crags. I had been out bouldering, and at the end of the day gave the sixteen-year-old lad a lift back to Guiseley. It turned out that we were almost next-door neighbours, and that he was mad keen to climb, and over the next two years we climbed a lot together. As he grew up his ability developed dramatically; he was small and compact but very strong, and his greatest assets were his fitness and determination.

In the summer of 1975 Tim came with my family and me to the French Alps. I had not then realised how good he was, but I do remember having difficulty keeping up with him as we walked up to climb the South Face of the Meije in the Dauphiné, and in following him when he led a pitch off route on the South Face of the Aiguille Dibona. From the Dauphiné Alps we headed south to Die, an epic drive over the Alpine passes in my Russian-made car, 'Bessie' (big and fat, and very slow).

Tim Leech leading Quark at Caley Crags. (Photo: Mrs R. Leach)

Two Rock and Ice friends, Gordon Smith and John Midgeley, were out on a major climb on Mont des Trois Becs, known as 'La Pelle', and only arrived back at the campsite at about midnight. The next day they were full of praise for the beauty and line of the route. They had climbed the artificial sections (graded in the guidebook as A2/A3) by free climbing, but this had taken a long time and they had only avoided a bivouac on the summit because the descent was so easy – they had walked down by the light of their head-torches. The whole outing had taken them about fourteen hours.

'Sounds good,' I said enviously. 'I think we'll have a go at it!'

Midge looked at me quizzically. 'You and who?' he demanded.

'The Apprentice!' I replied, and from that moment this name for Tim stuck.

Discussing the route with Tim, I was at pains to point out that if Gordon Smith, known to all and sundry as 'Speedy', had taken a full day on the route, we had better be prepared to bivouac! So, the next morning, as we drove up to Saillans and then Col de la Chaudière, we had cooking equipment, food and lightweight sleeping bags with us. We parked high on the road below the face of La Pelle, a mirror-like wall over 1,000 feet high. It looked impressive as we walked up towards it in the soft morning light of a beautiful day. As we roped up Tim suggested that he lead for the first sections and then hand over to me. On such terrain you are soon overtired if you lead through for you get no breather between pitches, and you are continually switching over rucksacks and equipment so that the second carries most of the load.

The rock was firm, white limestone, set at a reasonable angle; the French description had stated the route to be entirely overhanging, but we could see that this was not so. Almost as soon as Tim set off, I could tell that my young apprentice was something special on this kind of ground. He climbed with such speed and fluency that within the hour we were a long way up the wall, and below the first crux, a traverse left across a slab to gain a flake. It was graded Alpine VI in our description. At that time, climbing in boots and carrying heavy equipment, this grade used to make us apprehensive to say the least, but I was astonished by the ease with which my companion overcame the obstacle. He was across and up almost as fast as I could play out his rope. Following with our equipment, I felt clumsy, and at one point even had to grab a piton to stop myself swinging into space.

We soon reached the corner which our friends had said was the crux of the climb, graded A3 in the French description, and I was made to feel a bit like a supernumerary as Tim shot up the pitch with ease. 'Either this is the wrong route or it's time to hang up your boots, lad!' I thought to myself as I gritted my teeth and free climbed it, without too much fuss, but thankful for the secure rope.

'Do you want to lead, or shall I keep going?' Tim asked anxiously at the end of this pitch. I could see he was enjoying it all immensely, and he was making a much better job of it than I could have, so I declined the lead. He kept on climbing, making short work of a Grade VI wall which followed, and soon reaching the overhanging chimney which is a feature of the upper part of the face. The guidebook told us that this was a good bivouac site; we were much amused by this – it was still only 8 o'clock in the morning! The pace became faster and faster, and soon we were faced with the final real difficulty, a large, loose, yellow overhang, graded A3 with seven pitons for aid. Once again, the Apprentice climbed it free, although with much grunting and panting. Following, I needed a very tight rope to emulate my leader. I was becoming more and more impressed, but said nothing other than,

'I'll lead from now on!', for only easy climbing remained and I was worried that Tim might be getting tired.

Our pace slowed after that, and it took a couple of hours to finish off the route, but before midday we stood on the rock summit of the Trois Becs, looking out over a range of striking peaks and glistening rock faces. The descent was easy. We ran down a grassy couloir on the south side of the wall and half an hour later we were in the car, and then back at the campsite in time for lunch. Midge greeted our return with good-natured incredulity. 'Either you're climbing bloody well, or you've only been up on the col sunbathing!

'Neither,' I replied. 'I just used my secret weapon!'

'What's that?' demanded Midge.

'The Apprentice!'

Over the next few years I was to enjoy many fine days' climbing with Tim – at Easter 1976 we climbed 101 routes in a day at Stanage – but his ambition quickly outpaced mine. He had his sights set on the hardest rock and ice routes, and the following winter he climbed the North Face of the Matterhorn and the North Face of the Verte with Steve Bell. At 19 he climbed the North Face of the Grandes Jorasses, wearing crampons for most of the climb, and later the Nose of El Capitan. He then took up hard solo climbing and made the first British ascents of the North Face of the Droites and the Super Couloir of Mont Blanc du Tacul. He was also able to perform at the highest standards of the day on rock and pioneered the first 6c rock route in Britain, Moonshine at Curbar Edge in Derbyshire. In 1979 he was with Peter Boardman on Gauri Sankar, making the first ascent via the West Ridge, and in 1981 he and Nick Colton made an impressive series of climbs in Alaska. That same year Tim led an expedition to the South-East Pillar of Annapurna III, accompanied by Steve Bell and Nick Colton. Nick and Tim reached a very high point which many subsequent parties have failed to emulate, but were beaten back by sickness and bad weather.

On his return from this rare failure, the Apprentice set about pursuing his architectural studies, marriage, and then his career. Technically as a mountaineer he was one of the best, but he is also immensely likeable, without any pretence, modest but forthright, and with his feet firmly on the ground. I like to think that it was on La Pelle that he realised for the first time what he might achieve in climbing.

Much of the fringe rock climbing available in Western Europe is on limestone, with the notable exceptions of the granite in Scandinavia, the conglomerates at Meteroa in Greece and Montserrat in Spain, and the sandstone at Fontainebleau, but for variety Switzerland is outstanding. When Peter Boardman was working at Leysin, I went to work as a guide for him, leading parties up the Tour d'Ai and the Miroir of the Argentière. These are good limestone areas, but the very best rock climb I have ever enjoyed in Switzerland was on granite at the Eldorado Dome, a place that few British climbers have visited. The Dome is at the extreme east of the Bernese Oberland, and is reached from the top of the Grimsel Pass, via a path alongside the Grimsel Dam into a high valley below the peak of the Finsteraarhorn. The setting is superb – you look up the valley into an icefall, and around at high jagged peaks, and the Dome is found amidst the greenery below, an hour's walk from the dam. The huge, 1,550-foot face was opened up in 1981 by Claude and Yves Remy.

Tim Clifford climbing The Glen Arete, Shipley, West Yorkshire.
(Photo: Dennis Gray)

In July 1984 bad weather had forced us – my son Stephen, Tim Clifford, and I – from Chamonix into Switzerland, looking for better conditions on the rock faces of the Handegg area. There we met Erik Henseleit, a German climber who later died tragically on Shivling in the Himalaya; from that first encounter he and I were to be firm friends. Erik told us that the climbs on the Dome had at that time a fearsome reputation amongst Continental climbers for difficulty and, after supplying topo descriptions of Motorhead and Septumania, declined to accompany us. 'The routes are too bloody hard!' he declared.

It was hot and sticky as we walked up towards the rock face. I was apprehensive, for my two companions were very young – 14 and 16 – to be attempting such a long climb. Still, Tim Clifford had already shown himself to be one of the best rock climbers in West Yorkshire, despite an accident at Caley Crags resulting in a serious operation to a foot, with all the bones being pinned and wired together, and a prognosis that he would never climb again. When I had visited him in hospital, he had told me, 'I will climb again, and I will climb the hardest routes!' His determination both to recover and to become proficient were rewarded when, within two years, he was able to climb problems at our local outcrops that many of the adult climbers could not overcome. He had an ideal build for rock climbing, flexible and light, and was quiet and self-contained, showing little or no emotion. Thus he was possessed of that essential quality of low anxiety and arousal which allows good control in serious climbing situations. Perhaps I had no need to worry.

At the foot of the Dome I was struck by its beauty. The rock face was made up of metallic-looking slabs of red and grey granite, much wider than I had expected (there are now about a dozen routes up the wall). There were two ropes of two climbers on Motorhead when we arrived at the base of the face. This seemed to follow a series of corners and depressions until near the top, where it traversed right and climbed a steep wall to the summit. It looked a fine climb, but we decided to see if we could locate the start of Septumania, not keen to follow behind other climbers on a major route. A single careless stone dislodged from above can spell disaster if you are on the receiving end!

We found the start of Septumania, reputedly harder than Motorhead, and, according to the topo description, 'un patine désespérant mais sublime'. It was too difficult for Stephen, and he happily agreed to look after the equipment at the foot of the face, and bring it round to meet us on the descent route which lay on the right. As soon as we set off the climbing was demanding. Tim led the first rope-length, and then I set forth up a glassy slab with no protection. I became more and more unnerved. As we progressed we found that, apart from the occasional piton and bolts for belays, it was very difficult to place more than a minimum of nut protection, and much of the climbing is what is best described as 'bold'. By the time I reached the top of the second pitch I was drained. The sun was hitting the rock, shining out of a hazy blue sky, and I was sweating and gripped by the possibility of a bad fall. As I wondered whether we should retreat or not, Tiny Tim led out 150 feet of rope almost as fast as I could play it out. The climbing was solid 5A and 5B standard, and when I joined him on a good stance at the end of the pitch I had to suggest that he lead until he was tired.

The next section turned out to be even harder – a thin traverse, followed by some easier climbing leading into a very smooth scoop in the rock face. This was badly protected and required long stretches to reach small incut holds; I have to confess that I could not have led it. I began to wonder if we were off route. The topo indicated that this pitch was 6B, and in our vague way we had 'translated' this into British 5A. Later we learned that of course it meant nothing of the kind, and that it was actually 5C!

Although the climbing was slightly easier after this, the heat gave an exaggerated impression of difficulty, and it was hard to grip the small holds, despite clouds of gymnastic chalk. I led for a short while, but then was stopped by a desperate wall. I belayed and brought Tim up, and he climbed it as easily as if he had been on a boulder problem at our beloved Caley Crags. He reminded me as I watched of Joe Brown, for with neither of them could you ever tell whether the climbing was easy or hard; they simply went up without comment or fuss. The short wall led up below a roof split by a crack, under which Tim had belayed. 'Looks bleeding hard to me!' I said, but Tiny Tim was obviously in his element, and he was up and over this obstacle without difficulty. It turned out to be the other hardest section of the climb, and I had to take a tight rope in following my young leader.

Above this, slab pitch followed slab pitch. I began to tire badly in the heat, and even Tim was slowing down, but he kept climbing doggedly on upwards in the lead.

The granite sweep of the face was superb. Suddenly we heard a cry. The leader of the first party over to our right on the top wall of Motorhead was off! He fell a long, long way – about 70 feet – and then there was much shouting from both him and his party. He had fractured a leg, and when we returned to the foot of the face we saw the party slowly descending by abseil, and a rescue team climbing up to reach them whilst they waited for a helicopter.

The final slab pitches of Septumania were superb, compact red granite, and five hours after starting out we reached the summit of the Eldorado Dome. It was a climb to compare with any such route I had done in Yosemite in the USA, for I had counted sixteen pitches in all, many of them the full length of our 150-foot rope. We rested on the summit, and took in the view. Of all the people I was ever with in the mountains Tiny was the most undemonstrative; he never talked unnecessarily, nor ever remarked that it was all so bloody wonderful, but I am sure such experiences did affect him.

We traversed airily along the summit of the Dome and descended to meet Stephen, a tiny figure climbing slowly up to meet us in the late afternoon with our training shoes and other equipment on his back. After meeting up with him and changing, we quickly descended to reach the path which led us to our car waiting at the Grimsel Dam. At the campsite in the Hasli Valley, Erik greeted us with a brew. 'So, what was it like?'

'Like? . . . er, bloody easy,' I told him, tongue in cheek. In fact it was probably the most demanding climb I had ever done on the European fringe.

Running:
Winning by Losing

If you can pant and run, run and pant, pant and run, and
run and pant some more, then you can run the Marathon
my son!

Eric Beard

Consider two models: the first, a solitary figure moving along, running through deep woods, the other, a person striding around a tartan track set inside a sports stadium. It is the same physical movement of putting one foot in front of the other, but they are as far apart in reality as the lone hillwalker scrambling along the Grib Goch Ridge and the participant in a modern rock climbing competition, set indoors on an artificial wall in front of an audience.

Running, as in the first model, is like walking (and, to a lesser degree, climbing), a natural activity for human beings, and as the runner moves along through open countryside that activity possesses a primitive dimension that cannot be understood by those who have never indulged in it. You start out carrying a burden of cares from the daily round, but then, particularly if you are running through open country or woods, some magic can happen; an 'automatic pilot' takes over and you can find yourself in a trance-like state, moving along as if in a dream. The therapeutic effects of this are not to be underestimated. I have often set out for a run worried, distraught and fearful about the future, and returned feeling serene and relaxed, my anxiety abated.

The challenge and appeal of competitive running is something else, and its satisfaction is found in measuring yourself against some known yardstick – other runners, a distance, or a clock. There might be nothing material at stake, or there may just be fame and fortune for those who can outrun everyone else, but the competitive urge in running is always driven by the same wish to attain some pre-set goal. In this, athletes are no different from climbers.

There is now such an overlap between mountaineering and athletics, particularly in orienteering, fell running and marathons, with so many climbers taking part, that the connection between the two is not seen as unusual. When I started to climb at the end of the 1940s, I had never been on a run, indeed, my first climbing companions would have sneered at any such suggestion! Although games were compulsory at school, with soccer, cricket and rugby, I had never taken part in a cross country race. (Incidentally, although I was a cricket and soccer enthusiast at school, I was not so keen on rugby, having been stretchered off after an encounter with two bigger boys – Gerald Larner, now a famous music critic, and the well-known dramatist Alan Bennett!)

When I reported for National Service in 1954, one of the first things I had to do at the inception centre was to take part in a cross country run. Being a non-combatant, I had been made to feel none too welcome in the barrack room. The night before the run I was reading Anderl Heckmair's *Les trois derniers problèmes des Alpes*, when our Corporal, a small bully of a man, came in. 'Gray! What are you fucking reading?' he demanded. When I told him, he strutted up, grabbed the book out of my hand, took one look at it in amazement and hurled it across the room. 'Get yer bleeding boots bulled instead of reading such tripe. You consci's are all the bleeding same; soft, bleeding soft, reading dirty French books!' he declared. Of course, I should have done a *Loneliness of the Long-distance Runner* on him, and deliberately come last in their silly cross country race, but I was so annoyed at his daring to criticise my hero Heckmair that I decided next day I would show him!

They had set a hard course, through woods, hilly ground and muddy fields. It was January, with snow on the ground, and, typical of the Army, we were made to run fully clothed, carrying a pack and wearing boots! To cut the story short, I quickly found that most of the Pay Corps personnel were so unfit they could not keep on running continuously, but there was a core of about six runners who could. Although it hurt like hell, particularly in my legs and chest, I remembered my resolve of the night before and kept going, trying to take over the lead. As soon as I did so, a tall, angular figure strode past me, then slowed the pace down until I passed him again. And so the race went on, with the process being repeated. I knew nothing about running or tactics, so I had no idea what this guy was up to, and every time he slowed the pace down I sped it up again, much to his obvious annoyance. We kept this up all the way round the 6-mile course.

As we came up the hill to the finish I was in the lead, when suddenly the tall chap came past me as if I was standing still and easily finished first. I staggered in, absolutely knackered. The winner waited for me, and demanded to know which athletic club I was from in Civvy Street. I was rewarded with a look of blank amazement when I announced proudly, 'I'm not a runner, I'm a climber!' He walked away shaking his head. Later I discovered that he was a member of the national cross country squad, and that the four or five who had come in immediately behind me were members of the Pay Corps cross country team, who were the Army champions. This meant nothing to me then, but it did mean that my Corporal stopped calling me a 'consci' and the other lads in my barrack started talking to me!

Once I arrived at my 'permanent' Pay Office posting in February 1954 in Manchester, I started to run. The memory of that race at the Army inception centre stayed with me, for I had experienced for the first time the mesmeric feeling of moving along at speed through a snow-covered landscape, and like an addict I wanted to repeat the effect. A fellow member of the Pay Office and I joined the Manchester Athletic Club, and started training one night a week, then two, then three, until within a year I was running ten miles a day six times a week. This was mainly cross country, but when the summer came we took to the cinder track at Fallowfield, where the club had its headquarters. My climbing friends were amazed at my new-found enthusiasm, and I had a painful meeting with Joe Brown one night in 1955 when he demanded to know what his gentleman's gentleman was doing 'rushing around Manchester instead of climbing'. But I was not to be deterred, and for the next two years during National Service I trained and raced whenever I could. My dedication began to pay off when I came third in the Manchester and District Cross Country Championship, and second in the Leeds.

About the only positive thing I can say about the Army is that if you are good at sport, you are given every encouragement. Because everybody had to do National Service at that time, even the best sportsman had to sign up for a while, from First Division footballer to Olympic runner. I was therefore often running both against and with some of the best athletes of the generation. One of these was Stan Taylor,

Eric Beard – 'Beardie' to all who knew him – on his record-breaking Ben Nevis to Scafell run. (Photo: Dennis Gray)

who, I believe, did the very first four-minute mile. He was timed at four minutes exactly and, who knows, with modern electronic timing to hundredths of a second accuracy, if he might not have been the first to run *under* that magic time? Although I was never in his league, I got a great kick out of beating him a short while later in a road race held in Liverpool over 7 miles. Because of my athletic interest I was allowed special training leave at home, and on one of these occasions I met an athlete who has since become a legend in British climbing and fell running circles.

I was out training on the roads outside Leeds and panting away up a steep hill in Meanwood – I considered myself to be a bit of a man on the hills and was putting my heart and soul into it – when I became aware of another runner panting behind me. I put on more and more speed but I could not shake him off, then he passed me in a long, loping stride which appeared slow and easy. He waited for me at the top of the hill, and before I could get my breath back was demanding to know, 'What's your name, and which club are you from? I'm from the Leeds Athletic Club myself, and I'm Eric Beard.' I thought him pushy and did not take to him, but as I came to know him better, I realised this was extreme good humour and boisterous spirits. Long-armed and long-legged, dark, with a hawk-like face and a barrel chest, he had tremendous potential as a long-distance runner and was slowly climbing the ladder of athletic fame, after only a couple of years. Without any formal qualifications, his was the classic profile of a misspent youth, although he had never managed to become 'street-wise', and retained the essential simplicity of a child.

From that first meeting we trained together whenever I was at home, and he often came to my parents' house to meet my climbing friends. My father took to him as to a son. Unlike me, he was keen to learn the craft of being an entertainer, so my father taught him all the tricks of the trade of the stand-up comedian, and the rudiments of music, and Eric took up the guitar and developed his strong voice for singing. He had his sights set on the marathon race, and worked during the day as a greenkeeper on a golf course in order to have enough time for training. Completely dedicated, his job had to suit his running, and he had already given up the higher pay of a tram conductor, despite being voted Leeds' number one by the travelling public! Eric's ambition was to build up a team of road runners, and wanted nothing to stand in his way. Through him I joined the Leeds Athletic Club and we began to compete in road events, although I was still officially a junior.

On my demobilisation in January 1956, and subsequent return to Leeds, I introduced Beardie (as he became known to everybody) to climbing and my friends of the Rock and Ice. His impact was immediate. I remember one of his first climbs in the Llanberis Pass, when he had Joe Brown leading him, and Don Whillans climbing up behind solo, pointing out where he had to place his hands and feet. The rest of the club were watching from outside the tents in the Grochan's field when a car pulled up. A young climber jumped out and shouted across to us, 'Who are those two guys up there climbing with Beardie?'

Although Beardie never developed into an extreme rock climber, he quickly developed a keenness for mountaineering and a love of the hills, and his athletic prowess found a new outlet in feats on the British mountains which have made him a legend in fell racing circles. By 1969 he held the record for the Welsh 3,000s, the round of the Mountains of Mourne, the Skye Main Cuillin Ridge, the Cairngorm 4,000s and the Ben Nevis to Snowdon Summit, running all the way. He also held the Lakeland Fells 24-hour record, almost the blue riband of British fell running, but in retrospect his Cuillin record was the most outstanding for it stood for twenty-one years. These may read now as mere physical feats by a fanatic, but nothing could be further from the truth; throughout this whole period the one thing I do recall is that we laughed a hell of a lot!

One amusing incident happened in the summer of 1958, when Beardie, who was not then as good at impersonations as he was to become, was doing his Elvis Presley, standing on a table in the Bar National in Chamonix. The weather was atrocious outside, and the pub was packed with British climbers who were all joining in on the chorus, when in walked Whillans! He had an effect rather like the fastest gun in town in the old Wild West, and a hush descended as the whole crowd stopped singing, except for Beardie, who kept on belting it out.

'Beardie, is that song hard to sing?' rasped the Salford hard man. The singer finally stopped.

'Er no, Don. Why?'

'Well it's bleeding hard to listen to!' Then, punching his fist hard into a table, the Villain swung round and disappeared out into the rain-washed streets.

After National Service I found that I could not study, work, climb and run, so I had to cut down on the latter. Instead of training every day I used to go out for a spin once or twice a week, and of course in any races I entered this quickly showed. Unlike climbers, athletes in the late 1950s had a high standard of fitness and unless you had almost total dedication you were not going to win many prizes. I did have

Crossing the stepping stones in the Dovedale Dash. (Photo: Dennis Gray)

one moment of glory on the track when I won a mile race in 1956 at Headingley, running on the grass of the cricket pitch. My time of 4 minutes 34 seconds was eventually changed to 4 minutes 27, due to the lanes having being incorrectly measured! I had no illusions of grandeur from this performance, however, for athletic friends in Manchester – Geoff Lowe, Stan Taylor or Mike Berrisford – would have been half a lap ahead of me. I decided to become a recreational runner only, and simply keep up a reasonable level of fitness.

When I moved to live and work in Derby in 1959, Beardie came to share my lodgings at Nat Allen's mother's house for a while. She looked after us like two sons. We joined up with the local climbing groups, like the Oread Club and through Nat Allen met the Mercury Cycling Club. Every November the Mercury held a Bonfire Night event at Ilam Hall Youth Hostel in Derbyshire, including a panto- mime on the Saturday night and a run on the Sunday morning. In 1959 Beardie, the Rock and Ice, some other local climbers and I attended this weekend, as we saw it, for a laugh! Before the pantomime on the Saturday night the members of the cycling club challenged us to a competitive games session, and we were soon to find out that in wall squatting, British bulldogs and Indian wrestling we were no match for these two-wheeled champions; no wonder, perhaps, since they had members who had competed in everything from the Olympic Games to the Tour of Britain. We were cheered up by the hilarious pantomime which followed, produced by Tinsel Allen, Nat's wife, and with acting of a high order from certain members of her cast.

To wind up the meet, a cross country run was held on the Sunday morning on a course through part of famous Dovedale. This had been a feature of the Mercury calendar for several years, but 1959 was the first year that an outside group took part, and this became the first of many memorable 'Dovedale Dashes'. From that small beginning has grown up the most famous event of its type for cyclists, hikers, climbers, cavers and athletes, a must on many a climbing club meets list, and thousands are drawn to Derbyshire for the nearest weekend to 5 November each year. The run is still organised by the *Derby Mercury* who try to ensure that the original spirit of the race is maintained – it is an event for the super-fit athlete and the least fit of unfit climbers. The climbers are not really interested in who wins the race, but in personal challenges to climbing acquaintances: 'I'll beat you, unfit as I am!'

At that first open race in 1959 the cyclists beat the climbers hollow with Beardie being beaten in a sprint finish to the tape. It did not help that we did not know the course for it was not then marked out; I took a wrong turning and ran in the opposite direction altogether, adding an extra mile to the four-mile circuit! We vowed to gain our revenge in the Dash the following year. By then we were all good friends, and I helped with the pantomime, while Beardie became its star.

In November 1960 the river Dove was in high flood and the rain fell in torrents, driven by a cutting wind. The route of the Dash crosses the river by some stepping-stones and these were submerged under at least a foot of swift-flowing water. For safety's sake the race marshals had placed a climbing rope across the river, belayed from tree to tree, and competitors had to monkey over with the lower half of the body in the freezing water. The Rock and Ice were determined to win the team race (the first three home counting), and as we raced up to the stepping-stones Beardie was lying third, behind the Derbyshire schools champion, I was fifth, and our third man was a short way behind me. As the schools champion reached the water's edge and grabbed for the rope, Beardie overtook him to seize the rope on the outside. The champion, of tender years and small in stature, bounced off the rope like a fish jumping the line and plunged into the torrent. In true athlete's style, Beardie never looked back; he swung across the river like an ape and tore after the leader with barely a mile to go to the finish. Unknown to him, the schoolboy was in danger of drowning, struggling against the current, and several people had to jump into the river to help him. Derby climber Hank Harrison got the lad to the bank and I gave a hand to haul him up on to terra firma. By the time we had sorted ourselves out many runners had passed us, but the boy was a tiger and, spitting water from his lungs, he muscled across the rope in pursuit, with me close behind.

We passed runner after runner, the lad taking me with him as he cut a path through the wind and rain. I felt a bit guilty when I passed him in the drive of Ilam Hall, the two of us finishing fifth and sixth, but then he didn't stop. It became apparent why he had run so hard from the stepping-stones, for he tore straight at Beardie, who had won the race for the first time and was cheering in the other runners as they raced up the road. The boy obviously thought that the incident at the stepping-stones had been no accident, and Beardie was flabbergasted as the youth ran at him, fists flying and yelling abuse. It took three or four burly adults to restrain the angry boy. Eventually he was persuaded that his near drowning was by accident and not design, good humour was restored, and the Rock and Ice won the team race by a single point! It was a triumph for Beardie, who picked up both the winner's medal and a team one as our captain.

The 1960s rolled away, and Eric and I went our separate ways. Nat's mother and I had both found him a hard man to live with, for his single-minded dedication to his running meant that the kitchen and living room of her house were always either full of clothes drying, or mud from the fields. His diet took some keeping up with too, for his appetite was staggering. He could out-eat anyone I have ever met, and on one winter's night during an eating competition in the CIC hut on Ben Nevis he devoured seventeen pancakes! And that was after eating soup and stew first. He mellowed as he grew older and developed other talents – singing and entertaining, working with handicapped children, and mountaineering, at which he was no mean performer – but it was always running that dominated his life. For him running was like a drug; he had found what he could do best and he had to keep doing it. Some of his training routines were phenomenal and at one point he was running 240 miles a week.

One night in November 1969 the phone rang at home late on a Sunday night. I picked up the receiver and a voice said: 'This is Sergeant Burke here, Wigan Police. We have an unidentified body in the morgue, a victim of a car crash on the M6. All he was carrying is an envelope with a letter inside from you.' At first I thought it was Beardie, for he used to phone us from all corners of the country and pretend to be everyone from Tom Patey speaking in broad Scots to Don Whillans with his nasal Salford accent. But as the policeman went on I realised with growing shock and grief that this time it was no joke, and that it could only be Eric lying in the Wigan morgue.

Thus ended the career of someone who is remembered with great affection and respect by all who knew him. His records speak for themselves, but what they cannot tell is how good he was at making people laugh, and how he brought happiness to others simply by his presence. In those last years of his life he had grown into a great character and entertainer and his 'Beardie's Sing-Song', held twice weekly in the Cairngorms in the ski season, were attended by hundreds. He would persuade the most unlikely people to take to the stage, tell a story, sing a song or play an instrument, while he acted as MC of the evening, and undertook everything from playing the guitar and folk singing to fair impressions of Elvis Presley, Little Richard and Buddy Holly. I drove him to the 1969 Dovedale Dash on 2 November, the last race we were to run in together. We enjoyed the outing immensely and afterwards I dropped him on his way to Liverpool where he was going to prepare for an attempt on the world record for a 24-hour run. 'So long, pal,' he said, pulling a large monster's hand over his own and waving a typical comical farewell that had my young son in stitches. 'See you!' We never did see him again.

Despite training a lot over the Lakeland fells when I had lived at Coniston, I did not run in a race event there until 1974. I had accepted an invitation from the Manchester-based climbing club, the Karabiner, to become their President, and the holder of that title was naturally expected to take part in one of their major social events, a fell race held in September. My first outing was held in the area of the Lake District that I thought I knew best, the Coniston Fells. It began in the Coppermines Valley, crossed the Old Man of Coniston, then went across and down into the Duddon Valley. From there it came back round behind Dow Crag, up to the summit, then down again to Goats Water and from there back over the Old Man of Coniston to finish in the Coppermines Valley. The weather was good, and I had persuaded Tim Leech to accompany me. Although I had kept up running, and introduced Tim to this activity to improve his fitness, we only ran twice a week for about two or three miles each time, so we expected to be tested.

All went well for the first part of the race, but by the time we had reached the Duddon Valley we were shattered – we had been running for over an hour and still had another couple to go! It is terribly difficult to run at speed in such terrain, and we kept twisting our ankles on the tufted grass of the high fells or the boulder fields of the Old Man, or tripping up in the bracken down in the Duddon. We grew more and more tired but kept struggling on. By the time we had reached the top of Dow Crag we were in no state to appreciate the magnificent views, and hoping for some input of energy, I begged a block of chocolate from the person manning the checkpoint. This kept us going for a while, but the final steep scree slopes of the Old Man of Coniston took their toll. On reaching the summit all I wanted to do was lie down, but Tim insisted we keep going and we stumbled into the Coppermines Valley.

'I'll kill that Ken Beetham,' I snarled, 'he's a bloody sadist!' – Ken had set the course.

On the way down into the valley Tim shot off in front, whilst I shambled along behind, still uncharitably cursing the poor course setter, until I painfully reached the finishing line – at a walk. Tim and I had to agree that this had been the hardest outing ever. It was not until later that I discovered it need not have been quite such a trial; I had made a mistake, and the double crossing of the Old Man had not been intended by Ken! I had wondered why we hadn't seen any other runners since Goats Water! Somehow, I thought it was better to keep this revelation to myself, and declined to tell my young apprentice what I knew ...

Two years later we faced another gruelling experience together in our first Karrimor International Mountain Marathon. The Karrimor began in the late 1960s, a combination of fell running and orienteering, held in a different mountain region every year. Navigational skills are crucial to a successful completion of the course in any of the classes – Elite, A, B and C (based on distance and difficulty of navigation). The event is held over a weekend and participants must camp out on the Saturday night, so a tent, stove and food have to be carried. By 1976 the event had grown in size and importance, and I was flattered to be invited to present the prizes. The location that year was the remote Galloway Highlands in Scotland, and when Tim Leech and I arrived an astonishing number of tents had already been put up at the campsite in Glen Trool. More and more came during the night, and we tried in vain to sleep, continually disturbed by the rain beating down and by the noise of the new arrivals.

Early the next morning I sauntered over to the officials' tent to meet Mike Parsons, the boss of Karrimor, and Gerry Charnley, the driving force behind the event.

'Got your gear ready, Gray?' demanded Mike.

'Er, no. No lightweight tent, no stove, and we're not entered anyway. I thought you just wanted me here to present the prizes. Tim and I are just going up the Merrick, that's all.'

'Rubbish! I'm doing the A class, and you're in the B. Gerry and the boys will kit you out!'

Fifteen minutes later, in driving rain and sleet, carrying borrowed rucksacks and equipment, and wearing heavy mountaineering clothes and boots, Tim and I lined

The first ever Chevin Chase in 1979. (Photo: Dennis Gray Collection)

up with hundreds of others for the start of the B class. Everyone else was wearing lightweight fell running clothes and we felt conspicuous amongst all those fit athletes. From the first, however, it became obvious that we were lucky to be wearing our heavy clothes after all, for the driving rain turned to a blizzard once we reached the high ground of the Merrick (2,776 feet). Many of the runners were in danger of severe exposure and were forced to return to the start. There was a BBC camera crew there, filming one of their daredevil presenters who had recently been thrilling her viewers by parachuting, ski jumping and other acts of derring-do. She came staggering the other way, in full retreat, declaring, 'You're all bloody mad.' I had to agree with her.

We took great care over our map reading and this became the only Karrimor (of four) in which we made not the slightest navigational error. At times it was difficult to see the ground at all – the mist was down and the driving snow made it hard to look up – but worst of all was the fact that there were no paths. On the lower slopes, wading through heather and bracken became increasingly tiring as the day wore on. I was frankly surprised at the speed some participants attained – if you came across one of the Elite teams either crossing your route or moving along a part of it, they were like hares in comparison to our tortoise-like progress. It was a revelation how good these runners had become at this relatively new sport. Tim and I staggered along in our big boots, pleased to find that we were, nevertheless, overtaking party after party. We reached the overnight campsite, on the side of a windswept lochan, shortly after four in the afternoon. It is traditional that, although all the classes have different routes, they camp together on the Saturday night, and it was an incredible sight to see 2,000 people in lightweight tents camping in the heart of some of the wildest country in Scotland.

That night we found that our borrowed, single-skin bivouac tent leaked like a sieve. The rain poured through it and by midnight we were soaked to the skin. The wind howled and shrieked and blew down tents and made sleeping impossible. I

Rob Uttley, who died so tragically in the Himalaya in 1983. The Chevin Chase is now a memorial to him. (Photo: Mr and Mrs Uttley)

dozed off just once and was awakened by the noise of Tim's teeth chattering. 'This is worse than a bivvy in the Alps in winter!' was his only comment.

We packed up to the skirl of bagpipes and were away at first light. We had plenty of time to finish the course, and the weather had improved so much that by nine o'clock the sun had come out. We simply sauntered along, walking and jogging, whilst runners criss-crossed around us like bees going in and out of a hive.

The finish was a glad sight to see and we trotted in happily. We were still soaked to the skin despite the improved conditions, and as we sat drinking a cup of tea Tim and I both admitted that we had never dreamt this new sport would be so demanding. Later, I had the greatest pleasure in making the presentation to the winners of the B class, one of my oldest friends, Jack Bloor, and his teenage son Robert. Jack had been Arthur Dolphin's closest friend, and I had shared my first climb on Clogwyn Du'r Arddu with him when I was only 14.

In 1979 Leni and I decided to found our own race, a northern equivalent of the Dovedale Dash. It was to be a Christmas event, not to be taken too seriously, and aimed at everyone from the youngest of runners to the oldest of climbers. We soon found out that organising such a competition is no picnic; there is the course to be prepared, the marshalling, the changing, starting and finishing arrangements, the timing, and the catering, for it is essential to have refreshments available at the end of a winter's run. I spent days planning the route, running around it across Otley Chevin, close to my home in Guiseley, and on Boxing Day 1979 the first Chevin Chase Run was held. The course was quite tough, nearly seven miles long, with short sections of road, some big hills, some woods and a lot of moorland. Within a decade the Chevin Chase had become so popular that there were almost 1,000 entrants for the senior race, and 200 for the junior section (introduced in 1980 with its own, shorter and less demanding course).

At that first event we gave prizes for every category we could think of – the first three home, the first under-21, the first under-18, the first lady and the first local runner, among others. We had opened a small retail outdoor shop by then, and simply plundered the stock! Of course, we also awarded a prize to the first climber, and the winner that year was Rob Uttley, a young friend who boarded at the local public school. I used to take him climbing with me on Sundays at Almscliff, Caley or Brimham, and he developed into a brilliant climber, being short, powerful and thick-set. After school he moved to Sheffield University to study, and to be near the good rock climbing in the Peak District. He quickly made his mark in the local climbing circles, and in the Alps, where on his very first visit in 1981 he ascended the North Face of the Grandes Jorasses.

In October 1983 he joined a British team, made up of young climbers in an attempt on a new route in the Annapurna range of the Himalaya. In a forced descent from a high camp in a blizzard he became ill with what must have been a pulmonary infection. Unable to move him, his companion, Trevor Pilling, descended to alert Nik Kekus and Jon Tinker for a rescue bid. The weather turned savage and, try as they might, they could not get back up the flanks of Annapurna 11 to reach Rob. Thus he perished. This sad news reached me via the Foreign Office at the BMC. When I spoke to Rob's mother, she seemed unable to accept that it could be true. Her son had been 21, with so much to look forward to and such a powerful personality; once again we had lost a friend in the mountains. At Nik Kekus's suggestion, we agreed that the Chevin Chase should become the Rob Uttley Memorial Race, in tribute to Rob, who had been one of its keenest supporters.

In 1987 I handed the Rob Uttley Memorial Race over to the Guiseley Sports Centre (which had become a Mecca for climbers with its large artificial climbing wall), and a local running club which met there, and they have continued to organise the event with great success every 26 December.

The 1980s ushered in mass participation in running, particularly in marathons. I had never wanted to take part in one, although I often saw John Disley, Course Director of the London Marathon, at Plas y Brenin meetings, when he ribbed me about entering, and even offered me a guaranteed place. I had always declined, until one particularly stormy meeting about the centre's future, when I thought, 'What the hell!', and agreed to run in the next event. Within a week details of my entry in the 1982 race landed on my desk in the BMC office. It was literally only a few weeks away. I had done no training, busy at that time with BMC affairs. Had I known what was in store I would not have had the arrogance to think that I could jog a marathon any day I cared to try!

When I arrived in London in April the scale of the event took my breath away. On the Saturday I climbed at Harrison's Rocks and then drove up to Greenwich where I slept out for the night, to be awakened in the early hours by the first runners arriving. About 20,000 of us started out at 9.30 am in cold, drizzly conditions and I realised after five miles that I was going to be lucky to finish, although it was heart-lifting to see all the supporters as we ran through the rain-washed streets – the route was lined every inch of the way with cheering people. Jazz bands, West Indian steel bands, and military bands gave a tremendous feel to the whole thing, and there was a warmth of atmosphere; many of the runners around me were obviously as unfit as I was, and were running simply for charity. Some were dressed in clown outfits, or monkey suits, and there was a pantomime horse, an emu, and a goose. There were also many disabled people taking part and I was glad to be in their midst.

Stupidly I had stripped down to shorts and T-shirt at the start, and the wet and cold soon began to eat into me. At fifteen miles I nearly gave up, and by twenty I was almost in a trance. I had never known it was possible to hurt in so many places at once. I never hit the famous 'Marathon wall', which you are supposed to do at about 22 miles; I had it all the way, from about the first hour onwards. I crawled home over Westminster Bridge in over five hours, and I can remember resolving as I ran past Buckingham Palace never to do anything like this again! I arrived home with my head down, but carrying a finisher's medal.

'What time did you do?' Robin asked me as soon as I came through the door on the Sunday night.

'Oh . . . *hours*,' I replied.

'We watched for you on the telly,' said Helen, 'but you never appeared.'

'They only put on the first 15,000 and I finished 16,343,' I told her.

'*16,343!* You must be hopeless!' was her comment.

This rankled, so, despite my resolve, I decided to do the London Marathon again, and this time I did some training. I was back in 1984, when the weather was cool but dry, and my time improved dramatically. I came in in just over 4 hours. When I arrived home this time, Helen's observation was, 'If you keep on improving at that rate, Dad, another two runs and you'll win it!'

I have now been running for over thirty years, and in semi-retirement I can indulge myself more than in times past. My next aims are the High Atlas Marathon in Marrakesh, the famous race in Boston, and the Friendship Marathon in Eastern Europe, not to see if I can record a good time, but just for the fun of it. Running has given me many happy memories: of the lanes around Nairobi, where I had to run with a stone in either hand to ward off the vicious wild dogs, of the desert south of Tiznit in Morocco on the fringe of the Sahara, and of Chamonix with Eric Beard, when we ran up the Montenvers railway track to arrive in the early evening in time to catch the Aiguilles Drus and Verte aflame with the setting sun. I have never really cared much whether I have won or lost, but I have at times experienced a certain ecstasy in running through open countryside, either with friends or alone. Like climbing, I have found running to be life-enhancing, an antidote to modern urban living that is an important discovery for everyone who makes it.

The Eastern Bloc

He tried to bridge the gap that lies between the West and East, that climbers might all brothers be in the kingdoms of the snow.

From a song by Tom Patey

One of the positive aspects of mountaineering is its internationalism. It is practised in almost sixty countries around the globe, and one of its strongest heartlands is Eastern Europe. In Poland, East Germany and Czechoslovakia, for example, are to be found some of the best climbers and climbing in the world, while in Russia are some of the highest mountains and a large number of adherents to the sport. Because of political difficulties there have been long periods of isolation between climbers from these areas, but in the west we have always been aware that the mountaineers of these countries are no different from us in their love of the mountains. In my forty years of climbing there have been periods of political hostility and periods of detente between East and West, times when it has been possible to travel to countries like Bulgaria and times when this has not been the case. At official government level contacts were maintained, and at the BMC we had a policy of positive discrimination to try to help climbers from the Eastern bloc visit Britain. In the 1970s and 1980s, under our twice-yearly international visits programme and at our Buxton conferences we often met climbers from Russia, Poland and Czechoslovakia who had come in a group or as speakers.

During the 1950s and early 1960s such exchanges between East and West were much more rare. John Hunt led two British parties to Russia, one to climb in the Caucasus, the other in the Pamirs, and in 1966 a Polish party visited Britain. This led to a return invitation being made for a group of British climbers to visit the Tatra mountains in the summer of 1967. I had always wanted to go behind the Iron Curtain, and as soon as I heard about this invitation I wrote to John Hunt, who had contacts with the Poles, and to the Klub Wysokogorski in Warsaw. Within a few weeks I had back official permission to take a party of four British climbers to the High Tatra mountains in July and August 1967, and a request to give some lectures on my expeditions to Alpamayo, Yosemite and Gauri Sankar.

At about this time I suffered serious injuries to my hands from rope burns, and nearly had to have my right forefinger amputated so badly was the tendon damaged. Luckily a climbing surgeon I knew examined my injuries and suggested immersing my hands in wax baths, which worked miracles. Six weeks later I could use all my fingers, including the worst one, but it did leave me with permanent scars, and a certain lack of skill in manipulation. I was not to be deterred by these problems and felt that even if I could only make some easy climbs the trip to Poland would be worthwhile.

Near the end of July 1967 four of us – Jim McArtney and me in one vehicle, and Jimmy McDowell and Tom Morrell in Tom's car – set out in convoy over the Continental roads. We were two Scots and Yorkshiremen, a typically disorganised group of climbers, who soon lost each other somewhere on the German autobahns and didn't meet up again until we got to Zakopane, the main centre in southern

Poland for the Tatra. At that time there were no diplomatic arrangements between the DDR and Britain, and Jim McArtney and I had an incredible time getting in and out of the country. We could have been characters in a cold war spy thriller. Jim was an Aberdonian, the strongest ice climber and hardest drinker of his generation, built like the kilted man on the front of a packet of Scot's Porridge Oats, a great singer and an ardent Communist. His tragic death on Ben Nevis in January 1970, combined with the loss of Eric Beard, Tom Patey and Ian Clough all within a few months of each other, marked the saddest period of my climbing career.

Jim thought his membership of the British Communist Party would open all the DDR doors for us, but the grilling we received for hours on end by a woman from their State Security (the spitting image of James Bond's friend Rosa Klebb) soon dispelled his illusions. He was a dangerous revisionist, I was a tool of the capitalist system, and we were not welcome in this land of pure and undiluted socialism. We were, however, allowed a 24-hour transit visa to drive across the DDR to Poland, with the route prescribed and with no variations allowed. Jim could not give a damn about such things, and insisted that we drive here and there to talk with and stay amongst the East Germans. For five days we travelled around the country, and were surprised to find that this was no Utopian socialist state, but a policed country with the Soviets as overlords. The people were incredibly friendly and Jim won their hearts by drinking all the beer they placed before him, and singing Scots airs – off key!

We camped outside Karl Marxstadt amongst a group of young students by a lake, and were astonished to discover that we were the first Westerners they had ever met! They listened avidly but secretly to the BBC, and some of them spoke excellent English. They seemed frightened to discuss politics with us, but after a few beers it became obvious that they longed for more freedom. They lived in state-owned concrete multi-storey flats, and everything, from the kind of music they could listen to on the radio to their schooling, was regulated by the Party. We travelled south and visited the sandstone cliffs in the Elbe valley, and some impressively hard climbs, and then headed for Poland. When our retribution came, it was swift. At the border with Poland we were sent back by the East German guards to where we had come from – Berlin – where we faced stern questioning. 'Where had we been for the past five days? Who had we spoken to?' They seemed unhappy with our answers, and we then spent a whole day trying to get back into the West. We wandered back and forth between the posts at Checkpoint Charlie; the Soviets were booting us out, and the Allies would not let us back in! It was a bad time for spies, it seems. Finally, a kindly Canadian Colonel took pity on us, saying, 'I was a backpacker too in my youth!' (the first time I ever heard the term), and let us back into the West.

We then had to face Rosa Klebb again to try to get another transit visa. Pleading stupidity and ignorance, and dressed in his kilt, Jim put on a performance that would have melted ice. At one point he even jumped up and kissed Rosa, taking my breath away; I was sure that we would be in the Lubyanka for the rest of our days. With Jim you had to expect the unexpected, and there was method in his madness. Rosa's attitude suddenly changed, and she became convinced that we were not spies but utterly deranged – nobody ever kissed senior officials in the State Security Police! We were given our visas and warned about what would happen to us if we did not get to Poland in the allotted 24 hours this time. We needed no second bidding, although, travelling with Jim, it seems surprising now that we ever reached journey's end.

Poland in 1967 was much freer than the DDR, but it was obvious that some major political upheaval was going to take place soon, either there or in Czechoslovakia. Once we were in the Tatra mountains we mixed freely with the climbers, and through our interpreter, Taduez Jankowski (appointed by the Klub Wysokogorski), we learned of their hopes for more freedom and for democracy. The Tatra mountains lie on the borders of southern Poland and northern Czechoslovakia, in a national park, with camping and access routes strictly controlled. They are amongst the most visited mountains in the world, providing good granite climbing in summer, demanding winter climbing, excellent ski facilities – a magnet for hillwalkers and tourists alike. Unlike its neighbour Czechoslovakia, Poland has little climbing apart from this range, so that Polish climbers tend to be hardy mountaineers, rather than rock gymnasts, and in the last decade they have been a major force in Himalayan exploration.

We either camped or stayed in the network of climbing huts around the range, and during our month-long stay the weather was atrocious – as wet as Glen Brittle. We found that the rock had good friction when dry, but soon became like soap when wet and was almost unclimbable. We spent most of our days in the Morskie Oko Valley, staying at the Klub Wysokogorski campsite, and marvelled at the resilience of our Polish and Czechoslovak friends, most of whom simply slept out in the open without a tent, whether it rained or not! The Morskie Oko Valley is beautiful, with two large lakes trapped between granite walls and, towering over the Morskie Oko lake, the 3,000-foot face of Mieguszowiecki, one of the highest summits of the range at 7,518 feet. Mirrored in the lake are the pine forests and the reflection of Mnich, the Matterhorn of the Tatra, can often be seen too. The faces were easily accessible from the campsite and attracted us strongly. My hands were troubling me whenever I attempted any of the major climbs, and the folly of being too ambitious too soon after my accident was brought home to me early in our visit. I was on a climb with Jim McArtney, leading a pitch of V superior (the Poles use the Welzenbach system as in the Alps). I had led out perhaps sixty feet of rope, obtained a good thread runner and could see a large ledge about fifteen feet up; between this ledge and me was a corner groove split by a thin finger-width crack. I started to jam up it. This hurt my hands but I had almost reached the ledge when my fingers suddenly cramped. I could no longer feel the rock, the pain was acute, and I was in danger of somersaulting out of the groove backwards. I was wearing heavy boots and luckily on the corner of the left wall was a small, sharp-cut hold; I stuck my foot on this and balanced across swiftly without any hand holds, the kind of thing you might do on a boulder as a 'no hands' problem! Shaking with fright, I grabbed the edge of the ledge with the palms of my hands and threw myself into a mantelshelf to land, panting but safe, on the balcony. This taught me a lesson and from then on I was mainly content to traverse the ridges, which offer superb but easy scrambling on the knife-edges of firm granite.

During our stay I gave lectures in Zakopane at the National Park Headquarters, and at the Mountain Rescue station, and finally at the Morskie Oko hut. I then left the other three, and departed to give talks in Cracow, Oswieciem (Auschwitz) and Warsaw. Those last days in Poland made a lasting impression. I arrived at the Auschwitz concentration camp on my own, by car from Cracow. I thought I knew about the atrocities of war, and had been a pacifist since I was young, but nothing had prepared me for anything so terrible. I could only gaze in horror at what is preserved there, appalled at the scale of it and wonder that nations professing to a Christian faith could have spawned such an evil. Most frightening was the fact that it had all been planned by architects, engineers, scientists, administrators and doctors, some of whom, for all I knew, might have loved the mountains just as I do.

On a beautiful morning I wandered around the deserted barracks, the ruins, and the gas chambers. I sat alone beneath the massive, stark, stone sculptured memorial to the dead and wondered who I was and what I was doing there.

My trip to Warsaw was no less edifying, staying with the only Jew in the Polish government in her small flat in the beautiful old town. This area was completely devastated in the war, but has now been totally rebuilt. I had learned from Tadeuz Jankowksi about the Warsaw uprising – as a twelve-year-old boy he had fought in it and been badly injured – but from my hostess I heard for the first time about the fate at the end of the last war of the Jews in the Warsaw ghetto when her family had been almost annihilated. I was moved by the sights and terrible memorials she took me to see.

My lectures were greeted with great enthusiasm, for at that time Polish climbers had little first-hand knowledge about climbing in the Andes and the USA. I was struck by the way in which the climbing fraternity was as it had been in Britain after the war; they were close-knit and friendly, and although few had any material wealth, what they had they shared. I was impressed by the numbers of Czechoslovak and Polish climbers I met who were involved in the dissident freedom movements. The following year this was to be their undoing, as the unlucky ones among them were killed or faced prison in the Prague Spring. There was even a show trial in Poland known as 'The case of the dissident mountain climbers'; these people were implicated in supporting the Czech Uprising in 1968. As I drove out of Warsaw for home in early September 1967, there was student unrest and riots in the streets, and soon once again the Soviet masters were to regain their iron grip and contact with the West was to become more difficult.

Against all the odds, two climbers, one from Poland, the expert Himalayan mountaineer Janus Onyszkiewicz who I had met in the Tatra, and Alison Chadwick from Cornwall, met, fell in love and married. From March 1968 Janus became a prominent figure in the dissident movement in Poland and now twenty years later, after a life that could provide enough material for several books, he is a member of their first Solidarity government. Alison was an art teacher, a graduate of the Slade and Warsaw art colleges, who met Janus whilst studying in Poland. In 1971 Janus came to Britain to claim his bride, and they returned to live in Warsaw. Over the next few years, with the Klub Wysokogorski, they were to take part in expeditions together and in 1975 Alison and a team of Polish women climbers made the first ascent of Gasherbrum III (26,090 feet), and Janus, with a men's expedition to nearby Gasherbrum II, was able to join them on its summit. Gasherbrum III was the highest mountain ever to be first climbed by a woman.

In 1977 tensions in East/West relations had eased sufficiently for Janus and Alison to come to Leeds University on an exchange visit. They immediately became a part of our local climbing fraternity, and would visit us regularly at Guiseley. Janus had a real rapport with our children. A laughing, blond man, he was a real contrast to Alison, who was statuesque, with long dark hair, and almost Madonna-like. They were a love match and we were always happy to see them, to share a meal and to have interesting discussions about politics, climbing and the Eastern bloc.

Janus was convinced even then that change must come sooner or later, for he knew that 'the people want more freedom'. In 1978 Alison was invited to join an American women's expedition in Annapurna 1, whilst Janus was to take part in a British trip to Himalchuli. We said our goodbyes at the end of the summer, and never saw Alison again.

Alison was killed on Annapurna on 17 October 1978, in a mysterious fall with her companion Vera Watson at an awkward step around 24,000 feet. Comparatively unknown in Britain at the time, because so many of her outstanding climbs had been made in the Polish Tatra, she was probably the most accomplished British woman mountaineer. After her death Janus returned to Warsaw where he became more and more active in the Solidarity movement. Because of his Western connections, and his outspoken reports to the foreign press on Solidarity's behalf, he was an immediate target whenever the political situation became tense, and when martial law was declared in 1981 he was interned in the notorious Bialoleka Prison for over a year. Some British climbing friends and I organised a campaign to try to secure his release, bombarding the Polish President with personal letters expressing our concern, but not to much avail. Six months after his release he was back in jail again, and then again as recently as summer 1988 when, after a wave of strikes by the workers, he had given interviews to the BBC, Radio Free Europe and the Voice of America, and been convicted of 'disseminating false information aimed at fomenting unrest'. Jail seemed to hold no terrors for him and in a letter to a mutual friend he once confessed that, compared to the bivouac he had survived high on K2, it was an easy life! The fairytale ending came about with Solidarity triumphant in Poland and Janus a member of their first government. Every time I see him on the television speaking on their behalf, I feel proud to know that he is a friend and a fellow climber.

In 1974 I was invited to take part in a climbing meet in the Rila mountains of Bulgaria, and Michael Butler and I flew to Sofia not knowing what to expect. Although almost all the Eastern bloc nations had joined the UIAA by then, including Russia and Bulgaria, no one seemed to know anything about the climbing possibilities in the smaller country. We were treated with great courtesy and, as we were guests of state, no expense was spared in providing hospitality. We stayed in a plush hotel in Sofia, then were driven in mini-buses to the Rila mountains on the southern borders of Bulgaria with Greece.

We were astonished to find a large, modern complex in the Rila mountains called the Bulgarian National Mountaineering Centre, rather extravagant, we thought, in a country with only a few thousand climbers. We were even more impressed to meet the world's first Professor of Mountaineering, who was in charge of climbing arrangements there, and attached to Sofia University. Exactly what his duties at the university were we never found out, but his main climbing experience seemed to have been in the Pamirs and he ran the Bulgarian meet in the same way as Soviet mountaineering camps are run. The meet participants had to decide which climb they wished to try and were given a start time; if they were not back at the centre in an allotted number of hours, a rescue team would set out to look for them. The mountains were on about the same scale as our homeland hills, and the longest climbs about 800 feet in length! All the other climbers at the meet, mainly from the Eastern bloc, meekly accepted these restrictions, as did those from other Western nations who were there. We, however, caused an international incident by refusing to sign in and out and declare which climbs we were going to attempt. From then on wherever we went we were conscious of mountain rescue personnel dogging our footsteps with two-way radio, reporting on our progress.

The area around the Rila mountains is beautiful, verdant green in the valleys, with jagged rocky summits, and some fine ridges, but the rock is basalt, loose and not very good for climbing. In the valley above the centre was a large rock face, the biggest in the area, perhaps 1000 feet high, declared by 'The Professor' to be 'out of bounds', as it had not then been climbed. Michael and I had to have a go! Our whole visit was beginning to take on a cops and robbers slant as we crept out of the centre early one morning and raced up to the face. From its base it was rather like Sron na Ciche on Skye and about the same scale; we picked out a line of corners and grooves and Michael led up the first section. He is a high standard free rock climber, impressively strong, and one of the people I know who can do one-arm pull-ups.

All went well for the first pitches, which provided some good crack climbing at about Very Severe standard, but we soon found out why the face had not been climbed, for the higher we went the looser and dirtier it became. In the Rila mountains, even on the popular climbs a sort of black sludge oozes out of the cracks every time it rains, and many of the holds are covered with oily dirt when it is dry. Not for modern rock jocks . . . no sir!

Though easy, the climbing became more and more serious, and I took over the lead near the top of the route, to climb a series of terrifyingly loose blocks piled one on top of the other. 'This is no bloody joke Mike, do you think we should shout for help?'

'No way! The Professor will have your guts for garters if you do,' was his advice. So fear of the wrath of one man kept us going, climbing up some of the loosest basalt you could find anywhere. Just below the top I was stopped on a ledge below a square-cut corner of firmer rock, and try as I might I could not bridge up it.

'I'll have to bring you up, Mike,' I shouted down to my second. When he arrived at my belay he took one look at the corner, and swung round its left side and out on to a steep wall. With a few grunts, and a 'Watch me!', he had climbed up it. An impressive effort, I had to admit, as we sat on the summit ridge of the crag, eating a Mars bar and wondering what our punishment would be for making this forbidden ascent. 'Maybe we'll be forced to enrol next term at Sofia University to study mountaineering?' I suggested.

On the way down we met the inevitable man from the rescue service with his two-way walkie-talkie, reporting in to base on our movements, but back at the centre no one said a word about our illegal climb. At the end of the meet there was a prize-giving ceremony, hosted by the Professor. 'The hardest lead' was won by a young Czech, 'fastest time' by the Soviets, and then 'best climb of the meet', the new British route which Michael and I had made! We were very embarrassed about this, but the plaques were well meant and proffered in a spirit of genuine friendship.

Even if the rock climbing was none too good, in the Rila Mountains, this spirit was always evident. The local people were marvellous. On our last evening, we had a great sing-song in the local tavern and a drinking celebration that left us the worse for wear the next morning as we sped to Sofia to catch a plane back to London. We both agreed that the best thing about the meet had been the chance to meet climbers from other countries. In a bouldering session one of the young Czechs had been so impressive that we had discussed with him at some length the climbing possibilities in his country. He was a sandstone climber and spent every weekend he could on the towers of the Bohemian Paradise near to his home in Turnov, and as we said goodbye to him, I resolved that one day I would go to see these climbing areas for myself. If they could produce a climber such as Tomas, they must be something special!

In March 1984 I attended a UIAA meeting in Prague and persuaded Jiri Novak to take me climbing. Unlike the climbing areas of the DDR, which are spread out over many miles, the Czech routes are in 'towns' of hundreds of pinnacles grouped together; indeed, at the biggest centre, Adrspach, there are over a thousand summits. The three areas in Czechoslovakia are all set in the north of the country, and the nearest to Prague is the Bohemian Paradise, about sixty miles away towards the border with the DDR. The weather that March was snowy and cold, so we could not climb in the sandstone areas; the rain and snow permeate the rock and make it soft and unreliable, and wet sandstone is almost the worst possible rock for friction. However, on the edge of the Paradise, one rock face, the Suchych Skala, overhangs so much that it stays dry whatever the weather. This is where we decided to climb.

This was very much a fleeting visit, for I had only one day to spare, so we left Prague very early in the morning. As we drove north it began to snow. What do climbers from worlds apart, thrown together like this, talk about, with little common language, and different political systems and educational backgrounds? We talked about climbing, of course, about the Himalaya, about mutual climbing friends and, despite linguistic problems, got by in an odd mixture of pidgin German and Italian.

The Suchych Skala is a most unusual wall of rock about 200 feet high at its apex, with stone more like limestone than sandstone. As we walked up to its base in the snow, I asked anxiously, 'Will we climb?' 'Si, si,' Jiri replied. And climb we did, despite the blizzard which set in shortly afterwards. Once on the face and climbing we were sheltered and totally isolated from the elements. I watched with interest as Jiri climbed, for all the protection he placed was by knotting slings of various thicknesses and jamming them in cracks as we moved up. The Czech and East German climbers have developed this unique system of protecting themselves because of the softness of their rock. They also use small thread runners which are to be found in the sandstone, seeming to rely on them totally; I must say I am sceptical of their ability to hold a really serious fall.

After we had climbed two classic routes, Jiri took me off to show me around some of the climbing areas of the Czech Paradise. It was impressive, the more so because the snow emphasised the architecture and isolation of many of the towers – a forest of skyscraper-like rock pinnacles, many 400 feet high, ranged in serried ranks, glimpsed through whirling snowflakes.

'You must come to Adrspach and Teplice for the mountaineering film festival some year, in September,' Vera Millerova, the Secretary of the Czech Federation, told me as she drove me to catch my plane the next morning. 'I will try to get you an invitation to bring a party of British climbers to it as our guests.' In 1987 she kept this promise and three climbers and a 'coach' were invited to Czechoslovakia as official guests of her federation. Toby Kelsey, Craig Smith and Tony Ryan were the climbers, and I was the inevitable 'official' demanded by the old Eastern bloc regimes – the coach.

We arrived at Teplice in early September 1987. The film festival is very much the brainchild of Czech climber Miri Smid, a huge bearded bear of a man who lives in the area, to the north-east of Prague. We went to see him as soon as we arrived, and found him on crutches, recovering from a parapente accident in the Caucasus. 'If you go to the USSR to climb and have an accident, for God's sake don't let them take you to one of their hospitals. Catch the first plane you can back to the West! I nearly died in the Crimea, their hospital was so badly equipped,' he warned. I laughed. It was good to see this old friend again. 'I am including you in the Rest of the World side to play the Adrspach eleven,' he confided to me as we were leaving. So, I had been picked for the traditional football match held on the final night of the festival. 'Oh, thanks ... ' I mumbled, without much enthusiasm.

The weather was terrible during the festival at Teplice, pouring with rain and very cold – 'the worst summer we have ever seen', Vera assured us. In between the film shows (some of the worst anyone had ever seen), we were involved in much socialising – guided walks around the rock towers, meeting other climbers and drinking sessions with crowds of locals. After one of these I distinguished myself by sliding down a steep mud slope, and spearing my right palm with a lopped-down tree branch like a dagger. It went right through the flesh and the blood spurted, much to Vera's consternation. In the evenings, by which time the weather was usually fine, there were celebrations on the football ground: one night a rock concert, another a country and western festival with vigorous swing dancing, and on the final evening the winning film shown on a giant screen. There was also the famous football match – with 5,000 spectators – where I found myself at right

The Kings Tower at Adrspach – Czech sandstone. (Photo: Jiri Novak)

The author playing right back for the Rest of the World at the Teplice film festival. (Photo: Dr J. Wolf)

back, with a mixture of climbers from Poland, East Germany and Romania. The pace was fast and furious, but very friendly, and the Czechs even let me score a set-up goal to square the match in its dying seconds. At this the spectators threw their pilsen in the air!

After such levity, it took me some time to recover enough energy to get stuck into the climbing. At last, when the festival finished, the promised good weather conditions arrived and remained with us for the rest of our stay. Toby and I teamed up to climb classic routes, whilst Craig and Tony went for the hard climbs. We were intrigued to find out about the history and methods of climbing in the region, and about their grading system. The climbs are protected by knotted slings, threads or huge ring bolts which are all placed on the lead. You belay on the latter, often just hanging in space. Adrspach/Teplice is the biggest of the Czech sandstone climbing regions, with famous climbs such as Paprika and the Valley Crack, on superb rock. Surprisingly, probably because of its remoteness and the difficulty of access, the region was not opened up for climbing until the 1920s when Fritz Wiessner climbed the Kings Tower. The other sandstone areas were developed long before this, with the first climbs being recorded on the German side of the border in Saxony, and those in Czechoslovakia being made in 1888. The Czech Paradise was first climbed on at the turn of the century and there were Grade VII climbs recorded in both Germany and Czechoslovakia by that date which were then undoubtedly the hardest rock climbs anywhere in the world.

The Czech grading system is complex, for the hardest routes are all graded the same – VIIc – and this has stood for decades. The East German system, however, is open-ended, currently up to Xc, so when a Czech tells you the grade of a hard climb he may say, 'It's VIIc and 9a,' or 'VIIb and 8a'. We found it very confusing and on many of the climbs we were not sure what we were allowed to use, but we knew wherever there was a ring bolt it was usually possible to stop and rest . . . somehow! Our general inclination was to try to free climb everything, and there were many times when Toby and I would not have found the solution without our Czech guides, who climbed ahead of, behind or, on occasion, with us. This was the case when we were climbing the Mayors Tower, one of the highest and most famous of the towers of Adrspach, with Milos Noseck and Mr Laorch. I called him 'Mr' because I never knew his first name. He was a giant, perhaps the tallest man I have ever climbed with, and at a large cleft in the rocks the solution was for Mr Laorch to fall across it, with feet on one side and palms against the other, and for us all to climb precariously over him, using him as a ladder! We then pulled him up after us. The upper lip was six feet higher than the lower one so it would have taken a prodigious leap to clear it.

I have never been anywhere where the climbers use such unusual tactics, and sometimes the combined moves require four climbers to stand one on top of the other before they can be overcome. It is the leaps that are the most impressive, however. In some places the only way to make progress is to leap through the air on to an adjoining pinnacle or wall, and climb up it, and sometimes you have to use this method in descent. The leaps are graded I to IV, ranging from the plain crazy to suicidal! Jori, one of our guides, attempted one of the latter where you had to climb to the top of one pinnacle and, 100 feet off the ground, swallow-dive across the gap between that and a higher pinnacle behind it. On this second pinnacle, slightly down the wall, was a huge jug and as you screamed down the wall you either had to grab it, or go on to certain injury (which is what happened to Jori, who broke a leg and an arm!).

On another occasion I was climbing with Mr Laorch and, having completed our route successfully, we arrived at the top of a pinnacle. 'Wow', I gasped, as he simply jumped off this on to an adjoining tower from which we had to abseil to the ground. Then it was my turn. A hundred feet of space between the rock walls; certain death if you made a mistake . . . and no rope. The longer I looked, the further the landing on the other side appeared. 'O God,' I moaned to myself, 'and it's only grade I.' I could not bring myself to do it, and began to feel I was letting our party down terribly. In the end a bit of cunning saved the day, and I climbed up a bit higher on the side of the pinnacle and managed to bridge across in a series of complicated hand and feet pushes. I almost split in two, but I was able to grab the summit spire of the second tower and pull across on it. Mr Laorch stood, ready to field me, his laughter lightening what was for me a pretty desperate situation!

It took me the whole two weeks to come to terms with the seriousness of the sandstone climbing. Several times I set off to lead a pitch, and had to back off and hand over to Toby or one of our Czech friends. I had little or no confidence in the protection methods – sometimes the ring bolts were 80 feet apart. One day we had

A Czech climber leading a difficult route wearing the traditional slippers on his feet. (Photo: Jiri Novak)

a go at Valley Crack, a superb off-width route on a par with anything that Yosemite Valley has to offer, except that the rock is rough and not smooth and plays havoc with your clothes! I soon retreated when I found out that the first ring bolt was about 70 feet up, and I could not see any other form of protection between there and the ground. 'The landings are good at Adrspach, Dennis,' Miri Smid declared, laughing. 'You can jump down from 40 feet up on most climbs and be OK!'

'I'd rather not try. My bones are getting bloody brittle with old age,' I rejoined.

On the very last day of our stay I led the whole of a two-pitch VIIc, the Czarda route on one of the Adrspach pinnacles, a teeth-gritting exercise for me, especially on the second pitch when I could look down between my legs at Mr Laorch hanging on a large ring bolt belaying me 60 feet below, with only three small threads between us and the crux of the climb in front. This entailed a very high step with my left foot, on which I had to do a rock-over. 'For Christ's sake, watch me,' I implored, I don't know why, since he had no idea what I was saying. He must have guessed by the tone of my voice that I was desperate. Pulling on a tiny pocket with my right hand, I made the move and immediately reached a good hand hold ... I was up, and felt like I had conquered Everest. This was as hard a climb as I have ever led in my life.

The pioneer of this climb, Thomas Czarda, had been to Britain in 1986, and had led some of our hardest climbs with the brilliant young Slovak climber Svetozar Polaczech. Svetozar was climbing in carpet slippers, the Czech *bochkary*, with the soles cut off and car tyre rubber glued on to replace them! To see him solo outcrop routes like Downhill Racer at Froggatt Edge in them was most impressive.

I met Thomas and Svetozar again in 1988 in Prague, and whilst I was there I tried to help Thomas get permission to visit the West a second time. We had some fun and games trying to outwit the system, but at one point I completely cocked up our story. The money Thomas would use to fund this visit had been bought on the black market, then I was to hand it over to the State bank official, saying it was a gift from me to Thomas to pay for his travel and living expenses abroad. 'I'm Thomas's uncle from England!' I blithely told the official. Unfortunately, the bank man spoke perfect English, and by the time we had been through my supposed family geneal-ogy, it was rather obvious that I had no connections with Thomas. I was travelling on a special visa as a guest of the state, and I think he was afraid to call my bluff, so I got away, and Thomas and I fell about laughing outside the building. Thomas assured me that he would not get into trouble, 'It will be OK, Dennis. It will be OK.' He was recently married and he wanted to take his wife climbing in France and Italy; how sorry I felt for him that they had to go through such a charade. He was one of the best rock climbers in the world, but unable to travel freely. It makes me so happy to hear that their situation might at last be improved.

After the Prague Conference I had been attending, Steve Bollen and I travelled south to Bratislava to meet Svetozar. We spotted the fair-haired, blue-eyed, tall and athletic young Slovak straight away at the airport. A brilliant rock climber, he too has suffered under the regime by not being allowed by the authorities to represent his Federation in the World Cup UIAA Competition series in 1989.

There is friendly rivalry between the Czechs and the Slovaks. Not only do they speak different languages, but they have an entirely separate rock climbing back-ground, with the Slovaks climbing on limestone. In Bratislava there is a crag in the very middle of the town, about 40 feet high, but nevertheless a good training ground. The day after our arrival in Bratislava, Svetozar and his constant climbing companion and mentor, Alan, took us all the way across the country from west to east almost to the Soviet border in Svetozar's mother's Skoda. The drive took all day, even though Alan, at the wheel, behaved like a demented rally driver. We arrived at a limestone climbing area in eastern Slovakia, the Zadiel Gorge National Park, and when we walked up to the rock faces we could not understand why we had never heard of it before! It is far more impressive than some of the well-known French limestone centres, with its centrepiece a huge pinnacle, the Sugar Loaf, about 500 feet high. The rock on this was firm, but our climb of the tower proved to be difficult. It was like all Czechoslovak climbing – bold, and with minimal protection, only poor nut placements and the odd rusty peg. I would have had real difficulty leading it, but we were assured that it was one of the easier ones.

We stayed with a woman climber in her tiny one-roomed flat in Kosice. This place appeared to be open house to all climbers in the district and more and more arrived as the evening went on. We had a communal meal, lots of beer and then a sing-song, and afterwards thirteen of us bedded down in the one room! Svetio's girlfriend turned up, and we gave the two of them a pair of rock boots each that we had brought with us. The next morning, on a nearby limestone plateau with superb crags all around its edges, our hearts were in our mouths as Svetio solo climbed all the local test pieces in his new boots. After he had been climbing in Bochkary for so long, perhaps the Mega boots would make it all too easy for him! In between his solo forays, he led me up climb after climb, until after ten routes I had to declare, 'I'm buggered! I just can't do another, Sevetio.' Although he does not understand English, Svetio seems to know what you're trying to say if you use enough expletives.

Below the plateau was a large complex of buildings, and coming from that direction from time to time were the most indescribable human screams, drowned out immediately by loud music played through speakers: '*Scream, scream . . .*' then '*All you need is love!*' 'What the hell is going on?' we demanded. Alan looked at us for a moment, serious for once. 'It is a mental hospital, and the people who are screaming are most likely dissidents and political prisoners held here by the State.' Steve and I exchanged shocked glances. 'Bloody hell! The bastards!' I knew exactly what was going on; using the latest methods of psychological torture, like disorientation techniques, they could break anyone, however physically and mentally strong. The nations of the world should agree to ban the use of such methods immediately, for they are as degrading and inhuman as slavery.

After this visit to East Slovakia Steve flew back to Britain, and I went climbing with Svetio and Alan north of Bratislava. First they took me to a cliff on the border with Austria. At that point it literally overlooked the barbed wire border, and the block houses spaced out every hundred feet or so with a menacing armed man in each one. 'One of our friends jumped off the top of this cliff with a hang-glider,' Alan told me. 'He escaped to the West and ever since we have not been able to climb here!' We travelled on to an area of rocks and castles to the north, where Alan led me, in an ancient pair of patched rock boots, up a climb which, he told me, only four years before had been 'the hardest route in Slovakia'. Its head wall had several long stretches on it, and reaching for little side holds in the overhanging limestone, on the end of a very tight rope, I fell off several times before managing, with a little help from my friends, to scale it. This was perhaps a 6B standard climb. What worried me most was Svetio soloing behind me. When I fell off into space, dangling on the end of the rope, he would reach out and pull me back into the rock face – we were 200 feet up off the ground! I was really worried about knocking him off his holds, which were minute.

My last night in Bratislava began with a session on an outdoor climbing wall, actually a concrete bunker with holds cut into its surface, and I then took my two friends to the best restaurant in town for a meal. Alan proved interesting, speaking several languages, and well versed in literature, art, music and physics. Tall, dark and mysterious, he was obviously very much into student dissident politics and after a few glasses of wine engaged me with stories of their activities. Being in the company of people like him, and Janus Onyskiewicz, there is a great sense of fun. They were engaged in a game which could spell life or death for them, but the stories of their reverses and triumphs were told with much humour. That night in Bratislava we laughed until the tears ran down our cheeks, and Svetio, who could not understand a word of our conversation, also laughed, happy that his friends were enjoying themselves. He was a child beside his older companion, and revelled in his association with Alan, despite probably being barred from the national climbing squad because of it!

The events of 1989 will never be forgotten, and with *Perestroika*, Poland, East Germany and Czechoslovakia are working towards social democracy. It is interesting to consider that some of the influences on this have also touched on my own life. When I was at Brantwood I read John Ruskin's great work on social democracy, *Unto this Last,* in which he denounces economists for not conceiving economics in terms of human welfare, condemns the poverty and injustice which industrialism brought or intensified, and extols the virtues of a simple life, in which work should be the joy of existence, not a slavery. It was this book that confirmed Gandhi, a young man in South Africa, in his views, which he extended to include the principles of non-violent resistance to change such evils. Gandhi, above all others, is the man to whom many of the dissidents look in their ideals. We in the West could do with re-examining our own performance in this respect. I hope that from now on all climbers can move around the world more freely, meet each other informally and simply get on with enjoying their sport.

North America and
Israel

A land flowing with milk and honey.
Exodus

At the end of the 1950s the climbing world was largely parochial compared to today's international scene, but word did begin to filter across the Atlantic about climbing developments in a place called Yosemite Valley in California. The nature of these communications, by word of mouth and the odd mass media article, meant that we had a completely false picture in Britain about climbing achievements like the first ascent of the Nose of El Capitan in 1958. We believed the climbers had simply engineered their way up the massive granite face, using siege tactics and erecting a kind of aerial staircase of bolts, ropes and stirrups; from what we heard, they moved up hardly ever touching the rock. These myths were not dispelled until the mid-1960s, when Californian-based climbers started visiting Europe regularly. The impact of the techniques and more particularly the equipment they had developed for Yosemite climbing, including hard steel pitons, was immediate, and the names of Royal Robbins, Yvon Chouinard, John Harlin, Gary Hemming and Tom Frost became familiar to European climbers as they made many new and spectacular ascents in the Alps.

It is hard now to convey the air of excitement and the 'brave new world' feeling which accompanied these developments, but for the next decade a journey to visit the scene of the crucible of these initiatives – Yosemite Valley in the Sierra Nevada mountains to the east of San Francisco – was akin to a pilgrimage to Mecca for the faithful. Although the peaks in the valley are not high (Half Dome is 8,852 feet), they rise in immense sweeps of smooth, clean granite with the 3,000-foot face of El Capitan, above the Merced River, the centrepiece of a host of awe-inspiring walls equally impressive to climber and tourist alike.

Shortly before I left for South America in 1966, Royal Robbins and his wife Liz came to stay with me in Yorkshire, and in between bouldering and climbing sessions on our local gritstone outcrops (at which the Californian excelled), he told me about the latest achievements in 'The Valley'. I was fired with enthusiasm to visit what had now become the most influential rock climbing centre in the world, and that is how I came to be walking slowly down a tarmac road towards Camp IV in Yosemite in August 1966. My mind was swimming with the impressions and contradictions thrown up during my days on the road hitch-hiking from Mexico City. I had been struck by the generosity of some of my fellow human beings – one driver gave me a lift from Fresno to the Yosemite National Park boundary, *ninety* miles out of his way – and appalled by the meanness and nastiness of some of the others, like the racist who had given me a lift and, talking about the Watts riots in Los Angeles, had insisted on calling all coloured people 'niggers'.

The last three miles down the road to Camp IV seemed to take an eternity. The heat was getting me down – in mid-August it is too hot for comfort, with midday temperatures of 90°F and above – but I kept trudging along, my mind switching to impressions of my last few days wandering in Arizona, Nevada and California. What contrasts these states presented! There was such beauty in their deserts and canyons, yet Man's effect on nature as manifested in cities like Los Angeles had staggered my senses. The people had been as interesting as the scenery. It was the height of the hippie 'flower power' era and, with long hair and a beard, carrying a banjo and masses of luggage, I was one of them myself. I had some great conversations on everything from Beat poetry to gay liberation during my long journey, and only one anxious moment.

I had been hitch-hiking rather stupidly at around midnight in Fresno, on a street corner in the middle of town, when a young beefy guy came up to me and demanded, 'Give me some chocolate, man!' Not quite getting his drift, I offered him a square of the Cadbury's bar which I carried in my rucksack all the way from Peru. Instead of being grateful, he knocked it out of my hand to the ground. 'You being funny, boy?' he hissed through clenched teeth.

'No, no, I'm English. I don't understand,' I stammered.

'From England! Do you know the Beatles?'

'Well, not personally, but my mother's mother lives just across the road from Ringo's mum in Liverpool 8.'

'Jeez man, that is cool, really cool,' and he ambled off, chuckling to himself.

I stopped for a breather beside the Merced river to watch some naked blonde-haired girls diving into the glinting water and giggling; I could see that Yosemite was something more than a centre for rock climbing. Despite such distractions, however, and the myriad signs of man's presence and work in the National Park, the visitor is never far from impressive views of rock faces. I limped on past a campsite, wondering how the Americans managed to move their masses of equipment and caravans to such a place, then, as I drew level with Yosemite Lodge, I saw Sentinel Rock on my left and El Cap directly ahead. El Cap made me gasp at its scale and line and swept away my thoughts of the last few hours.

I turned into Camp IV, the Yosemite climbers' campsite, and found it very different from how I had imagined it to be. It was full of trees, dark and dank, and overrun by cats, dogs and the other animals that Americans keep as pets, including a full-grown baboon on a chain. At that time it was the only site in the valley where you could bring pets, and it looked rather like a zoo. Shortly after my visit it also became a summer gathering place for beatniks but the authorities took a strong line against the 'beautiful people' and closed the place down for a while. This was a pity, for the mixture of climber and hippie might not have proved too incompatible.

My reception by the locals was embarrassing, to say the least; Royal Robbins had forewarned them of my arrival, and I was treated like a cross between Don Whillans and Mick Jagger. I hardly had time to get my pack off my back before they had me out climbing on the boulders dotted around the campsite. Physically I was at a very low ebb, and my weeks on the cargo boat, then the trips in Peru and Ecuador, and hitch-hiking from Mexico were no preparation for a competitive session with some of the best boulderers of the time. I was well and truly outclassed, and had to fall back on the ploy of declaring myself a 'mountaineer', looking into the distance and telling the young rock jocks that 'it's all a different story above 20,000 feet!' No sooner had I failed on one problem than I was marched to the

Chuck Pratt leading on the Lower Cathedral Spire, Yosemite Valley 1966. (Photo: Dennis Gray)

next, to fail yet again, until finally I couldn't even get started at Kors Wall and gave up my feeble attempts in disgust.

Exhausted by the heat and by the ordeal of well-meant but incessant questions, especially about the truth of some of the Whillans and Rock and Ice stories, I advised them to 'believe all the legends!', excused myself and wandered over to the bar of Yosemite Lodge. Propping up the counter was a round-faced, bearded, squat guy, with twinkling eyes and a ready chuckle. This had to be Chuck Pratt, by common consent the valley's best free climber, responsible, with Royal Robbins and others, for pioneering great classics on El Cap like The Salethe and North America walls. I introduced myself and immediately took to his jolly personality, vastly different from the youthful inquisitors I had just left behind. 'You stumbled on the out-patients department, boy. They're just so close in they are wanting to burn you off!' he laughed. I had heard how competitive they could be in the valley, and the treatment a stranger might receive in the wrong hands. Chuck suggested we go back to camp and make some Teton tea, a brew of wine, cloves and other secret ingredients stewed up on the fire in a dixie, to celebrate my safe arrival in the valley.

By the time the preparations for this had been completed it was dark. We sat round a fire in Camp IV, drinking and talking, when suddenly there was a shouting

The author leading a 5.9 on Glacier Point Apron, Yosemite Valley 1966. (Photo: Dennis Gray collection)

and roaring, which could surely not have come from a human throat. Into the flickering light which illuminated our vision leapt a figure, as wild-looking as imaginable, with long, jet-black hair, madly flashing eyes, a face that had really been lived in, and a body that would not have been out of place on the son of King Kong. 'It's OK,' Chuck assured me with a laugh, 'it's only Warren.' Warren Harding, pioneer of the Nose route of El Cap, proceeded to jump about wildly, over and into our fire, snatch the Teton tea and gulp vast quantities down his gullet, then disappear roaring back into the night.

'Is he always like that?' I gasped in amazement.

'No, not always, just some of the time!' I later got to know this madman well, and found him to be a one-man laughter show who refuses to take climbers, climbing, the park authorities, character builders, climbing magazines, training and the ethical mandarins seriously!

'Watch out for the bears tonight,' Chuck warned as I crawled into my sleeping bag, lying out in the open under a tree. Up above my head was a bundle strung from a climbing rope, the only safe way to leave our food. Bears would wander into camp and, if they smelt foodstuffs within reach, would rip a tent open and even attack the occupants if they got in the way. That evening, a full-grown grizzly did come into our camp, and caused panic with climbers and tourists alike. I awoke to see an enormous creature up on its hind legs, pawing at the bark of my tree – it could smell the food hanging from one of the branches. It took a while to persuade the bear to leave our meagre groceries alone and turn its attention to a nearby tourists' frame tent, where we guessed there were plenty of supplies stacked in the larder.

I enjoyed some superb climbing over the next ten days in the valley, first with a young Californian called Mark Klemens, then with Chuck and later with the irrepressible T. M. Herbert, who fully lived up to his reputation as the funny man of American climbing. Tall, dark, gangling and noisy, with a sense of humour that turned each of our outings into a farce, he is very much a part of the Yosemite climbing story. Named 'T.M.' at birth, and T.M. ever since, he was responsible for, or had a part in, the pioneering of many new climbs, including the Muir Wall of El Capitan. Some days we managed a single long route, on others we climbed three or four short climbs. Both the slab climbing and the cracks were outstanding, with the former being ascended mainly by edging and the latter, particularly the notorious 'off-widths', using every form of jamming technique possible – fingers, arms, legs, my whole body and on one occasion my head!

I wanted to stay to live and work in the USA for a while, and I had hoped to be in Yosemite all season before moving to New York where I had a promise of work in the Harlem ghetto on a community project. After a short time, however, I received a message that the effects of my mother's incurable illness had much worsened. My American friends were marvellous in this hour of need and ran me immediately to San Francisco airport to catch a plane back to London. T.M. saw me on to the flight and his words still ring in my ears: 'Now you come back here boy, or we'll flay you alive, you goddam Limey, you.' I still have not made it back to the valley, but those ten days were some of the best of my climbing life, and I was pleased that I was there during the golden era. Many of the innovations developed in Yosemite, like the grading system, have become universally accepted throughout the States, while the 'Big Wall' techniques have proved to be applicable from Patagonia to the Himalaya. I can't wait to go back to Yosemite; the quality and diversity of its granite climbing is unique in my experience.

In August 1975 I went on a month's climbing tour of the Eastern States of America. By this time the sport had really taken off throughout the continent and many of the climbers were based in the Eastern States, where there is some magnificent rock climbing as well as wilderness areas, in the Appalachians, and the Green and White Mountains. I flew to New York on the cheapest charter – Laker before he went bankrupt – and arrived with the equivalent of 50 dollars in my pocket to travel throughout an area as big as Western Europe. With me was another impecunious English climber, Ian Parsons; we both agreed to get around by hitch-hiking. We travelled first to the Shawangunks, north of New York up the Hudson river above New Paltz, on up to North Conway, the 'Yosemite of the East', in New Hampshire, south-east to Boston, where we climbed close to the city and visited a friend at Harvard, then back West, down to the 'Gunks again, and then back to Kennedy airport for our flight back home. It was a total distance of a couple of thousand miles, with some hairy experiences – one guy pulled a gun on us in a pub because, as he said, 'I don't like Limeys!', and then we were picked up late at night by two young boys high on drugs in a stolen car, which they proceeded to crash into a wall at speed. Hitch-hiking in the USA is much more dangerous than climbing!

We climbed first at the Shawangunks. Before leaving New York I had phoned Fritz Wiessner who lived in Vermont and, although he was then 75 years old, he agreed to show us around. I had met Fritz often at UIAA meetings and we were close friends. He was one of the outstanding mountaineers of his or any other generation, and when he died in 1988, the climbing magazines were fulsome in their praise for his climbing achievements, from his early first ascents on sandstone in his native Germany, through his great climbs in the Eastern Alps, to his pioneering efforts in North America, after his emigration in 1928. He had made outstanding climbs, including the first ascent of the Devil's Tower in Wyoming, and the first climb of Mount Waddington (13,177 feet) in British Columbia, as well as taking part in Himalayan explorations and almost making the first ascent of K2 in 1939 on an expedition which ended in tragedy and controversy. In 1935 he had also discovered America's most popular rock climbing area, the Shawangunks, and made the first climbs there. For some reason he had fallen foul of the American climbing establishment, and even at his death, by which time he had been honoured and feted throughout his adopted land, there were still hints that he could be difficult, that he was not easy to get to know and that he 'teemed with conflicts and contradictions'. My own experience of him was entirely different. He was warm and avuncular with me, and our meeting in the Shawangunks in 1975 was typical.

'Ve are going climbing, Dennis, you and I only,' he insisted the moment we met, as he climbed out of the car after his long drive down from Vermont. 'There is a climb on the Near Trapps I will make with you. It is a classic, the Yellow Ridge it is called, but it will be easy for you. It has three pitches; you can lead the middle pitch, I will lead the other two.' There was no arguing with Uncle Fritz, and how I admired him as we roped up at the foot of this climb, after crossing the Trapps road and scrambling up through dense vegetation. He was 75, but still bubbling with enthusiasm for climbing; a short, powerful man, with a bald head and a moonshaped face, and always laughing. 'Is it wise, Dennis, to climb only in shorts and vest? Vot about ze animals?' he demanded as he set off. He was dressed in a woolly sweater, and long leather breeches, and the temperature was in the low 80s.

'I always climb in shorts when it's hot,' I assured him, admiring his neat footwork and quick movements as he climbed up to a nose out on the right of the base of the rock face, which was about 200 feet high. On following him I found out what was really behind his question. Suddenly, my leg felt as if someone had inserted a red hot needle into it! 'What the hell is it?' I shouted out, in excruciating pain, and only just holding on to the rock face.

'Hornets, it is hornets!' Fritz shouted down. No wonder he had donned his leather trousers for this route! When I joined him he was almost beside himself with laughter: 'I told you this climb is full of animals!'

'I though you meant marmots or mice,' I admonished. 'If I'd known it had hornets all over the first pitch I wouldn't have come near it.'

'It is really a beautiful climb though, Dennis. I do want you to do it.' I agreed to lead the next pitch, which was superb, up a series of steep corners to a belay on a ledge below a large overhang above. Fritz came up swiftly then set off up this top pitch which must have been around 80 feet of climbing. When he reached the large overhang, I was surprised when, after stopping for a moment, he pulled straight over the roof, his feet dangling free. To say I was impressed is an understatement. Later that night, after he had entertained Ian and I to dinner at the Minnewaska hotel, he took us up to his bedroom to show us his training routine. We were both amazed at a demonstration of his weight training and stretching programme. He had brought with him from Vermont a set of weights, a chest expander and a Bullworker and he was still at 75 as strong as either of us! 'You know Dennis, every year beyond 65 is like ten years before that in terms of physical decline. I have to work much harder these days to stay in shape, otherwise I would not be able to climb at all," he emphasised to us.

I found out later from the guidebook that Fritz had made the first ascent of Yellow Ridge in 1944, and that it was graded 5.7, which would be a creditable lead for any climber at any age. It was typical of him not to mention it. Equally typical was his action when we planned to move on up to North Conway; he sent his son Andy down to the 'Gunks to pick us up and drive us there, despite his being a busy senior legal adviser to one of the senators in Washington. Where Fritz was concerned, climbing and friendship were more important than work, and as we profusely thanked Andy when he dropped us hundreds of miles to the north in New Hampshire, he grinned and said, 'Don't thank me. You know my pa; when he gets an idea into his head there's no arguing with him!'

We had a good time climbing in North Conway in the White Mountains, on Cannon Cliff, the slabs of Whitehorse and the Cathedral Ledges. One afternoon in particular was exciting: when American Pete Gilbert and I were climbing the famous Sliding Board route on the Whitehorse Slabs. This is a great classic climb of the area, but it mainly relies on friction, so if you get caught on the 800-foot high face in a storm it usually means that you have to be rescued on ropes from above. We had set out in perfect weather, and Pete had led me up the crux pitch with no bother at all. Above this we had run into trouble, for suddenly the cloudless sky had turned black, there had been a couple of frightening lightning flashes, and spots of rain had begun to hit the rock within seconds. Pete ran out our 160-foot rope as fast as he could and by the time I followed up the quartz fault in the slab, it was raining hard. Before I could join him this had become a flood, and I was soaked to the skin. The Sliding Board is as smooth a slab as any I have come across, and I had to shout to Pete to take the rope tight for it was impossible to friction up the wet rock. When I joined him, he too was wet through and, despite it being summer, the air temperature had dropped and we were both shivering. Our position looked serious, for we were still a full rope-length below the top of the slab and it was impossible to climb, with water flowing down it in a constant stream. 'I think we will need to be rescued,' Pete confessed.

'Bugger that.' I dismissed the idea and began traversing about to see if I could find some way off and out of our dilemma. Over on my right, many feet above me, was a small tree growing out of the cliff face. 'Untie,' I said to Pete, 'I'm going to try to lasso that sapling.'

'No kidding?' was his surprised response. I tied a round, ball-like stone I had found on the ledge into our rope and, almost throwing myself off with it, I caught the tree first shot! 'You should be in the rodeos,' was my companion's comment at this effort, which I tried to pass off as if by design, when in fact it was sheer bloody luck. Or perhaps all that practice throwing a cricket ball at the wickets when I was young had finally paid off ... ? I climbed up and grabbed the end of the rope hanging down the slab with the stone in it, then hand over hand swarmed up followed by Pete. From the tree we lassoed a branch on a stouter tree above the first and then traversed off to safety and the valley. On the strength of this performance I became known for a short while as 'Dennis, the Limey Lassoer'!

All too soon it was time to leave and return to the 'Gunks and then back to Britain via New York. I had seen enough of New England to want to go there again, and in October 1979 I returned in time to catch the autumn colours on Mount Washington in all their glory. The rain teemed down in buckets and climbing was out, but as I walked alone to the summit of that peak, I was almost in tears of ecstasy looking down at the sight below me, a wonderful panorama of golds, browns and reds. And while the day drew to a close as I descended, shafts of sunlight came down through the trees, which seemed to catch fire before my eyes and turned to a blazing intensity. New England in the Fall is certainly as spectacular as its reputation implies.

You could spend a lifetime wandering over the vast area of North America rock and mountain climbing, and still not manage to see it all. In the 1980s I climbed at Boulder in Colorado and at Calgary in Canada, two areas that are vastly different and further apart than Britain and the Alps. Despite the soaring rock walls of the Eldorado and Boulder Canyons, and the steep impressive white limestone faces of the Rockies, my keenest memory from these two trips is of a short climb I soloed near to Calgary.

Outside Calgary, in a cornfield, stands a large boulder. It is situated in a crater, so that from the edge of the field it is almost hidden from view, but on closer inspection it turns out to be around 40 feet high. On the left-hand side of its largest face is a steep corner called Greenwoods Corner. Just as Joe Brown and Don Whillans are legends of British climbing from the 1950s and 1960s, so Brian Greenwood is a byword in Canada. His brilliant first ascents of such major routes as Mount Temple's North Face in 1966 were at the cutting edge of that era, and I was keen to investigate what standards he had achieved, having known him as a young man in Britain.

My companion as I stood at the bottom of the boulder in September 1988 was Murray Toft, a mountain guide from Calgary, and a good friend. He warned, 'It's hard, even though when Brian climbed it first he was wearing gym pumps. I'll give you a top rope on it if you like.'

'No way. If Brian could get up it in sneakers, my sticky boots will murder it.' Twenty feet later I was eating my words, for I was pushed to my limit and nearly falling off in trying to bridge up the smooth corner. 'Bloody hell, Murray, I'm in trouble,' I shouted down. The rock was smooth, volcanic, crystalline, and my feet were marking time. Below on the ground were some nasty boulders waiting for me if I tried to jump off. Murray ran round to the top and began to shout down instructions.

'There,' he kept insisting, 'out on your left there is a big jug for your hands.'

'That's no bloody use. I'm facing right,' I moaned. I realised I had to do something, and quick; bridging at the top of that groove, legs akimbo, my limbs were shaking with the strain. I half turned, and in doing this began to slip. 'Jesus!' My hand curled over the jug, and the very next moment my feet shot off and I swung wildly across the wall. Desperation made me keep hold with my left hand, then get my right on to the same hold and pull up over the roof to easy ground and the top.

'That was impressive,' laughed a relieved Murray.

'Impressive? It's solid 5c. You tell old Greenwood next time you see him his corner nearly killed me!'

Peter Pan Livesey, the man who changed the face of British climbing in the 1970s. (Photo: Denis Gray)

Brian Greenwood and many emigrants like him are just part of the important British contribution to climbing world-wide, and representative of Britain's high standing in a sport we did not invent. This position in international circles was emphasised for me in 1980 when Pete Livesey and I, on behalf of the BMC, were invited to Israel to organise an instructors' course for the world-famous Wingate Institute of Physical Education in Tel Aviv. I had been to Israel on my own in 1968, to travel and investigate climbing possibilities, but also to see what was happening there, believing at the time that the future of world peace was dependent upon their political situation. The fate of the Jews had begun to interest me the year before when I had visited Auschwitz, and I also felt that Jewish thinkers like Einstein and Freud had made a tremendous impression on my life.

In 1968 I found that the whole of Israel was on an unthinking high – their victory in the Six Day War the year before had made the Israelis the heroes of the world, and had bred an arrogance and a belief that they could solve all their external problems by force of arms. This belief was later reinforced by brilliant commando exploits like the raid on Entebbe, but by the late 1970s they had begun an inevitable drift to the right, involving stronger and stronger measures against the Arabs living in their country, and particularly against the Palestinians in the occupied West Bank territories.

My trip in 1968 was magical. I travelled widely, climbed on a small limestone crag near to the walls of Jerusalem, and sat for hours at the Wailing Wall, watching Jews from all over the world crying out to God for his mercy. It was one of the most impressive religious observances I have ever seen, and strangely intriguing (although perhaps not as odd as a Pathan ceremony I saw outside Peshawar in 1989, with dancing and singing by a troupe of male eunuchs. The youngest were about 16 years old, and the oldest about 35, neutered when young with the agreement of their parents; they are assured of a good living for many years, for only eunuchs are allowed to entertain at certain ceremonies, including weddings and the circumcision rites).

By May 1980 Pete Livesey had almost single-handedly changed British rock climbing standards. Originally an outstanding young athlete, he had brought to the sport a totally new concept in fitness training, and become the archetype of the new breed of dedicated, trained and superfit rock climber. He was tall and bespectacled, and we used to rib him that he only climbed so well because he was so ugly. Indeed, one of our favourite topics of conversation at the time was the fact that in the future only sportsmen so blessed would be able to climb truly hard since they would be sufficiently at odds with the world to be aggressive on the crags! This was of course toungue in cheek ...

The meet in Israel took place in the Wadi Amud valley, set above the sea of Galilee and we were quartered at a nearby kibbutz, eating our meals with its members. We also had to rise at the same time as them, about 5 o'clock in the morning, for by mid-morning it was too hot to climb. Our aim was to help set up a group of active rock climbers who could act as instructors for the Israel Alpine Club, by 'testing' participants who had come from all over the country, noting their techniques and commenting on their suitability or otherwise. There was a real cross-section, from students from Tel Aviv University and a professor from Jerusalem, to a housewife from Jaffa and a Colonel who was head of the Israeli paratroopers.

The Wadi Amud cliffs are very much like the Derbyshire dales, or some of the modern French limestone areas, but the pride of the valley is a free-standing pinnacle called the Amud, about 200 feet high, and overhanging on its shorter side which abuts into the steep slope of the dale. On our first visit Pete and I both solo climbed up the long side of this pinnacle, then sat wondering if the rope we had carried up would reach the ground to abseil off down the short side. 'Only one way to find out!' declared Pete and off he launched into space. It did reach, just, but I had stupidly left all my equipment on the ground, and had to abseil classic fashion to follow him. The last sixty feet, spinning through the air with the rope running round my thigh and through my bare legs, left me with a high-pitched voice and a rope burn which took weeks to heal!

Once the course started it was all action, with climbing from six in the morning until midday, when a halt would be called for lunch and a rest in the shade out of the crushing heat of the sun. Another two or three hours in the afternoon completed the day. As the week progressed, the more I liked and admired Pete. He was no show-off, neither did he strike you as being outstanding immediately, but he was solid and really knew technique and rope work intimately. The Israelis were very impressed with his attention to detail; certain of their belaying methods were not recognised safe practice. They took criticism with good grace, and accepted that they all needed more experience before they could run climbing courses on their own. When it came to enthusiasm and application, however, our charges took some beating, and some mornings we would do five or six climbs before lunch then three or four more in the afternoon, some of them multi-pitch.

High up in the Wadi was a mirror-shaped wall of perfect, steep, grey limestone about 80 feet high, set above about 120 feet of easy rock. It was concave, with a shallow groove up its centre, and had been top-roped innumerable times, but no one had dared to lead it for there was no protection on the top wall. A fall from it would have had dire consequences. One lunch-time Pete slipped away unnoticed and, wearing only a pair of shorts and his rock boots, in the searing heat had climbed the easy first section of this unled challenge before we spotted him. As he traversed out across the concave upper face, solo and with no protection of any kind, we spied him and a buzz of excitement went round our circle sitting in the shade below. I hardly dared watch. He had no idea as to how hard this climb might be, and was now apparently stuck in the middle of the face. But no, after a few moments of carefully assessing the problem, he began to move precisely and confidently, and in complete control. Move followed move until it was soon over and he was on top! We all cheered. A brilliant first ascent behind him, he later assured me it was 'only about 5b', but I was not deceived by this and bought him a whisky to celebrate that night in a pub on the shore of Lake Galilee. A Yorkshire-man buying a fellow Tyke a whisky is almost unheard of, so you might guess how impressed I was at his feat!

Living on the kibbutz gave us much food for thought. In this experiment in socialism, everything is owned by everyone on the camp, the children are brought up communally and everyone shares in the chores of cleaning and cooking. We spent evenings with some of the kibbutzniks, talking about their past and their future hopes, and I was struck by one man in particular. He had been a famous portrait photographer in Switzerland, and now worked as a labourer in a banana plantation on a trial basis to see if he and kibbutz life were mutually acceptable. If he proved himself to the other members, by dint of hard work and self-sacrifice, he would be set up with the best photographic equipment and able to use once again the skills which had made him famous in his earlier life. I spent an evening poring over his photographs; his colour work was good, but his black and white prints were masterpieces.

'Don't you feel that 18 months working in a banana plantation is a waste of your like and skills?' I asked him.

'No, not at all. It has taught me many things, and if I am to live the rest of my life here on this kibbutz I must earn my place like everyone else has done,' he replied.

At the end of the course Pete and I bade farewell to our new-found climbing friends and then travelled around the country for a while, visiting the Dead Sea, Jericho and finally Jerusalem. Inevitably, there outside the city wall we met up with local climbers on the fine small limestone cliff I had first been to in 1968. Pete solo climbed almost every existing route on the cliff and pioneered one or two new climbs, but stuck on one problem and, despite repeated attempts, could not solve it. Several years later at a BMC Youth Meet in the Peak District a brilliant young climber from Israel, Joav Nir, quizzed me about our visit. 'Yes, we have now climbed the route that Livesey could not climb at Jerusalem,' he was able to report. 'It is called *Peter Could Not Climb It!*' Such is the fate of every leading pioneer of every generation in our sport for, as Mummery so rightly observed, 'Today's impossible climb is tomorrow an easy day for a lady!'

The Fairest Cape –
South Africa

Free me, free me, the people are calling.
Zinzi Mandela

Early in 1981 I was invited by the Natal section of the Mountain Club of South Africa to visit their country, to take part in a Mountain Rescue exercise and a climbing meet in the Drakensberg mountains, and to do a lecture tour. The Mountain Club is one of the oldest climbing clubs in the world, with sections in many parts of the Republic. My initial reaction was to refuse their offer, but I decided first to consult a South African friend in Britain. He had every reason to hate his country's iniquitous regime, for the apartheid laws had prevented him from marrying in Cape Town. He and his girlfriend had moved to more liberal Durban, and lived together for three years, until one night police battered down their door, beat him up and took his girlfriend away. Through the action of some of the climbers in Durban who had now invited me, they had eventually escaped via Mozambique, and come to Britain, and were now happily married.

I knew that as General Secretary of the BMC a visit by me to South Africa could be misinterpreted, and might even be used by that country's regime for propaganda purposes. Although I hate apartheid, and was well aware that many many people (Whites as well as Blacks and Indians) were involved in the freedom fight, I wanted to form for myself a true picture of life and climbing in South Africa. This consideration, and my friend's advice to go, made my decision. I was advised to travel only as a private citizen, and to request that my lectures should be open to all races – the activities of sports bodies in South Africa are emancipated from the apartheid laws, although this fact is often misunderstood. Finally, my tour was to be set up so that I would receive sufficient payment from my talks only to cover my expenses.

My liaison man in Durban was Adolf Flockemann, a lawyer and the Chairman of the Natal section of the Mountain Club. He was not only most understanding, but also quickly proved to me that many of my preconceptions about South African climbers were wildly awry. They care little about the colour of a man's skin, or his background and, as is the case with dedicated mountaineers everywhere, the climbing and the climber matter more than anything. Many of them have been unable to accept the rule of apartheid, however, and this cancer has forced some of their best mountaineers to emigrate.

On the morning in February 1981 when I left our home in Guiseley, it snowed heavily. Most fortuitous, as it turned out, for a chip pan caught fire in the kitchen, and I had to use snow to douse the flames before the Fire Brigade arrived! It caused quite serious damage, and I felt very guilty at leaving Leni and the children to clear up the mess, but my need to travel and to climb was too great. This need was starting to create a gulf between my wife and me; she understood my craving for such experiences, but this did not help her with the reality of being left on her own to care for the children.

I flew to Durban via Johannesburg. Durban is South Africa's principal sea port, famed for its beaches, sharks and industry. It is a city of almost a million people of mixed races and religions, with Hindus and Moslems as well as Christians, and known as the most liberal of the major cities in the Republic. Because of its proximity to the Drakensberg Mountains, lying several hours' drive to the north-west, it is from there that all rescues in these 11,000-foot peaks are co-ordinated. The Chairman of the Mountain Rescue was Doc Ripley, a legend in Drakensberg climbing circles, one of the great pioneers of climbing in that range, and my host while I was in Durban. He was a wee, gnome-like man, with a grey beard and a wizened face, and it was clear that when he spoke, either with the authorities or with his team, he was in charge.

It appeared that the Mountain Rescue had had to contend with difficult problems. Each time there was a serious accident requiring an evacuation, a team had to be organised to travel from Durban by road, sometimes in the middle of the night or in the rainy season of the winter. It was a tricky journey. Recently, however, they had been given the right to call upon the helicopters of the South African Air Force, and we were to take part in an exercise aimed at co-ordinating this action. The flight to the foothills of the Drakensberg, with the whole team on board, would be made in a large gunship helicopter, but for the work in the mountains a small lighter version would take over. The Doc toiled over these plans late into the night.

The Doc lived in an old bungalow on the edge of town, and up on a hill above were some of the finest houses I have ever seen. I wanted to have a closer look around, so I decided to go out for a run up to the houses and then out into the open country beyond. The beautiful lawns and gardens of the houses in this 'whites only' section of town contrasted sharply with the buildings outside the city, the homes of Indians. I reminded myself that it was here amongst these people that Gandhi had begun his career, and discovered the power of non-violent resistance, and then was heartened to fall in with two Blacks out running. They were training for the Comrades Marathon, one of the most demanding athletic events in the world, run from Durban to Pietermaritzberg over a distance of about 56 miles. The marathon alternates in direction each year, for starting from Durban is uphill and starting in Pietermaritzberg is down hill! I assumed because of the apartheid system that these runners would be diffident in approaching me, but we talked as we ran on together, and they told me that they were forced to stay in a township nearby, but they were able to work in Durban.

At first light next morning a gunship helicopter landed on Adolf Flockemann's lawn, and the Rescue Team and I piled aboard. On the flight was a large Afrikaner, a cameraman from the national television organisation, who was reluctantly accompanying us into the mountains to cover the exercise. He gave me my first experience of a no-holds-barred white supremist South African. He was appalling, but he was honest and made no bones about how he saw things – his ancestors had built this country and the 'fucking kaffirs' were little more than animals who had to be kept in their place. I was careful not to let this guy rile me too much, but was heartened by the good-natured support I had from the rest of the team, one or two of them also Afrikaners. They joined in and ribbed the guy mercilessly.

We could see nothing during this hour-long flight but we landed at a farm in the foothills of the Drakensberg, from which the whole operation was to be co-ordinated by radio. On stepping out, I could see to the north the Dragon

Mountains, glistening like a giant's teeth across the horizon. They looked impressive and difficult to climb. After quickly transferring into light helicopters we were soon up amongst them, and they looked even more impressive close up to the rock walls, although I saw with dismay that they were mainly of basalt, a terrible rock for climbing, loose and friable. The Zulus called the Drakensberg 'The Barrier of Spears' and sitting in the front of the chopper I could see why. We flew around the Cathkin Peak and the Monks Cowl, where Richard Barry, an outstanding Springbok climber, had been killed in 1938.

I was familiar with this type of rescue exercise, in which a casualty was evacuated off a cliff face in a remote part of the range. Everything depends on the skill of the pilot and the courage of the winchman, and the South African Air Force showed themselves to be as good as any in this field. The process worked like clockwork and within an hour or so the casualty was down and the exercise completed. I was one of the first to return to the farm, and I wandered down the valley below to stretch my legs a little. As I poked about, I found a shallow cave with paintings on the walls by bushmen, the original inhabitants of the area perhaps as long as 20,000 years ago. This race were prolific artists, using pigments made from iron and zinc oxides, and I marvelled at their technique. They knew about using perspective, and the antelopes on the rock walls really seemed to be moving through time and space, as realistic now as they were when the unknown artist painted them. I was astonished that this fantastic art treasure was left to the wind and rain unprotected, where anyone could touch, photograph or deface it, and returned wildly excited to tell my companions of my find. I felt a bit deflated when they assured me, 'You'll find them everywhere, all over South Africa! There are thousands of them and only the very best are protected.'

The Bell in the Drakensberg Mountains. (Photo: Paul Fatti)

After a debriefing session, one of the Afrikaner climbers and I set out for the Cathedral Peak area of the range, to join up with the climbing meet which was already under way. My companions guessed that those attending this event would probably be bivouacked under a peak called The Bell, a striking summit like an inverted tea cup, a little under 10,000 feet high, and one of the hardest summits to reach in the range.

'Would you like a lift up there, Dennis?' asked the pilot of one of the helicopters, who had heard of our plans. I needed no persuading, for it looked like at least two day's march from where we stood to reach The Bell. In minutes we were off and away, with our large heavy rucksacks at our feet, whirring first across the high veld under the mountain faces then up into the Cathedral Peak range. Soon the winch-man crawled in to tell us we were nearly there – he knew the place where the climbers were bivouacking from an earlier flight that day. 'We can't land you at the exact spot – it's in a narrow gully and dangerous with cross winds – we'll drop you out on the face and you can traverse across to them.'

'Thanks,' I gasped, as I glimpsed some terrifying rock walls tearing past out of the helicopter door. The chopper slowed down, then hovered about 15 feet above a sloping ledge.

'This is where you have to jump out,' the winchman told us, pointing out of the door.

'You're joking?' I suggested, hopefully.

'No, not at all,' and before I could stop him he had grabbed my rucksack and thrown it out of the opening! My companion was equally disturbed at this news, and showed visible qualms about letting his rucksack be thrown from the aircraft. One moment I was standing at the door, my knees knocking in unison with the vibrations of the helicopter, and the winchman shouting 'Jump! Jump! Jump!', the next I felt myself propelled through space. The ledge below me was sloping, and underneath it was at least a thousand feet of space! I hit the ground like a boulder falling from the sky, and clung to its wispy grass and rock for dear life, only to realise that it was absolutely safe, a gentle incline and really quite wide. Seeing me safe on the wall, my climbing companion threw his rucksack at me and followed it down.

We recovered our dignity and waved the chopper crew farewell as they sped off south, back towards their base. We traversed slowly across the cliff face and climbed up a gully. At its head, bivouacking in a rocky defile, we found the members of The Mountain Club, about ten in number. I had secretly to admit that this was a hell of a place, with soaring rock walls all around, and massive drops at our feet – an eagle would have been in its element there. After introductions all round it was agreed that two ropes of two would attempt to climb The Bell the next day, and I was included.

I settled into a small cave in the rock face, and with two of the South Africans sat watching the sunset behind the summits above our heads. From them I learned about some of the history of the climbing in the region, and that The Bell had been first climbed in January 1944 by Hans and Else Wongtschowski, and was a serious route on which several climbers had subsequently been killed. It was graded E, according to the Drakensberg alphabetical grading system, which begins at A for the easiest ascents.

Early next morning we were on our way. I led an easy first pitch, and realised immediately that the grass was the firmest thing to cling to. The exposure was acute for the ground around the start of our climb masked rock faces, now below my heels and providing hundreds of feet of immediate height. My companion Brian, one of the leading Drakensberg climbers, led from there because, as he said, 'It takes a while to get used to the loose rock', and I saw with relief that he kept the rope tight between us as I followed him up a steepening wall – by the time we reached the crux pitch, it must have been vertical. I could only marvel at the pioneers who had first succeeded in overcoming this obstacle, climbing blindly up on loose rock, and heading into an ever more serious situation. It is hard to explain why basalt feels so bad; I think it is because it is not uniform, sometimes firm and sometimes brittle, sometimes downright bloody loose, and holds often break without warning. You must always have your weight spread, for to rely on a single hold is to invite disaster. The accident rate in the Drakensberg is frightening, in proportion to the limited numbers of people climbing there.

I breathed a sigh of relief on reaching the top of the pitch; although it was about Very Severe by British standards, the looseness of the rock was beginning to unnerve me, 'Do you want to lead?' asked Brian.

'Er, no thanks. I'm finding it too bloody gripping,' I had to reply. Brian laughed.

'I used to feel the same when I first climbed here, but you do get used to it!' he assured me, and led off with speed up the next pitch. The angle began to go back as we climbed up the slope of The Bell formation, and soon we began to climb together with coils. I immediately felt more confident, perhaps because this was a familiar routine for me, and was able to lead up a last steep step before the summit. Although I found it frightening pulling up on huge jugs which might break at any moment, and climbing in the South African style with a minimum of protection, I reached the top of the pitch and brought my companion up to join me. We unroped and raced up to the summit. Sitting on top of The Bell I realised for the first time how beautiful the Drakensberg is. I had never seen so many shades of blue in the sky, and all around were impressive spires and summits – the Inner and Outer Horns, the Pyramid, the Column and Cathedral Peak itself looming above us.

We descended by abseil and as we were going down, mist began to envelop us, creeping over the Barrier of Spears from Lesotho, the harbinger of bad weather to come. I was most worried about the anchors for the belays on our descent, and it was a relief to reach the comparative safety of the base of the climb, despite having to dodge the falling rocks dislodged by our companions descending after us.

That night the bad weather arrived and we awoke to the crashing of thunder echoing around the rock walls above us. The noise alone made sleep difficult, but then it began to rain and sleep became impossible. 'Began to rain' is an understatement; I mean that a flood poured down on our heads, and soon we were all wet through. Streams ran down the rock, and everyone got up and wandered perilously about the rock faces trying to find a drier place to hide. Brian, sheltering with his girlfriend and some others in a larger cave, decided he had had enough. On the other side of a col to our north there was apparently a bivouac hut. 'Do you want to come with us and try to find it?'

'No way,' I told him. 'I'm staying here until it gets light. It's too bloody dangerous moving around this lot in the dark.' My wet and cheerless cave seemed a safe haven compared to wandering around those rock faces by the light of a head-torch.

The night passed as all such nights do, shivering, wet and miserable, my Afrikaner companion in the cave seemingly impervious, and keeping a continuous supply of coffee and tea shared out around the party. At first light Brian returned with his friends; they had not found the hut, and had spent the night sitting out in the open on their rucksacks. We packed up, and set off carefully down the gully in a strong wind and driving snow – I had to remind myself that this was the height of summer in a country with one of the most amiable climates in the world. It was some time before we reached the gulley's base, and gained a path leading on down to the valley and eventually to the Cathedral Peak Hotel. On the way down we met Adolf and some more Durban climbers who had set out at first light to check we were OK. As we all descended together the weather improved and soon we were coming down quickly towards the Mlambonja river. There was no bridge.

'How do we get across?' I demanded, for it was roaring in a flash flood from the storms in the mountains, and since nearly drowning in Nepal I have been fearful of such obstacles.

'We'll swim across!' Brian volunteered.

'Will we hell. You won't get me to even try it!' I responded. Brian dumped his pack and, fully clothed, dived in. I had to admit to myself that these Springboks were hardy characters, but the next moment he was fighting for his life and being swept downstream by the speed and force of the water. Fortunately, he had tied himself on to a climbing rope and had a belayer on the bank, and we all yanked on the rope, pulling him in to the shallow water downstream like a fish on a hook.

'I've never seen it like this, man,' said Adolf. 'We're bloody here until it goes down.' Stalemate . . . but then once again enter the 'Limey Lassoer'! I tied a boulder on to the end of a climbing rope and at my first throw caught a stout tree across the river, dozens of feet away. The stone wrapped itself around, I pulled the rope tight and announced triumphantly to my amazed companions, 'That's how we'll get across.' We could not get the rope tight enough from that angle to clear the water, so the first person would get wet, but Brian was already soaked to the skin and seemed totally fearless, so we volunteered him. He started to monkey across and, despite our hanging on to the rope, and his being fastened to it with karabiners, he almost drowned a second time, going right under before snatching the rope in desperation where it was out of the river. He climbed up it hand over hand to reach the safety of the opposite bank, and we all cheered. He moved the rope round to set up a safe route for us all to follow, and each was pulled across by a rope attached to a harness with a snaplink fastened to the fixed line.

The drive in Adolf's car back to Durban was fascinating. First we passed along dirt roads, made difficult by flash flooding after the storm in the Drakensberg, and saw the Ngwane, Zulu and Nguni people living as they have done for generations in mud huts in their tribal family units, then on to Escourt to join the modern motorway leading to Pietermaritzberg, founded by the Voortrekkers. There I gave a talk to the local climbing community at one of the lecture halls of the university, before heading back to Durban and a welcome bath, meal then bed at Doc Ripley's. The next morning a young climber was waiting for me in the Ripleys' kitchen. He was to be my guide for the next few days, and he had parked (literally at the front door) our means of transport, a multi-cylinder motorbike. Soon we were roaring through Durban's traffic and an hour later, dusty but excited, we arrived at Monteseel, a limestone escarpment out in the Zulu country to the north of the metropolis. My shy young companion began to chat. He was 19 years old and of English descent, fair with blue eyes, of lithe build, and a student in Durban. Soon we had roped up and had completed our first climb together, of about Hard Very

Severe standard, with a face about 100 feet high. My companion climbed so fast in the lead that I had difficulty in playing out his rope for him.

'Watch out for the snakes,' he warned. 'They are deadly here and sometimes the place is crawling with them.'

By 11 o'clock the sun was high, it was becoming hotter and hotter and, although I was dressed only in running shorts, a T-shirt and rock boots, I was sweating profusely. Still, no sooner had we coiled the rope at the top of this climb than we raced to the bottom to start on our second, and no sooner was this successfully completed than we were on to our third. By the time we had finished five climbs, each one harder than the last, my arms were aching fit to bust. I called a halt.

As we walked a little way down the back of the crag we talked. I found out that Cape Town was where the biggest number of active climbers were, and that the rock was superb. Below us was a shanty town with tin roofs, obviously inhabited by Blacks. I looked at these, then at my companion, and realised that he was ashamed of this example of the way in which many of his fellow countrymen were forced to exist in that rich country. We said nothing.

As we prepared to descend a gully to start our sixth climb, my young friend trod on a snake! It had been sleeping in the dense undergrowth which filled this cleft and struck at him, but he leaped out of its reach with tremendous agility. He seemed badly shaken. 'I am very frightened of snakes, Dennis!' he confessed. 'I won't be able to do any more climbing today.' I bit back a 'Good!' – I was tired out. He looked so white and drained that I feared he might faint, and I made him sit down for a rest. He slowly recovered. 'That was a viper!' he said. 'If you get bitten out here on the crags, you're in serious trouble – the nearest anti-snakebite serum is back in Durban!'

We called it a day and decided to have a wander around before riding back to town. The more I talked to this sensitive white South African the more I liked him, and over the next few days we became friends. He told me that he hated his country's apartheid regime, and that as soon as he had finished his studies he would emigrate, probably to Canada. Later, he took me to the climbing wall at Durban University. I was surprised to see how big and extensive it was, a brick-built structure, set out of doors on the campus of the university and available to any climber who wanted to use it. It was in a beautiful setting, and I could only envy the South Africans their marvellous climate; with a hot summer and mild winters an outside climbing wall can be used all the year round.

I gave one more lecture in Durban and then flew south-west to Cape Town, a long flight which made me realise how big the Republic is. As we came in to land I saw one of the most famous landmarks in the world, the Table Mountain, and below us the Cape, reaching out like a giant finger into the glistening seas – the meeting of the Atlantic and Indian Oceans. These were magnificent views which lived up to their reputation. John Moss, an old climbing friend from Leeds University and now a Senior Lecturer at Cape Town University, met me at the airport.

'Would you like to do a climb?' he laughed, as we shook hands.

'Where? On Table Mountain?' I guessed.

'No, here on the edge of town on the Lion's Head.'

'OK,' I agreed, 'if there's enough daylight left.'

I had not seen John for many years, and as we drove out to the Lion's Head he filled me in on his movements. After a spell teaching in Canada, he had taken up an academic post in South Africa on the coast near Port Elizabeth, where he had become involved in ocean sailing. The job as lecturer at Cape Town University meant that he could now pursue both his favourite activities – climbing and sailing. I turned the conversation around to apartheid. How did he see it? What was going to happen? 'Mmm, let's not go into that now,' he said. 'Come to the university tomorrow and meet my students. I have more Blacks than Whites in my department, and you can talk with them, and see what they feel about the future.'

'You're on!' I replied, as we arrived at the base of the Lion's Head.

Speeding through Cape Town, I had seen modern skyscraper buildings, shanty towns, and wonderful houses with fine lawns, some with a Dutch neatness, others like English country houses. 'This is some place,' I said.

'Yeah, it's about the best place in the world for a climber to live – as you'll find out!'

The Lion's Head was bigger and more impressive than I had imagined, but was dwarfed by Table Mountain to its north. We roped up at the foot of the rock face and John led off. He had lost none of his fluency, and in following I found the climb was much harder than it looked. I struggled with a rounded gritstone-type crack: 'You bugger, this is hard!'

'Well, I have done it several times before,' John conceded. On joining him I saw above our heads a long steep wall. 'Do you want to lead?' he suggested. 'It's not as hard as it looks.' Off I climbed. It was a superb pitch and not at all difficult, composed of block type sections of granite with big holds on the crack edges. The next pitch was the crux, and was 'thin' rather than strenuous. John ran out the full length of the rope, climbing swiftly, as the day was now drawing to a close and we wanted to get up and off before dark. Below us the lights of Cape Town were coming on, and they presented a spectacular sight when we finally reached the summit by one last easy pitch. 'There aren't many cities where you can climb a 450-foot, classic Hard Very Severe after work are there?' John chortled at me.

As we started to descend I asked him what it was like climbing up on Table Mountain. 'Bloody brilliant!' he enthused. 'The rock is hard sandstone and there are dozens of good routes, but they are long – anything between 600 and 1,000 feet. You must climb Africa Crag. It's the best classic route I've ever done anywhere, and the best thing of all is that you go up there in a cable car and walk down to the foot of the routes!'

'Sounds like the modern climber's dream of heaven,' I observed as we ran down a road leading back to John's car.

My host in Cape Town was Geoff Ward, a South African who had lived, worked and climbed in Britain. He was a shop manager, and lived in an old wooden bungalow with his wife and two young children in one of the less prosperous areas of town. 'Everyone imagines that all white South Africans are rich, have coloured servants, two cars, and no need to work!' Geoff laughed as we sat in his front room drinking beer later that night. 'Many of us are as poor here as the coloureds; the cost of living and house prices are sky-high in Cape Town.'

Next morning it was not fit to go climbing for the 'Cape Doctor' was blowing, a feature of the Cape area at that time of year. I visited the famous Groote Schuur Hospital where the world's first heart transplant had been performed in 1967, and then went to see John Moss at the university, where he introduced me to some of his students. His department was very well equipped, and the university buildings were modern and beautifully situated on the edge of the city, with Table Mountain and the serrated summit of its satellite, the Devil's Peak, forming a spectacular backdrop to the campus. As I sat and had coffee with some of John's young friends, I had to revise my ideas about how apartheid worked; it is far more subtle than I had realised. I was with an Afrikaner youth and a black girl who were both students in the same department, and both reading for a degree, and I could almost have been convinced that the fight was won. But the people of all races were still not being allowed to learn to live together. The majority of the population – the Blacks outnumber the Whites by five to one – have no vote, cannot decide where they wish to live and which jobs they would like to do, and who they want to marry. Afterwards, a young student took me outside and pointed out into the Bay of Cape Town. 'Do you know who is being kept out there on Robben Island?' he demanded. 'Nelson Mandela! He is our leader, and some day he will be the Premier of this country.'

'I hope so,' I honestly replied. 'I do hope so.'

The Cape Town section of the Mountain Club is by far the largest in the country, and that evening I gave my first lecture to them in a large public hall in the centre of the city. I noted with some satisfaction that there was a small group of Blacks at the back of the audience, which numbered many hundreds. My lecture was well received, with the anecdotes from my early climbing days the high spot of the evening, and afterwards a large group took over a seamen's tavern on the edge of town. The singing went on and the excellent Cape wines flowed until late into the night. The company was mixed again; I only dwell so much on this because before visiting South Africa I had assumed that such socialising was impossible.

The next morning Dr Richard Smithers, one of South Africa's leading climbers, and I caught the cable car to the top of Table Mountain. The view out over Cape Town and the Cape Peninsula is stunning, with the same extraordinary range of blues in the sky as in the Drakensberg, and all the way around the summit rim are cliffs. We descended to the foot of the Africa Face, and my companion pointed out the line of the Africa Crag route. In the middle of the face is a steep arête, and the climb follows this direct after reaching it by an exposed traverse from the right. We roped up. 'The first pitch is the hardest,' Richard informed me. 'Do you want to lead it? You climb straight up the wall to that niche about 70 feet above us'.

I started up the rock face and was immediately impressed by the quality of the sandstone – it was rock uniformly solid and the friction was superb. The climbing was typically 'outback'; none of your nut-every-few-feet, or pegs and bolts to aim for, you just run the rope out and make damn sure you don't fall! The last few moves into the niche were hard, and very exposed, with no protection close by. Richard came storming up to join me. 'I've done this climb so many times, I've lost count!' he said with a grin. I asked him how many routes there were on Table Mountain. 'Hundreds,' he replied, 'maybe a thousand.'

'How good are the non-whites? Do many of them climb?'

'Climbers like Ed February and Ed January are bloody good, and there are two clubs made up of coloured climbers in the Western Cape.'

'Can they join the Mountain Club?' I ventured.

'Of course they can, but most don't care to because of peer group pressure. It's a real pity because they would gain a lot, like access to facilities and technical information.'

I led the next pitch, an easy traverse left along a wide break, but the next sensational section looked so hard I could not believe it was climbable. Richard swung out boldly across an overhanging nose on to the edge of the buttress, then around a corner out of sight. The rope simply hung in space. When I followed him, I found that each hand hold was so big and the friction so good that, despite the situation and angle, the technical standard was actually only about Severe; perhaps the addition of 'desperate' or 'magical' would do it more justice though. Richard was belayed in a little eyrie on the edge of the rib. Above him the arête looked even steeper than the rock below. 'Bloody hell, it looks hard.'

'It's easy, honest,' he assured me, but I insisted on him leading. Again it proved to be just as he had said, but the higher we climbed the more the situation impressed me. The final wall was a fitting finale, and as I led it, pulling up on jug after jug, I was shouting back down to my companion, 'This must be the best route in Africa', and 'Should be on any climber's list of routes to do!' so exhilarated was I by the atmosphere.

The other short routes we did that day proved an anti-climax after Africa Crag, and, looking at colour slides of climbing around the area in Richard's front room later, I was amazed to find out that the first ascent of this superb route had been made back in 1936. 'You wait until you get to the Magaliesberg,' Richard warned me. 'There are routes there that Dick Barry climbed around that time, like Red Corner at Tonquani, that are harder than Africa Crag. No kidding.'

'Bloody hell, he must have been some climber.'

Over the next few days I climbed with and met many of the local Cape Town climbers – Bob Gray, who had been a colonel in the Rhodesian Army at 22, and involved in the vicious bush war which had been a prelude to that country's independence; Ed February, one of the black climbers, who explained that the main problem faced by him and his black friends was lack of cash, which meant that climbing in areas away from Cape Town was often beyond their means; and Mike Scott, another well-known local climber, who took me around the Eastern Cape, to Stellenbosch, with its Dutch-style houses and lush vineyards and orchards, the pass of Du Toit's kloof, the Hex River area and then the Paarl Rock Dome.

My final lecture in Cape Town was a sell-out, with about 400 people there and as appreciative an audience as I have ever enjoyed, and then we had a party at Geoff's house. Before I left for Johannesburg and my last talk, I drove out with Bob Gray to the Cape Point of the Cape of Good Hope, through places whose names reminded me of my home and family – Seaforth, Bantry Bay, Scarborough – and were a lasting memorial to all those who had come from Britain and Ireland to settle in this far-off land. It is land which surpasses all others I have seen in the richness of its natural resources; it should be a paradise for all its citizens, and not a prison for the majority because of the colour of their skin. 'What do you think will happen to this country?' I asked Bob, as we sat gazing into the foaming sea where the two great oceans meet.

'God knows', he said, 'but I keep telling anyone who will listen that we must work towards a fairer society or die here, for this will not be another Rhodesia. If a war of liberation starts in South Africa no one will be able to contain the killing.'

I flew in to Johannesburg at night and enjoyed the glittering sight of it from the air. It is the largest city in Southern Africa with around one and a half million people, and the centre of the gold and diamond mining industries; a large, straggling place with skyscrapers and mines abutting modern housing developments. On the outskirts of the city, 17 miles away, is Soweto, made up of 26 African townships containing over one million people.

My hosts in Johannesburg were Tony Mills and his wife, two Britons who had gambled everything on a new life in the Republic. Tony took me on my first morning to meet some of the local climbing fraternity, and I then travelled out of town to visit one of the world's deepest gold mines. It was out on the Witwatersrand, the richest gold-bearing reef in the world, about 50 miles long and stretching east to west with its hub the city of Johannesburg. This was a singular experience. The shaft went down over 10,000 feet, and at 5,500 feet I decided I had seen enough, for the heat and smell of the workings were enough to make me feel sick. There, working almost naked in those conditions, cutting into the lode, were the black miners. They looked just how the racist Afrikaner cameraman I had met in the Drakensberg had described them – 'animals'. Degradation becomes self-fulfilling, and these migrant workers, living in a place like Soweto, almost had become 'inferior species'. I could not help but compare all this with what I had seen at Auschwitz and the way the Nazis had degraded the Jews.

The next morning I left the city early with Paul Fatti, a compact, powerful man, now a Professor at the Witwatersrand University, and one of the Republic's most travelled mountaineers. We drove out to the Magaliesberg, about one hour by car to the north-west of Johannesburg, a long escarpment of hills covered in rock outcrops rising up out of the veld above rich farms. We parked the car at one of the farms and walked up to a high plateau. Large birds were nesting in the cliffs. 'They are Cape vultures,' Paul informed me. 'We keep clear of their nests in the breeding season. They can be vicious and will attack you if you go near to their eggs or chicks.' We walked across the plateau and then descended into an idyllic deeply wooded valley, with a stream, a rock pool and many trees in its bed – Tonquani. Sitting on a granite boulder at the side of the stream I felt that it was as beautiful a place to rock climb as I had seen. Across the stream from us was an imposing rock face of red granite. 'That's where Red Corner goes.' Paul pointed out the line of this famous climb. 'Do you want to try it?'

'Well, Richard Smithers told me I must.' We wandered across to the base of the cliff and began to rope up, no one else in sight. In response to my question as to how many climbers there were climbing in the Magaliesberg, Paul laughingly replied, 'Not many!'

'Hundreds?' I ventured.

'Dozens. No more.' I whistled. This range was 70 miles long and littered with cliffs 200 to 400 feet in height.

'Watch out for the baboons. They will open your rucksack and eat your food if you're not careful,' warned Paul piling rocks on top of his sack before starting to climb. Paul set out in the lead on the long first pitch of steep wall climbing, and I watched carefully as he climbed up the corner then out on to its left wall. 'Not so fit,' he grunted, as he came to a more difficult section which was obviously very steep. Slowly the rope ran out, and Paul, protecting himself first by clipping an *in situ* piton, then by placing nuts, progressed up the wall and finally traversed a little to the left to reach a stance maybe 120 feet up. 'That looked hard!' I shouted up. There was no response from my leader, merely a 'Climb!' How many times have I responded to this monosyllabic command.

Within seconds of starting out I was engrossed by the climbing; the rock was firm, the sun was hot, and in only shorts, rock boots and a T-shirt, I felt liberated as

I moved up the wall. How lucky I was compared to those poor black buggers back in that mine in the Witwatersrand! This climb was hard and I marvelled at the standard the pioneers had reached; without modern equipment it must have been a desperate lead. I was glad when good cracks appeared near the top of the pitch where I could get some hand jams. On joining Paul I confessed that this was the hardest pre-war climb I had ever done. He offered to let me lead the next pitch, which followed the corner all the way to the top, and this was easy but excellent climbing. The whole route was abut 200 feet in length.

On descending I was amazed to find that my rucksack had been carefully lifted out from underneath its protective boulders, and my sandwiches had disappeared. Nearby was the wrapper. Paul laughed until he cried. 'These baboons are so intelligent, they knew which rucksack to open. They leave the locals alone and go for the bloody foreigners!' His rucksack was where he had left it, untouched. He did share his lunch with me.

We climbed some more routes at Tonquani and then headed back into the city, where Paul and his wife Janet had me to dinner. There I met Janet's father, a thorough-going Afrikaner, and engaged him over dinner in a good-natured argument about the future of his country. 'You don't understand at all. The Blacks are not ready to govern this country, it would dissolve into tribal warfare,' he advised.

'You ought to be educating them, getting ready for one man, one vote!' I countered, and by the end of the meal everyone had joined in and I was late for my lecture. The audience for my talk that night was small, but they were enthusiastic and keen to talk climbing with me late into the night. Paul's particular interest got an airing too. He was engaged in almost a one-man campaign to save the Magaliesberg from exploitation and development by big business. Everywhere, wilderness is under threat, and South Africa is no exception, but Paul's policy of purchase of the best areas of these mountains has paid off. Ten years on, there is now a Magaliesberg Protection Society, of which he is the Chairman, which owns many of the most beautiful, unspoilt areas of the range.

The leading rock climber in Johannesburg at that time was Clive Ward, and over the next few days I climbed with him. Clive, a tall, dark, quiet man in his late twenties, had been born in London, but had emigrated to improve his job prospects and, of course, his climbing experience. He was mad keen to climb and shepherded me up and down climbs in the Magaliesberg all day long, some of which were 300 and 400 feet in length. One in particular was a steep wall climb he had pioneered with two big pitches that were both hard and spectacular. The rock in some places was dirty and covered with lichen, but this was to be expected on almost virgin rock. (Climbers in Britain are used these days to climbing on clean, perfect rock and do not realise that when the routes were first climbed they might have been dirty and covered in vegetation.)

Before I left South Africa I wanted to climb Revolver, pioneered by the Barley brothers, the hardest climb of its era in the Magaliesberg area, and named by Tony and Robin after the Beatles record (keen fans that they were). On my last day in Johannesburg, Clive drove me out to climb this route, which follows a rightward trending groove and crack system for perhaps 300 feet up a steep face. I led the first pitch without too much difficulty but, on belaying below the second pitch, which Clive had warned was the hard one, I saw with concern that it was wet.

After my partner had joined me I tried for almost an hour to get started on the second pitch but, despite attempting it with many different combinations of holds, I just could not get any higher than a few feet up. The wet holds and seeping cracks completely undermined me, and I had to tell Clive, 'I can't do it! Will you lead it?' We changed belays and the local hard man then tried his best, but he too could not make it go. He tried and tried, but each time he got established on the rock his feet shot off the wet holds and he had to jump back down on to our belay ledge. 'We'll have to abseil off!' he advised. 'It won't go today. It's too wet.' He began to set up the ropes to descend when, with a flash of inspiration, he decided to have one more attempt and traverse in after climbing a couple of moves upwards on the left of the normal route.

We reorganised the ropes, and Clive pulled himself up off the ledge on what appeared to be good flakes, but then the traversing moves looked desperate and I cowered on the ledge expecting to have to field him at any moment. He stuck on, despite his feet coming off the rock and then he was into the groove and above the wettest part of the climb. 'Phew! That was bloody hard,' he called down. 'I've done this route twice before, but it's never been as hard as this.'

'You're getting past it,' I taunted, but ten minutes later I was eating my words. Those first moves were good 5c climbing, and when you reached the wet rock it was desperate. I have to confess that in following Clive I shouted for a tight rope! I redeemed myself by leading the top pitch, however, climbing up a steep reachy wall, a move sequence that was on perfect rock, and was scarce in protection but with good holds once you could reach them.

'The Barley brothers must be pretty good climbers?' Clive asked as we drove back to town.

'Not bad,' I replied, 'but not as good as Albert Smart!'

'Who the hell is Albert Smart?' my companion demanded. I felt I had to let him in on the joke.

'He was a fictitious climber Robin Barley and I invented. We used to claim he was the best climber in Yorkshire, which anyone with a bit of nouse will know means that he must have been the best in the world. I used to write his name up in climbing journals for making early ascents of the hardest routes. Then one day a climber did appear on the scene with that name, and he was from Yorkshire, but *he* had great difficulty in climbing the easiest routes. Still, the expression stayed with us.'

On the long flight to London the next day I had plenty of time to reflect on all that I had seen in South Africa; the situation experienced at first hand is far more complicated than most people understand. Before going I had known something about African tribalism and about how the European settlers had been responsible for developing the continent economically from my time in Kenya, but this does not give the descendants of the settlers the right to take advantage of a system like apartheid to use their fellow men as slave labour so that they can keep their economy going.

I have no sympathy with those who declare that sport should be above politics, and above such considerations as the freedom struggle in South Africa. If sport is about anything, it is about fair play, and giving our opponent or partner exactly the same chances as yourself to win or lose. Under a system like apartheid, whose real *raison d'être* is the almost limitless supply of cheap labour it provides for the Republic's industries, this is not possible. Therefore the true struggle in that country is for everyone who believes in the values of democracy, equality and justice. I am glad to report that, with one or two exceptions, the climbing fraternity in South Africa subscribes to these values.

Tanigawa-Dake –
The Killer Mountain

Some one from below
Is looking at the whirling
Of the cherry snow.
Hakugetsu

Which mountain would you least like to climb? Which route or face would you fear most in bad weather? Would you be more anxious being caught by a winter blizzard on Ben Nevis, or a summer thunderstorm on the north face of the Eiger? Would you rather be camped out high on K2 or lost in the Khumbu icefall on Mount Everest? Each of these situations is potentially lethal, and each of these routes and mountains has exacted a terrible toll of human life from the unlucky or the unwary. However, if I was an insurance broker, and had before me all the details of accidents world-wide, I would not be too unhappy about insuring any climber engaged in the sport in summer or even winter, except perhaps on one mountain. I would have to think of placing an exclusion clause in my policy when it came to Tanigawa-Dake!

Approximately 100 miles north of Tokyo in the North Honshu province of Japan, and known universally to Japanese climbers as 'the killer mountain', Tanigawa-Dake, an isolated and complex peak of modest height (6,380 feet), is statistically the world's most dangerous mountain. Exposed in summer to typhoons from the Pacific Ocean, and in winter to the extreme cold and massive snowfalls that prevail in the Japanese Alps, it boasts many ridges with deep ravines. Its lower slopes are covered in evergreens which act like ball-bearings in the winter, delivering huge avalanches. Its rock faces are very loose, and stonefalls are almost continual; boulders the size of footballs come hurtling down its couloirs and walls, and it is quite definitely no place for the faint-hearted.

The rock on Tanigawa-Dake is composed of basalt and on its northern flank there are huge faces, rising almost from sea level, with small glaciers licking at their base. They provide a challenging prospect in the summer, but in winter the conditions can be extreme. Normally it is so cold that masses of powder snow build up on every ledge, in every couloir and, lower down, on every bush! Although this North Face is an innocuous-looking place when first seen from the valley, a visit to the climbers' cemetery at its base would soon make the arrogant humble, for over 800 names adorn the memorial there and each year about twenty new ones are added.

This accident rate, the highest anywhere in the world, demands that a permanent rescue team be stationed at the base of the wall throughout the year. In summer, you have to present yourself to this team, and have your equipment, experience and objectives rigorously examined before you are allowed to proceed. In the winter, however, none of this applies; by some strange quirk of Japanese logic, the authorities feel that anyone who ventures up on to Tanigawa at that time of year must be competent and know what they are about.

In the summer of 1981 I was the leader of a six-man British party which visited Japan as the guests of the Japan Mountaineering Association. We travelled hundreds of miles in a relentless programme of sightseeing, hard driving, socialising and, of course, rock climbing, on Mitsutoge, a beautiful mountain close to Mount Fuji, a cliff called Joyama on the Izu Peninsula, Gozaisho, a superb granite range of mountains near Nagoya, then Rokko Mountain, behind Kobe city. There we also visited Japan's National Mountaineering Centre, and then sampled Kobe beef, claimed to be the best in the world, in Sukayaki. The hospitality and warmth of our hosts surpassed any we had previously experienced, and at each place, with the different groups of climbers, we toasted each other's health in *sake*. This always ended with a word of warning to us, 'Be careful on the killer mountain!', which seemed to act as a signal for everyone to burst into song! After several performances I realised that the refrain was always the same and, when completed, followed by the whole company of Japanese collapsing in gales of laughter.

My curiosity overcame me, and one evening in Kyoto, when the refrain had been sung to us yet again over a glass of *sake*, I took Takao Kurosawa our interpreter aside. 'What does the song mean in English?' I demanded. Takao grinned at me.

'Dennis San, it roughly translates as follows. "If you go fishing in the rivers of Japan you may catch a fish, but if you go fishing in the river which runs from off Tanigawa-Dake you might just catch the body of a climber"!'

'That's a bit too bloody macabre,' I thought, and decided that Takao, with whom I had become good friends, was having a joke at my expense. I was dumbfounded when I checked later with another of our Japanese guides, famous climber Naoe Sakashita, and he produced approximately the same translation!

Our progress throughout that visit was magnificent. Free rock climbing standards in Japan at that time were way behind Europe and the USA, and we were continually making first free ascents and even pioneering new climbs. The distances we travelled were immense and in every city we visited or at every climbing hut there was either a formal dinner or a party. Speeches were the order of the day, with the traditional Japanese politeness and courtesy combined with a natural reserve being slowly turned on its head by this party of raucous British climbers engaged in good-humoured tomfoolery. In the end our hosts began to outdo us! We hardly ever slept, and after ten days of this manic behaviour were definitely beginning to flag. We took a trip to Kyoto to recuperate and saw the ancient capital of Japan at its best in superb summer sunshine. There we experienced a communal bath, the *Cha-no-yu* tea ceremony and a Geisha play, the *Samisen*, and visited an art museum where I was thrilled to see a Ukiyoe woodblock print by Sharaku, the greatest-ever exponent of the art form. I could have spent weeks in this beautiful and fascinating town, but the Secretary of the Japanese Federation, Yoshikazu Takahashi, was determined we should keep to our schedule and accordingly we set out on the final leg of our programme.

We arrived by minibus at the base of Tanigawa-Dake on the evening of a superb June day. There was not a breath of wind, and towering above us was the huge north face of the mountain with tendrils of mist clinging to its ridges, emphasising the features of the wall. I suggested to Mr Takahashi that we take a closer look at the face. 'Yes', he said, 'but first we must pay our respect to the dead climbers. Then we can walk up and inspect our climbs for tomorrow.'

The party comprised Paul Dawson, Mark Vallance, Mike Trebble (the youngest member), Richard Haszko, Nigel 'The Corporal' Gifford and me. We had come together *ad hoc* via the BMC, after real difficulty in recruiting enough participants because of the costly air fares from Britain to Japan. However, it was a party that worked well; we all got on famously together, and the almost incessant laughter had rubbed off on our Japanese colleagues too. We arrived at the base of the mountain a happy bunch.

The jolly mood quickly became sober as we entered the climbers' graveyard below Tanigawa-Dake; we could not believe our eyes. It was like the cemetery of a small British town, with several sculptures tastefully arranged around a well-maintained site – a life-size naked climber wearing only a rope, a massive piton and a tomb containing an eternal flame as a memorial to every fallen comrade. Our attitude changed from laughing and joking at our own possible fate on this mountain to one of reverence and a sombre realisation of the truth. We spoke in hushed voices and glanced upwards apprehensively. I gazed up at Tanigawa and wondered, 'What the hell is up there on that mountain hidden in the mist that devours climbers like this?'

The majority of Japanese follow religions of acceptance, either Buddhism or Shinto, and our Japanese climbing friends held a simple ceremony, which we also observed, praying for the dead and our own safe deliverance. Then we walked up the road to where it ended, at the start of the glacier which runs up the foot of the face of the mountain. The mist dispersed and in the evening light the Ichinokura Sawa Wall looked benign; it was hard to imagine, sitting on a boulder studying the face, that anyone could come to grief on its slopes. It was a huge and complex mountain, however, and on its lower sections there was so much vegetation it looked almost like a jungle.

Naoe pointed out some of the outstanding features and possible routes that we might try. 'Up the glacier, then skirt that buttress to gain the easy angled spur, then climb up that until it abuts against the face proper. Then climb up the edge of the buttress direct until you can gain the easy slopes above. Once at that point it is easy, but dangerous, for the rock is loose and one has to be careful not to get avalanched either by the snow or scree!' This warning from Sakashita, delivered with sombre emphasis, had a real effect on me. He was still recovering from injuries sustained falling into a crevasse whilst trying to solo Annapurna. He had been down inside an ice cage for a week, and had managed eventually to climb out and crawl down the mountain alone. This was one of the great survival epics of mountaineering history. A climber like Naoe Sakashita would not use warning words lightly.

We stepped on to the glacier to get a closer look at the face. Walking up over its snout, we saw what appeared to be fishing nets made up from climbing ropes. 'Trying to catch a fish or two?' I asked innocently.

'No, Dennis San, they are to catch the bodies which emerge from the ice every summer. There are many dead climbers under here and every year at this time we recover some as they emerge from the melting glacier.' We gulped, stunned into silence by this information; by now the jokes had all stopped. We walked slowly back down the glacier like condemned men; the morale of the whole group had changed dramatically. I tried to cheer them up by pointing out that rescue was free here, and that we were all well insured through the BMC. Nigel Gifford growled, 'It's not bloody insurance we need, it's someone to tell whoever it is keeps hurling stones down the mountain to stop it – at least for tomorrow!'

That night we were guests of the Tanigawa-Dake rescue team at their head-quarters under the face. Around the walls of the hut were gruesome pictures of bodies they had rescued off the wall in winter and summer and I began to feel we were in some nightmare movie and not here to enjoy a climb. The hospitality, however, was excellent, and a huge meal was followed by toast after toast, first in *sake*, then in whisky, to the success of our climb. (Incidentally, we had been continually surprised by how much the Japanese drink, yet how fit many of them were; Japan has the greatest incidence of longevity in the world.) We became so merry imbibing that I forgot all about the lurking beast outside, but even inside we had to sit in our duvets, heavy climbing breeches, woolly hats and gloves, so up on the face, even at the height of summer, it must still have been freezing.

At first light we were trudging back up to the glacier where we split into our climbing teams – Mark Vallance and Nigel Gifford with Naoe, Paul Dawson with Mike Trebble, and Takao Kurosawa and me. Educated at Tokyo and Vienna University, Takao was small, dark and stocky, and apparently older than he looked. He translates books from German or English into Japanese and is a real enthusiast for travel and high mountains. Richard Haszko decided he would like to investigate our surroundings further and took off with a young Japanese for another side of the mountain, intending to try an easy route to the summit.

When we reached the foot of the spur, Paul and Mike headed off across the snow to try a route up steep slabs and walls, over to the left of a deep couloir, whilst the rest of us decided to solo climb up the ridge immediately above us. As we gained height it was possible for the first time to appreciate the scale; the spur contained perhaps 1,500 feet of climbing, but when we arrived at its head there were still hundreds of feet of steep rock face above. On every steep section of this first part of the climb, and at every awkward move, Takao would intone a ritual warning, 'Be careful here, Dennis San, for Mr So and So was hit by a stone at this point,' or a little higher, 'Mr So and So pulled a block off here on to his second man,' or a little further on still, 'Mr So and So fell from this place because of verglas to his death!' This was all delivered in the sort of calm and matter-of-fact voice that he might use to warn me to watch out for the traffic in Tokyo. The effect of these warnings was that we climbed up the rib as if it was Extreme in grade, and not Severe as in the guidebook.

We reached the top of the spur in good order despite our nervousness, then stopped at the foot of the upper steep wall to rope up. Here the serious climbing began and Naoe led off, with Mark and Nigel tied to his rope. Takao, who prefers the high mountains, winter, snow and ice climbing to rock, invited me to lead him.

We worked our way up the edge of the buttress, via some steep hard climbing on rock which became progressively looser. I was becoming jittery, for, as the sun climbed higher in its orbit, more and more stones began to fall down the face from the snowfields high above our heads. We were climbing up a pronounced rock nose, and most of these whistled away harmlessly down the couloir on our left, but when I looked down between my legs I saw a party of climbers climbing up the bed of this channel, exposed to the worst of the avalanches. 'Who the hell is that in the couloir? They must be trying to commit hara-kiri!' I shouted down to Takao.

'It's Professor Ohuchi and Mr Japan.' We had had real difficulty in pronouncing some of the Japanese names, so we had given them nicknames. 'Mr Japan' was one. He was a giant and a member of the rescue team, and we had christened him thus because he looked as though he could pick the archipelago up and carry it on his broad shoulders. Ohuchi was a distinguished Professor of Botany from Tokyo

University, and had been one of our guides and a generous host in the city. We had referred to him (behind his back) as 'Hoochy-koochy!'.

'They must be absolutely bleeding crazy,' I shouted.

The higher we climbed the more dangerous the rock became, the basalt being very fractured by the frost and ice. As I pulled on to a ledge where Mark and The Corporal were belayed, trying to look small under their crash helmets, I saw by the look on their faces that they were totally gripped. Above and to their left, Naoe was tussling in a groove with the crux of the climb, and as he moved up stones came whistling down around us. I have known Mark jump off the top of a crag into thirty feet of space, with only a single Friend as an anchor, to demonstrate his faith in the products he manufactures, but now he was anxious. 'If I could go down from this place with honour, without letting the side down,' he said tersely, 'I'd be off like a shot back to the valley. This place is bloody dangerous. I'm terrified!'

'Attention! A stone!' shouted Naoe and, as if in a Hollywood movie, as Mark finished speaking a boulder the size of a football crashed in between us. It smashed to pieces, and we jumped about like rats in a cage.

Naoe managed with some difficulty to lead this hard pitch – his leg and one of his arms were still causing him much pain from his accident in the Himalaya. He belayed and brought up first Mark, then Nigel, then it was my turn to lead this the hardest section of the route. I climbed up a steep wall, then traversed left into a fine hanging groove. After a difficult bridging move I was into this feature, and saw with relief that it had several pitons in place for protection. I clipped into the first of these, moved up, and nearly fell off as my left hand hold just pulled off the rock face when I put my weight on it. 'Must spread your weight,' I kept telling myself; this is the only safe way to climb such loose rock. At the top of the groove was an overhang and getting out over this was the hardest move on the pitch. I completed this section, and was resting in a bridging position, when a huge rock avalanche was triggered from somewhere above my head. Boulders the size of chairs came hurtling down, and I cowered into the rock face. Most of them bounced off the rib above us, and shot off down into the couloir where the two Japanese were climbing.

Looking down and across to my left I could see Ohuchi leading in the middle of that dangerous channel, and suddenly stones were falling all around him. I saw him hug the rock trying to avoid being hit, but then the inevitable happened and a rock struck him fair and square on the shoulder and knocked him off the cliff face! Horrified, I followed his flight, down, down, down, until he was out of my sight. I had seen him fall about eighty feet and, shaking, I screamed up to the others, 'Ohuchi's been hit! Ohuchi's fallen.' They had seen the accident and did not need me to draw their attention to the plight of the poor Professor. By the time I had joined them, after scrambling up the last few feet of the groove, Naoe was already arranging abseil ropes so that we could go to the rescue.

I brought Takao up on to my perch and, shouting, we made contact with Paul and Mike climbing out on slabs to the left of Ohuchi's couloir. They were almost level with the point where he was hanging unconscious on the end of the rope, and they traversed over to him. They shouted up that he was badly injured and we would have to lower him, but got him on to a ledge, out of the bed of the couloir and away from the worst stonefall danger.

We descended by a series of short abseils towards our goal, and then had to traverse the couloir to reach the injured man; we tip-toed at speed across this dangerous channel. By the time we reached the others, they had good anchors arranged, and Mr Japan hd made a seat or tragsitz from the rope. We hoisted Professor Ohuchi on to his broad back.

I have ben involved in many rescues over the years, and I have never seen anyone more competent than Mr Japan. We lowered him with his burden 150 feet at a time, leap-frogging each other, going out in front setting up the next abseil whilst those behind recovered the equipment from the previous lower. With our large party we could do this quickly, and the important thing was to regain the spur quickly, to be relatively safe from avalanche danger. Once we had embarked on the operation, I hardly spoke to my team-mates, but kept looking anxiously up the couloir expecting more stones to fall at any time. I was hit on the shoulder by a small one, and my scream would have done justice to any ham actor. Mr Japan was also struck, several times, but he shielded the injured man with his own body, and never made a sound when the stones found their target, calmly getting on with descending the couloir.

Soon we reached a place where we could traverse over to the spur, and Paul Dawson and I were now having to climb down solo to remove the equipment successfully. Carrying ropes, pitons, slings and Ohuchi's rucksack, I became stuck at the top of a groove. 'Bloody hell, Paul, I'm in trouble!' I panicked.

'No you're not, you daft bugger, you're off route. Climb back up. It's easy. The way down is on your left.'

'I thought it felt hard for Severe,' I grinned at him when, a few seconds later, I had slithered down the easy crack he had pointed out.

It took us some while to descend the Spur – 1,500 feet of lowering by tragsitz is a long way – but Mr Japan's strength was impressive. Usually, after a couple of 150-foot lowers with the weight of a man on your back, you are knackered and have to rest, but our Japanese rescue expert showed little sign of fatigue. Two hours later we reached the glacier and, as I leaped across the bergschrund between the rock face and ice, it was like being delivered from an open boat in a raging sea back on to dry land. My shoulder hurt where the stone had hit me, but I was over the moon to have escaped from this dangerous situation with such a minor injury. My team-mates were all fine, but we all agreed, as we carried Professor Ohuchi down the easy slopes of the glacier, that we would never, ever set foot on Tanigawa-Dake again. We were cowards, and you had to be a Japanese to enjoy climbing there!

We were soon met by the permanent rescue team who had come up to meet us. They transferred the injured man to a stretcher with runners, babbling excitedly in Japanese, and set off down the ice at speed as if in a slalom race. I asked Takao what had been said. 'They are very impressed with how British climbers made the rescue, Dennis San, and they say you would make very good members for their team!'

'No way!' retorted The Corporal, who was walking down at my side. 'We wouldn't go up there again, even to rescue Haszko. If he gets into trouble we'll definitely leave it to the professionals to get him off!'

We caught up with the rescue team as they were bundling Professor Ohuchi into a kind of mobile ambulance with tracks that had been driven up on to the glacier. He came round, and began to cry out, obviously very distressed. 'What's he saying? What's he saying?' I demanded of Naoe.

'He says his wife will be very annoyed with him!'

'Why?'

'Because, Dennis San, this is the third time he has been carried off Tanigawa-Dake as an injured man. She has forbidden him to climb upon the killer mountain,

Professor Ohuchi being lowered off Tanigawa-Dake. (Photo: Dennis Gray)

and she had no idea he was up here on the mountain. She thinks he is away attending an academic congress!'

'Poor bugger!' I sympathised, for the one thing a Japanese man fears is losing face with his friends and colleagues. We had met Mrs Ohuchi, who was a beautiful and charming lady but no mere chattel of her husband. In domestic and economic matters she ruled the roost, and I could imagine the scene when she was phoned with the news of his accident. Still, at least he was alive, and we were relieved to hear, once he reached hospital, that he would make a complete recovery.

This epic over, we anxiously awaited the return of Richard Haszko. He came back in the late afternoon, just as a storm was brewing, and was happy to discover that he had been the only member of our party to reach the summit of Tanigawa-Dake, having ascended by a route up its west flank. Whilst this route was on a less forbidding aspect of the mountain, he did confirm that it was loose and had been the most frightening outing of his life. The summit area was apparently very complicated, with many ridges, and the way off the mountain long and difficult to find, especially once it had misted over after midday.

We returned to Tokyo the next day as if we had been given a reprieve from a death sentence. I gave a lecture in the early evening at Seibu Sports, the largest sports shop in the world, to an audience of Japanese climbers. At the end our party formed a question-and-answer panel. A young Japanese lady climber stood up and smilingly asked, 'Did you enjoy your visit to Tanigawa-Dake, the killer mountain?' I thought for a moment, not wanting to give any kind of offence to our hosts, and then answered her with my favourite *Haiku* poem by the Shinto priest Chomei. It seemed to me to sum up our experience.

Charmed by the flowers, I seem to feel a love for them. How can this passion still possess my soul when, methought, I had utterly renounced the world.

On returning to the valley from Tanigawa, my perception heightened by the experience on the face, I had been struck by the exquisite beauty of the flowers on the meadow above the rescue team's headquarters.

In the Land of the Morning Calm

Life is but a drop of water set in a boundless sea
Go climb to the summits between heaven and earth
Join in constant harmony with an infinite nature
See the riches of your life, drop of water and sea.
Yi Un Sang – Epic poet and mountaineer

'Mr Dennis, please show us the mantelshelf again?' begged Miss Annapurna, a member of the thirty-strong course I was instructing made up of South Korea's leading climbers. This was most embarrassing – I couldn't tell if it was a big send-up or not! Surrounded by grinning Orientals, I decided, 'In for a penny . . . !' I walked up to the rock face and weighed up the problem, one of a series we had worked on the night before on the boulders scattered around the base of the Insoo Bong mountain. Placing the edge of the outside of my right palm at above waist height, on a small side hold, I pressed down hard and tickled the wall with my rock boots as I began to move up. I cranked away as hard as I could and, after a desperate struggle, got my left foot on to the edge of the hold my hand was on and rocked my body over. I stood up to the accompaniment of enthusiastic applause. After a sequence of two delicate movements, I had my hands on the top of the boulder, and from a second mantelshelf that was nowhere nearly as hard as the first I pulled myself on to the summit, to deafening cheers from below.

No. I decided they had not been sending me up; their attempts to repeat the problem were genuine enough. After several attempts and falls, and with a desperate struggle, one of their leading rock climbers managed to get up the mantelshelves.

Two days before I had flown into Seoul, the capital of South Korea and one of the biggest cities in the world to attend the General Assembly of the UIAA and also, at the invitation of the Korean Alpine Club, to run a course of instruction, and explain to their best climbers the training regimes involved in modern rock climbing. This request had been flattering to someone who is not even a Yorkshire first eleven (nor second, for that matter) climber, and my first response had been to refuse. However, I was interested in training methods, which were developing fast in rock climbing, and concerned that many young people were harming themselves either by using the wrong techniques or by subjecting their upper bodies to over-use leading to serious tendon and ligament injuries. I decided to help the Koreans if I could, and agreed to take part.

We travelled eastwards from Seoul in a taxi to the Bookhan San National Park, less than an hour from the centre of the City. There, at the road's end, all around a Buddhist temple set on a hillside in deep woods, were granite faces and peaks. After a forty-minute walk up to a climbing hut through the woods, we were sitting on its porch looking up at Insoo Bong, a mountain which could have been transported straight out of the Yosemite Valley, with superb grey granite faces, seamed with cracks and tinted yellow by the late afternoon sun. This was a first-class climbers' playground. Away in the distance to the east we could see Mount Dobong, equally impressive, whilst the lower valley walls boasted outcrops of rock, many several hundred feet in height.

I could see temples dotted on the hillsides and later found out that the whole area has a deep religious significance, a place of pilgrimage for Buddhists, Shamans, Confucians, Taoists and Tanguns. Tangunism and Shamanism are the original religions of Korea, at least 4,000 years old, although there are only a few adherents left in the country. Buddhism is now the major religion, followed by most of my present companions. Few of these could speak English, although one or two knew some French, and I was grateful to have Mr Oh, an interpreter.

On our first day in the Bookhan San we climbed the Chouinard 'A' route on Insoo Bong's South Face, a classic 5.8 (using the Yosemite grading method), 800-foot crack and chimney climb, one of two outstanding climbs pioneered by Chouinard several years before. The granite was good. It was immediately obvious that my companions were skilled climbers, but had little or no idea of how to use modern protection methods. They would run out 100 feet of rope up ground with perfect placements in which to put nuts, but each one they placed simply fell out again as soon as they climbed above it. We climbed in a large party made up of several ropes of three, for I wished to observe as many of them in action as I could, and from below we must have resembled a caterpillar slowly wending its way up the impressive wall.

Insoo Bong is a difficult peak with no easy way to its summit, a huge granite dome whose descent is by way of abseils down the western flank. The next day we repeated the exercise and climbed the Chouinard 'B' route on the south face of the mountain, over 1,000 feet in length and hard. It is graded 5.9, but I thought its crux pitch was harder – a thin slab set at the very top of the mountain, entailing 60 feet of tricky climbing. I watched one of the tiny Koreans (who I had nicknamed Yum Yum) lead safely up it, followed by his two rope-mates. Climbing in mountaineering boots, they had no problems, so I had great confidence as I set out in my Fire sticky rubber boots. The climbing became more and more reliant on friction, and after 30 feet I was worried stiff by the lack of protection. Just as I was about to flip, a bolt, invisible from below, appeared out on the slab to my left. Reaching it required an enormous effort and I was shaking as I clipped into it. There is much ethical debate amongst climbers about the use of bolts, and whether they destroy the sport's essential spirit of adventure, but I would suggest that one in 60 feet is not too many! Yum Yum was obviously an outstanding performer, but I had been terrified at the way he had run out 150-foot rope-lengths of climbing on the lower parts of the climb without placing *any* protection at all.

The autumn tints of the trees below the mountain, the firm granite, on a par with any I have ever enjoyed, and the warmth of friendship from the Korean climbers made this route memorable for me. Even now, in retrospect, I think it deserves inclusion in any book of the world's best rock climbs.

It was time to start the course, and when I met the group, 30 strong, there was not a novice in sight. Between them they had made many famous ascents, and I felt a fraud, believing there was little I could teach *them*. Still, at least I towered over them – unusual for me at five foot eight! Initially they all looked alike (as, apparently, we from the West do to Orientals), but I could soon recognise them all. Everyone was called Mr Lee, Mr Park, Mr Moon, Mr Oh or Mr Kim – in Korea first names are only used by those who are very familiar with each other – so, to avoid confusion yet not offend their traditions, I called them after the mountains they had climbed. Mr Makalu, Miss Annapurna, Mr Manaslu, Mr Ogre and best of all, Mr Eiger (which they all seemed to find hilariously funny) were no problem, but one of them had never climbed outside their country. I called him Yum Yum, and he is now universally known in Korea and Europe by this nickname.

The meet was centred on a large climbing hut, but most of the party preferred to camp because it is free. On the first night, as I lay in bed in the hut, I could hear from outside a noise such as Red Indians make in the Westerns – a chanting which went high, then low. I went outside into a cold, beautifully still, moonlit night and climbed a short way above the refuge; there before me was a group shuffling around a fire, dressed like American Indians and led by women priests. They were Shamans, following one of the original religions of the country. The priests live in the caves under Insoo Bong and at other sites in the mountains of South Korea, and are descended from exactly the same people who originally peopled the North American continent.

During the first few days I was relieved to find that rock climbing standards in Korea were not as high as Europe, and I felt less guilty about my position as teacher. I had trained like a demon before leaving home, running, bouldering and solo climbing on my local gritstone outcrops, and I found I could manage their most difficult climbs, then about 5c. The course members had never previously encountered double rope techniques, and their use of modern protection methods was inefficient and, although they rarely seemed to fall, when they did they usually hurt themselves badly. Yum Yum, for example, had fallen several years before on Insoo Bong – a route with perfect rock and bomb-proof protection possibilities on a crack pitch – and had suffered nasty injuries. They seemed more orientated to mountaineering and I had been impressed how on the top slab of the Chouinard 'B' they had fearlessly gone for it with no hesitation. At that time they were not into training for rock climbing (unlike now), although several of them were experts in Taekwondo, the Korean martial art. Mr Oh gave me a friendly demonstration one night of this 'way of the feet and fists' and, despite our height and weight difference, I was no match for his lightning speed and technique, spending most of the time on my back on the ground.

Around the camping ground there were many boulders, and I spent hours each evening working out a circuit of problems on these. Surprisingly, the Koreans had not thought of developing such activities, but once they had seen my example they soon took to it, and before the end of our course each problem had been graded, named and written up by the indefatigable Mr Oh. Doubtless there is now a guidebook to bouldering in that area!

Mr Oh was a marvellous character, and nothing was too much trouble for him where I was concerned. He was a small, round man with a moon-shaped face, who laughed a lot and sang traditional songs around our camp fire in the evening. He told me much about the country's history, and about climbing in South Korea. The first rock climb was made in the Bookham San area by some British climbers from the Legation in Seoul in the late 1920s, although Younghusband had made some exploratory journeys at the turn of the century. After the last war, and the end of the Japanese occupation, climbing had really taken root, and now there are more people going into the hills than in almost any other country in the world. The Korean Alpine Federation states in its current literature that there are 2,500,000 climbers! (How do you define a climber?) Every high school, university and college boasts a climbing club, as does every town, even the small ones. Seventy per cent of the country is covered by mountains, and there are hundreds of places to rock climb and, in winter, practise on ice. Mount Soraksan, for example, in the north-east of South Korea is 5,651 feet high and has on its flanks the most spectacular rock face in the country, almost two miles wide, with an average height of around 1,000 feet and made up of perfect grey granite. For winter climbing the Towangsong Waterfalls provide almost 1,500 feet of hard ice, and the most demanding route of that season.

Mr Oh also told me that there were long-established climbing competitions in South Korea. The oldest began in 1959, a mountaineering skills event involving everything from navigation and camping skills to some technical climbing – rather like the Karrimor Mountain Marathon event. More recently pure rock climbing competitions based on speed, style and difficulty had been established, with separate events for men and women. I had been encouraged by how many women I saw climbing whilst I was in South Korea; interestingly, they also have the largest women's university in the world.

Each night on the course we had lectures and question-and-answer sessions in the hut. I explained the rudiments of rock climbing training, and the latest developments in Europe and the USA in both equipment and techniques. Their enthusiasm to learn knew no bounds. Many other young climbers joined in the sessions and, via Mr Oh, I was able to find out what life was like for them. Few could be totally dedicated to climbing because of the social pressures upon them. For the youngest there was a school system with exams that made the British system seem like a sinecure, and for the older ones there was the need to make a living. In South Korea there is a six-day working week, with a ten-hour day the norm, and the competition for jobs is acute in a country which turns out more graduates than Britain. It was unheard of for a young person to pack in studies or work simply to climb; such an idea struck my companions as incredible.

Most Koreans start climbing at high school, and the system is such that an older climber will look after a young beginner. They form extremely close and deep friendships and climb as a team, usually in parties of two ropes of two. When they have grown up together each seems to have a sixth sense of what the other is doing. When a Korean introduces you to his rope-mate it can be most confusing, for he may refer to him as a 'brother', as well as calling him by his first name. This team structure, along with the willingness of major industries to sponsor expeditions, is the basis of their recent success in the Himalaya, where they have emerged as the main rivals to the Japanese.

The Koreans' attitude to climbing reminded me of ours in Britain in the late 1940s and early 50s. Their standard of living was similar and none of them owned a car. They could only climb at weekends, and travelled out to the crags after work on Saturday nights, slept under the rock faces and climbed on Sundays. Few could travel abroad to climb, and the members of the course had all taken part of their holiday entitlement to be there, coming from all over the country, perhaps spending a day and a night travelling by bus. I was most flattered.

Our course was covered by the national climbing magazine, which dealt with everything, from extreme rock and ice climbing to mountain flowers and conservation issues – the thickest I have seen anywhere in the world. Its editor, Mr Park, was a most interesting man, who could speak English and was a Buddhist. One evening he asked me to join him and his wife for a meal at his house near Seoul. We had drunk quite a lot of local wine when he asked, 'Do you practise meditation? I like to do this after a meal whilst taking tea. 'Would you like to join me?'

'OK, sure.' We sat, perfectly still, at a small table with the tea-set on it, our hands folded, and under his instructions I slowly relaxed my whole body and closed my eyes. I almost fell asleep, so serene did I feel.

'I would like to meet with you inside the teapot. Put your mind into it!' commanded Mr Park. 'Come inside the teapot with me!' This may sound ridiculous, and you may think I was intoxicated with drink, but I did find myself, or at least my senses, inside the teapot; and I was conscious of being there with another – Mr Park! It was a warm, friendly experience only broken when his wife came into the room some minutes later.

'How on earth did you do that?' I asked.

'There are some things which cannot be explained but must be experienced,' he replied enigmatically. The episode set me thinking about how meditation could be used by rock climbers, whose mental preparation is so important. As climbing develops in the East, perhaps their Buddhist tradition of martial arts training allied to mental control – focusing all the body's energy on to a single event or problem (the Focus of Ki), used by the Samurai – will bring about a revolution in rock climbing standards.

'I need to find a small cliff about 100 feet high which has never been climbed on,' I told Mr Oh towards the end of the course. 'Do you now of one?'

'Sure thing Mr Dennis, I know one.' As good as his word, he walked us up to a steep crag to the west of Insoo Bong, just off the descent path. Our entourage seemed to grow daily, and a Mr Young il Kim, who had been asked to take photographs of our course by the Korean Alpine Club, now joined us.

Mr Oh's cliff was in a kind of gorge and ideal for my purposes; I was surprised that no one had ever climbed there, for it was only half an hour's walk from the hut. It was about 80 feet high and I pioneered a climb up its walls, starting at the right-hand side then traversing across left for many feet, before tackling a difficult final crack by hand jamming. Exiting out of the top was tricky; a large loose pinnacle and a grass sod were blocking the way, and I had to hang from jams whilst I excavated my way over these, before a final strenuous pull on to the top. The aim of this exercise was to show the advantages of double rope techniques and the placement of nut runners in such a climbing situation, and the enthusiasm with which my effort was greeted was almost as if I had pioneered a new extreme. Literally dozens of ascents followed my own, with some of the male members of the course leading the climb half a dozen times. Miss Annapurna ascended the route in fine style and even gave me a kiss when she came back down! This was greeted by hoots of laughter by the party, and I blushed, not at this public show of affection but at the reaction to it.

On our final evening at Insoo Bong we built a large bonfire, and the cooks prepared *Bulgogi*, a Korean speciality of thin slices of beef heated on hot stones by a fire. We also drank ginseng, made from the mysterious 'man-root' (so called because it looks like a man's body), and served hot with honey as a refreshing and warming drink to keep the freezing night cold at bay. I looked up at where I knew Insoo Bong to be, then at the stars, and was sad that I could not talk with my companions. Apart from Mr Oh, none of them spoke English. However, when it was time to say goodbye the next morning, and I had made a speech which was translated by Mr Oh, we communicated well enough with handshakes, hugs and kisses. How we all need each other in this world!

Back in Seoul I attended the UIAA meetings. Some people see these forums as an excuse for wining and dining at someone else's expense, but the world is shrinking fast with mountaineering problems becoming ever more international, and concrete results are achieved every year. The need for closer co-operation between all the mountaineers of the world in the years that lie ahead, to help preserve the climbing environment, is now self-evident.

After the traditional final banquet at the end of the UIAA meetings the photographer Mr Young il Kim approached me. 'Would you like to visit my home, Mr Dennis, and meet my parents?' I readily agreed and after a short taxi ride we arrived. His mother and his father were both famous artists, his mother in graphics and his father in furniture design. He had been in North Korea before the 1950s, and had climbed in the mountains there, making first ascents on what he said were beautiful peaks. Kim junior had suffered a bad injury from a fall years before, and his ambitions in mountaineering terms were now very modest, but he was totally dedicated to his art of 'social photography'. He showed me some books by Diane Arbus, studies of low life in New York – people on skid row, drunks, prostitutes and transvestites. I was stunned into silence. 'Would you like to come with me and I will show you what I am working on. I hope to do a book about Seoul with the same theme.'

In Seoul (which in English simply means 'The capital'), Kim took me to the red light area, Itaewon, a garish, neon-lit world that never closes. It seemed that he was well known in this district, and as we visited various clip joints, a strip club, a gay bar, and sat and had a drink with some transexuals, I realised that he was keenly observing my reactions. I was fascinated, and the more I saw the more I wanted to see. I have always felt a sympathy with those on the fringes of society, and I am not alarmed by transvestism, nor judgemental about strippers or prostitutes (who are often more sinned against than sinning). Mr Kim seemed to accept me, and we sat in a bar and talked through what was left of the night about art and photography. I understood more and more of what he was saying as I became in tune with his idiomatic use of English as the night progressed. As we shook hands and said goodbye the next morning, we agreed to be friends always. About a year later I heard that he had been killed in a car crash.

On my last day in Seoul the boys from the Ahgoo Club appeared in a battered old minibus at the swanky Sheraton Hotel to take me climbing. I had not been to bed and with my head throbbing like a bee-hive, I regretted my temerity of the night before when I had laughingly agreed to meet them. They had come to the hotel to extract a promise that I would climb with them the next day before being ejected by the doormen. They were like the Rock and Ice in its 1950s heyday ('Ahgoo' actually means rock and ice!), a small group of outstanding climbers unconnected with the establishment. They earn their living by making mountaineering equipment in family cooperatives, with mums, wives and girlfriends all working at sewing machines in the front room on rucksacks or sleeping bags, whilst they hammer and file away in the back of the house making climbing hardware. Karabiners, tents and even a new rock boot with a sticky sole were developed in this way. I found out that many such groups of climbers are involved in the business of manufacturing like this. At that time the equipment market was flourishing in Korea, with designs copied from Western sources and often an improvement on the original product! Items like Friends were illegally manufactured too, but these were not as good as the real thing.

In the communal Aghoo van I was introduced to the members, and everybody was called Mr Lee, except Mr Wook. Mr Wook had the best climbing record in the country. He was dark, in his late twenties and a bit portly, but bigger than the rest with shoulders and arms like a weightlifter. He had been once to the Alps and climbed the Walker Spur on the Grandes Jorasses, the North Face of the Eiger and the North Face of the Matterhorn; he had led a new route up the Ogre in the Karakoram Himalaya; and he had visited the USA, where he had led some of the hardest rock climbs (some of them 5.12c) on sight, by flashed ascents. This had amazed the Americans. And he had an extraordinary training routine – he always drank about six bottles of hard liquor each day.

We arrived at their 'factory', their home, and I was impressed at the industry that was going on there. Everyone was hard at work making equipment, and I was indebted to the men who had taken a day off to take me climbing. They showed me the video of their Ogre climb, and I was full of admiration for their achievement. They had been to the mountain twice in successive years. On the first trip Mr Lee (the best English-speaker among them), had lost his eldest brother, killed in an avalanche. The idea that Orientals do not feel loss the way we do is nonsense, and Lee cried as he described how he had dug his beloved brother out from under the snow. The climb had involved some of the most difficult ice climbing yet achieved in the Himalaya; Mr Wook had to be something special, for he had led hard pitches up what appeared to be vertical ice for hundreds of feet.

The family left their work-benches for a moment to wave us goodbye, and we headed for Mount Dobong to the south-east of Seoul. The area was similar to Insoo Bong, but nothing like as popular. It was Mr Wook's favourite mountain, and on the face of Sunnin Bong he had pioneered the hardest existing pitch in South Korea, which he offered to climb with me. I had not been to bed and was hungover, but I wanted to take this last chance to climb in this area, so I agreed.

We climbed some boulder problems on the way up to the face, and it was immediately obvious that Mr Wook was a stronger climber than any who had been on my course. We then tried a single-pitch route on a small crag below the mountain, to clarify our rope-work and calls before venturing on to the bigger face above. It is hard to climb with someone you have never met before with whom you have not one word of any common language, and this hilarious experiment caused the boys from the Ahgoo to fall about laughing at us both. Mr Lee was rushing about like a lunatic, up to the top and then back down again, round the side, whilst I explained 'slack', 'tight' and 'pull'. The pitch was hard and it later transpired that only Mr Wook had ever led it.

The ascent of Sunnin Bong was a tremendous route, and Mr Wook's hard pitch proved to be a Direct finish to a classic 5.9 climb, undoubtedly a candidate for one of the world's best rock climbs. An easy first pitch was followed by a superb undercut flake crack, trending rightwards across the face, which my companion led with a minimum of protection. On his feet he had a pair of home-made rock boots with sticky soles which he had developed, and he protected the climb as he went by placing the odd Friend, which he had also made himself in the co-operative. The next pitch was the hardest on the original route, and after leading a thin traverse I swung into a wild off-width crack and very nearly fell out! I had little in the way of protection and, as I climbed higher, I realised Mr Wook was shouting to me to turn round and face the other way – I caught a glimpse of him across the face doing a kind of tribal dance and gesticulating in a turning motion. This was not going to be easy, but facing right there was absolutely nothing to help me exit out of the top of the crack. My left arm was locked across the crack, my left leg sunk inside and crooked up underneath me. I was tiring fast and shouted to Mr Wook to 'Watch out!', but he just kept dancing away and waving his arms about wildly. I held my breath and did a swift somersault around, whipping my right arm, right side and right leg into the crack just as I was about to fall. 'Bloody hell!' I shouted to the uncomprehending Mr Wook. 'It's easy this way.' There were big holds out on the left-hand side of the fissure.

After that excitement the climbing was easy, until we arrived at Mr Wook's Direct finish. I was impressed – a thin finger crack split the wall and disappeared from view about 60 feet above my head – and quickly made it plain to Mr Wook that I did not wish to lead it. He seemed unconvinced, but once I had tied myself down to about three belays he got the message and set off. 'Dramatic' is perhaps the best way to describe his progress, as he more or less pulled himself up on his jammed digits alone. Once again his home-made Friends did sterling service. I could not have led the pitch which was 6a/6b climbing throughout, and definitely the hardest route in the country.

We came back down the face by a succession of abseils, and I was astonished when at the foot of the face, Mr Wook pulled a bottle of vodka out of his rucksack! He offered me a slurp, and when I declined he seemed genuinely surprised. He shook his head and proceeded to drain half the bottle as if he was drinking water. Another Don Whillans! Such a training diet would kill most other climbers.

Next morning, just as I was about to take a taxi to the airport, the boys of the Ahgoo showed up. The doorman began to muscle in, but this time Mr Wook firmly caught hold of his arm and he seemed to realise that he was playing with fire. 'We have come to take you, Mr Dennis, to the airport,' announced Mr Lee. 'And our parents have sent for you some gifts!' He handed me a large bundle of stuff, with a rucksack, a pair of pants, a travel bag, a chalk bag and much more, all made in the family co-operative. I was touched and gratefully accepted. 'Please thank your parents and family and do give them my love,' I mumbled, choked with emotion.

Many of the members of my course also came to see me off at the airport. Some years before I had met Yi un Sang the Korean poet and climber and, as I walked away with a lump in my throat to catch my plane, some of his words came back to me: 'I am a poor man, but I am rich, for I have treasures, my country, my poems.' To this I would add, 'The friends I made in Chosun ... the land of the morning calm, Korea.'

Mr Wook leading the undercut flake on Sunnin Bong. (Photo: Dennis Gray)

North Africa

Into the mountains did I climb, so many paths I there did find
Who was to tell me: leave this one, take that one?
Berber Chant

In October 1987 I paid my first visit to Morocco. The year had been really difficult for me, with the finalisation of my divorce and the setting up of a new home on my own away from my family, and for the first time in my life I was lonely and sometimes depressed. I was also aware that there was a small faction within the BMC who did not agree with the way I interpreted my post as General Secretary and, behind the scenes, were running a campaign to try to discredit me. The majority of my colleagues made it plain that such criticism cut no ice with them, but the atmosphere made life unpleasant and added to my feeling of wanting to get away.

It was my good fortune that the UIAA General Assembly was held in Marrakesh that year, and my trip there affected me deeply. I had never been attracted by the North African Arab countries before, but I was enthralled by how exotic Morocco was; so near to Europe, yet so different with so unique a brand of Islam. In Pakistan and Iran I had observed the growth of the fundamental movement, and half expected to find North Africa in the throes of a similar progress of revision, but Morocco, with its majority Berber population and its many sects or confraternities (seen as heretics by the orthodox Muslim), is extraordinarily un-doctrinal.

On my first visit the weather was superb, with hot days and cool nights, but it was the light that really fascinated me. As you move further south towards the Sahara, it becomes more intense, until the blue above you and the sunsets make all other skies you have seen look like pale imitations.

I was won over, and I set about getting to know this wonderland. I soon found how cheap it was to get to North Africa from Britain. Once in Morocco or Tunisia it is easy to travel around by bus or group taxi, but without losing a sense of adventure. Travelling on your own, particularly in areas like the Rif Mountains, requires great circumspection and you are often faced with what Stevenson, travelling in another place and at another time, accurately described as 'the bright face of danger'. Ten trips later I feel I know Morocco and, to a lesser extent, Tunisia pretty well. Morocco is a mountaineer's country, with places that will become important in the future for all rock climbers. I have climbed Toubkal, at 13,750 feet the highest peak in the Atlas and the whole of North Africa, visited the great cliffs of Aioui to the north and the Todhra Gorge in the Central Atlas (perhaps an African rival for France's Verdon?), and discovered a bouldering paradise at Tafraoute in the Anti Atlas, sea cliffs at Mirleft on the Atlantic coast, and the cliffs at Elgeira in the Tel of Tunisia (including the scorpions and snakes that nest on them!). I have travelled from the Rif Mountains to the Sahara, often on my own, and during these journeys I have enjoyed many extraordinary experiences. Until I began travelling solo I was really 'little acquainted with true adventure!'

New Year's Day 1990, Dennis Gray in the clothes worn by Ait Atta tribesmen. (Photo: Dennis Gray Collection)

Mustapha

I was frightened, not for myself, but for my companion Mustapha. We were climbing up smooth, water-worn slabs set in a gully above the Ourika Valley, our objective, to reach a small summit, set on a grassy ridge high above us, which we hoped would be a good viewpoint from which to see Toubkal, the highest mountain in the Atlas.

In wonderful Marrakesh, at the side of the Koutobia mosque, there is a Cheshire Home, one of many throughout the world inspired by Leonard Cheshire, an observer in the plane which bombed Hiroshima, who was so appalled by the effects that he decided to devote his life to serving his fellow men. The Cheshire Home in Marrakesh, underfunded and terribly overcrowded, looks after boys who have been stricken with polio, many of them Berbers from remote villages. Polio is rife in North Africa and only now, with the help of the UN World Health programme and charities like Rotary International, is a mass vaccination programme under way. I defy anyone to visit the home in Marrakesh and remain unmoved. Children have to sleep three in a bed, two at the top and one at the bottom, but there is good cheer and song to be found there.

I was visiting an American friend there, a volunteer health worker from their Peace Corps, when I met Mustapha, eighteen and, unlike many of the other boys, an Arab. He had been stricken with polio at fifteen and, being a member of a large family had been left to beg in the streets of Marrakesh until the Cheshire Home took him in. He was very intelligent, with the upper body of an athlete, deep brown skin and dark eyes, flashing white teeth, a ready smile and wavy black hair. His greatest ambition was to climb the summits of the Atlas Mountains. He told me this as he sat in an ancient wheelchair.

Mustapha badgered me to take him into the mountains and by way of inducement acted as my guide around Marrakesh: he took me into the souks and the Saadian tombs, introduced me to the Gnaoua trance musicians, and dealt with the hustlers in the great Djemma Square. He swung along on crutches, moving so fast that I had difficulty in keeping up with him and in the hot afternoon sun he soon had me gasping for a glass of *thé à la menthe*.

Two days later we left Marrakesh by bus. We went first to the village of Dar Caid Ourika, about 40 miles out, where it was market day, and then got a lift with Berber tribesmen to Setti Fatma, high in the beautiful and surprisingly lush Ourika Valley. From here we could walk right into the heart of the high peaks of the Atlas range. We slogged up the valley in the heat of the day, surrounded by greenery, waterfalls and granite boulders, following a path along the banks of a cool, clear stream. What a contrast to the arid plains around Marrakesh! We had spotted a gully leading out of the valley and up to the summit ridges, which had seemed an easy means of ascent with its entry about 1,000 feet above us. From below it looked low-angled, and as we climbed the first steep slopes I marvelled at Mustapha's strength and dexterity; balancing on his crutches, he kept right on my heels as we climbed. On reaching the gully we could see higher up a difficult section, with a barrier of rock slabs right across our intended route. What should we do? Could we avoid this obstacle by traversing out of the gully or would we have to retreat? We were dressed in track suits and shod in trainers, and carried no climbing equipment and, although the slabs were not difficult by mountaineering standards, they were nevertheless technical climbing.

Whilst I was wavering and wondering, Mustapha took the decision for us, swung past me and began to work his way up the rock face. I held my breath and watched, fascinated. His left leg was atrophied and useless; his right leg could take his weight, but it could not be moved unaided. Using his crutches as a bridging device, he made progress up the rock face. When this ceased to be effective he used them as hooks, and when *this* technique began to fail he simply mantled up on them. It did not matter that he had never been on a mountain before; he knew how to climb instinctively.

After about 120 feet he had to stop, for his effort had been enormous and he was lathered in sweat. I climbed past him, anxious to see what lay above and saw that the slabs steepened near their top into a headwall. This was only a few feet high but I found it hard to climb, disadvantaged as I was by the altitude, the heat and my inadequate footgear. I tried to imagine what it might be like climbing up it on crutches, and I shuddered. A fall could have the most serious consequences with a bad injury almost certain, and our remoteness a problem.

I waited at the top of this obstacle as Mustapha climbed bravely up to join me. My heart went out to him as I saw him in difficulty, so I climbed down and grabbed hold. I was astonished at his reaction. He spat at me and cursed me in French, then hissed, 'Don't touch me! I am nobody's boy.' I left him and he dragged himself up to join me, the muscles bulging in his biceps as he pulled his body up hand over hand.

He did give me one of his crutches to hold, but I was helpless and felt that it would be my fault if he were badly injured. His upper body strength saw him up, however, and soon he was on the ledge at the top of the rock wall, and lying panting at my feet above the difficulties.

We struggled on up the rest of the gully together in silence, my mind in turmoil. I had hurt Mustapha and clumsily offended his pride, but when we reached the summit ridge he swung over to me and held on to me for a moment to show his gratitude for bringing him this far.

The view was magnificent; we could see many mountains, including Toubkal. 'Can we climb Toubkal, *mon père*?' Mustapha pleaded. I looked at him, amazed. He was a true climber, and I felt I owed him a promise that he could cling to back at the home. I hoped it might lift the black despair he often felt at his predicament.

'We will climb it together some day. I will come back next year and somehow we will get to the top of Toubkal, *Insh' Allah*.'

'*Insh' Allah*,' Mustapha repeated happily.

Six months later I was sitting in a café in the Tafraoute Oasis, watching television with Berber tribesmen who had materialised out of the night. The Casablanca marthon was being covered, and I shouted for joy when, ahead of many able-bodied runners and one of the first to cross the finishing line, I saw Mustapha in his battered old wheelchair!

On the Buses

The bus careered down a road somewhere in Spain, and all around me people were shouting and fighting with each other. The only person (apart from me) not caught up in this seething mass was an old Frenchman, who was travelling to his home in Marrakesh. He told me he was recovering from a recent heart attack and had been forbidden to travel by air. Travelling overland by coach seemed an odd alternative for someone who was not so well!

These four days and four nights on the road from Leeds to Tiznit in southern Morocco were a personal triumph for me. When young I had fallen off a high building and fractured my skull, creating a perception problem, and since then I had been unable to ride a bicycle or travel a long way on a coach. This journey had proved to be aversion therapy of an extreme nature!

Apart from the Frenchman and I, the bus was full of Moroccans on their way home for Christmas and New Year. Our difficulties began after an extended stop in the night at a Spanish restaurant, where our drivers had partaken in seasonal fashion of the patron's hospitality and indulged in some convivial drinking. Two and a half hours later we set out, heading for southern Spain and the ferry to Tangier. The driver seemed to want to make up the time spent imbibing, and as we roared through the night I must confess that, although I too was merry with wine, I quickly became alarmed. I had never travelled on a bus at such speeds, nor with quite such a drunken or mad chauffeur; as we zoomed along the lanes of Spain, he was cackling manically at his terrified passengers.

Without warning, a huge Moroccan jumped up from the seat in front of me and bellowed in French that the bus driver was not fit to be in charge of a child's perambulator, let alone a bus full of his compatriots. The relief driver, who had been collapsed on a seat at the front feigning sleep, stirred himself at this insult, staggered down the alleyway, stood over the Moroccan and demanded an apology, for the honour of 'La Douce France' was at stake! Our huge spokesman positively refused to retract his statements, so the relief driver swung at him. The punch missed its intended target – the bus was swaying around like a ship in a storm, the captain at the wheel still cackling in a high-pitched voice – but landed fair and square on the nose of a particularly attractive young lady. This was the signal for the whole bus to erupt, and passengers lashed out at all and sundry around them. Women were at the forefront of this mêlée and I watched, incredulous, as large heavy men were duffed up by slight girls. Being tipsy, I couldn't understand why the passengers were thumping each other and not the mad drivers, but the old Frenchman and I seemed well out of it, so I kept quiet.

Suddenly, Jean-Pierre, the old Frenchman, was up on his feet, shouting '*Arretez! Arretez!*' He was small and round, with a shiny billiard-ball head, just like Mr Magoo. 'Stop! STOP!' he commanded again in a basso profundo voice that, it seemed, could not possibly have emanated from such a small frame.

To my amazement, at this second bidding the fighting ceased. The pugilists returned sheepishly to their seats, and sat down, looking at their neighbours with embarrassment. One of their number loudly intoned some verses from the Koran, begging forgiveness for their actions, and five minutes later everybody was asleep and silence reigned.

I was impressed and a short while later I tip-toed up the aisle to where Jean-Pierre was sitting to congratulate him on his effective and safe resolution of what could have been a nasty scene. I confessed that I had been worried. 'Oh no, *mon ami*,' he advised, 'I have lived in North Africa all my life. The Moroccans would not have harmed us!'

'You could have bloody well fooled me!' I thought.

Away from the main tourist centres, Moroccans are usually friendly and courteous, although they are proud. Their country is fascinating and is the nearest place to Europe that is definitely different. In 1988 I travelled hundreds of miles by ordinary service buses, to Taroudannt, the magnificent walled city, the oasis of Tafraoute to its south, the valley of the Dades, with its kasbahs or fortified villages, and the Todhra Gorge. This gorge is set to become a major rock climbing venue. Pioneered mainly by the French, it is a huge cleft stretching for miles up into the high mountains of the Central Atlas into which you can drive a car, because its stream bed is like a rough road. The entrance is so narrow that you can stand and throw a stone from one wall to the other. In places the walls might be 1,000 feet high, in others they are only 100 feet high, composed of perfect red limestone. Sadly, the routes have rows of shiny steel bolts in them, denying the climber the sense of freewheeling adventure that seems to fit so well with Morocco and the African continent.

On that trip in 1988 I had a strange experience in the south of the country. Kif or cannabis is still grown in huge quantities in Morocco, particularly in the Rif Mountains. It is, of course, part of the populist hippie past of the country, but now dealing and possession are illegal with the penalties for a tourist being quite severe – a massive fine, a jail sentence, or both. I met a Frenchman who had been caught in possession and had spent some time in jail and the stories of his treatment there would certainly have put off any would-be dealer.

I had been running in the desert outside Tiznit, and as I jogged back through the town two young Berbers joined in and ran alongside me, following me all the way back to my hotel. (Moroccans are mad about sport, particularly soccer and athletics and you never get jeered at out running as you sometimes do elsewhere. Rather, there are cries of encouragement from all sides.) Just around the corner from my hotel were the public *Douches*, and when I went to take a shower the two young men were still waiting. Contrary to the belief of some, Moroccans are very keen on bodily cleanliness, and they also have an uncomplicated attitude to sex. Bisexuality is not taboo, and my two Berbers not only followed me to the shower, but tried to get into it with me! I had to physically stop them from getting into the cubicle!

When I came out, they were still waiting, and they insisted that I come with them to their father's hotel, as it turned out, the barest and cheapest I had seen in North Africa. They plied me with many glasses of mint tea, and then made me promise that I would return that night for a special dinner – they knew the importance to us Nazarenes of Christmas Eve! Surprisingly, despite the spartan nature of the hotel, this meal was delicious. When it was over they insisted that I go upstairs with them. I had smuggled a bottle of wine in with me and, from a hiding place under the table, had managed to drain it glass by glass without anyone noticing. I was feeling the effects and agreed to go with them, intrigued.

Waiting for us in the corridor was an evil-looking fellow – one-eyed, unshaven, wearing a turban and a stained djellaba – who, it transpired, was a kif dealer from the north. The young Berbers wished to give me a Christmas present, and from this man they had obtained a carrier bag full which they now presented to me with delighted grins! They were whispering in a mixture of Berber and Arabic, and I had not understood what they were up to, but now I panicked. I knew of how kif dealers sometimes set tourists up, unloading a pile on to them, then alerting the police. The tourist can be fined a large sum, the dealer gets a reward and, it is rumoured, the stuff back so that he can start all over again.

'*Je ne fume pas!*' I stammered, handing it back. The two Berbers looked at me in amazement. A hurt look came over their faces and they tried to make me take it, but I refused once again. They became agitated and even annoyed and, after shouting at each other, rushed off down the stairs, leaving me blocked in the corridor with old one-eye. 'Oh God,' I thought, 'they've gone for the police!' No, they were back in a few minutes with a bag about half the size of the original one. I realised then that they thought I had refused because it was too much for me to smoke on my own! This action seemed to imply that I was not being set up, so, not wanting to annoy them further (Berbers can be dangerous enemies), I accepted their gift, thanking them from the bottom of my sinking heart. I was terrified that they might insist we start smoking the stuff there and then in the corridor, but even they obviously saw this would be foolish and they allowed me to go back to my hotel where, I assured them, I would get 'liberally stoned' behind my locked bedroom door.

I said goodbye to them the next morning with real sadness. The fact that they neither feel nor think as we do might be no bad thing, and they certainly meant me nothing but friendship.

I spent the next four days on buses wondering how I could ditch the kif, constantly putting off the moment. I was budget travelling, so I was always in contact with other people (although the only English-speaker I met was a Scot who had spent six and a half years travelling around the world!). On the fourth day at Tinerhir on the edge of the desert, in a stifling heat, the bus was stopped by a police road block. This was heart attack time, especially when they climbed aboard and made a bee-line for the only European – me! I was travelling light and the sports bag I had with me was normally never out of my sight, but on this trip the driver had insisted that it must go up on the roof with everyone else's baggage. After a heated argument I had been forced to agree to this, and now it was up on the roof-rack, and wrapped inside my towel was the packet of kif with enough for about a hundred joints!

'*Passeport. Bagages*,' demanded the police. Fortunately, like all bureaucrats, I was carrying a briefcase and I thrust this into the *gendarme*'s hands. He searched it again and again, shaking his head at the contents: a couple of paperbacks, some toilet paper and my passport.

'Oh, God,' I thought, as I saw his reaction, 'they've had a tip-off!'

'*C'est tout?*' he asked.

'*Oui, c'est tout*,' I replied, seeing myself like the French kid I had met, in jail unable to lie down in an over-crowded cell. After looking at me with a huge smile for quite some time, whilst I smiled inanely back, the policeman suddenly handed me my briefcase.

'*Bonjour, monsieur, merci beaucoup*,' and he got off the bus, still shaking his head. He must have been thinking how odd this British tourist was, out in the middle of nowhere with nothing but a briefcase and some toilet paper!

On arrival at Tinerhir I walked into a side-street looking for a barber to have a cutthroat shave – I badly needed one and they are cheap in North Africa. Eventually I found one, a kind and friendly man who surprised me by refusing any payment. Apparently I was the first Nazarene he had ever shaved and he was happy to do it for nothing. On an impulse I took a quick look outside his shop and, seeing there was nobody about or waiting, fished the packet of kif out of my sports bag. I pushed it into his hands. He looked at me in bewilderment, smelt the contents, then looked at me again in absolute astonishment. I indicated that it was a gift and, cottoning on, he quickly stuck it away out of sight into a drawer.

'*L'hamdullah. Shokran.*' I grinned and quickly left the shop leaving the barber wide-eyed and amazed. The whole episode confirmed my belief that there are still plenty of adventures to be had travelling alone by bus in Morocco!

The Oasis

I lay on my back watching Ron Fawcett edge his way up the middle of a smooth slab set on a boulder above the Tafraoute Oasis in southern Morocco. It was a perfect March day, as the preceding five days had been. The temperature must have been around ninety degrees and, although it was too hot for me to enjoy the climbing, Ron was still full of dedication to his art and up there and fighting. He was a tall, powerful figure, and I had known him from boyhood, and followed his progress when he had first emerged as a star on the Yorkshire outcrops. He had moved on to the national scene and finally, in the late 1970s, had established himself on the world rock climbing stage to rest for a while on a pinnacle above the rest of the pack. Now, his well-muscled, angular frame, without an ounce of surplus fat and unmarked by the ageing process, carried him on up the Tafraoute slab and I heard a little squeal of delight from his lips – 'cracked it!' I marvelled at this show of enthusiasm; he was still as keen as he had ever been on climbing and had been out on the rocks since our arrival at the Oasis, from sunrise to sunset.

My other companion now balanced on the summit of a boulder opposite to Ron, his camera clicking as his model moved up. The wilderness photographer John Beatty was equally dedicated to *his* art. Before the sun rose or as it grew dark his tall dark, angular figure could be seen setting forth out into the desert. This desert was a wonderful subject for John. After the heaviest spell of rains which anyone could remember, which had only finished the night we arrived, every hour of the heat of the sun that passed caused it to come to life in greenery and blossom. The almond and orange trees were in full bloom, and flowers stretched like a carpet endlessly into the sand. It was a land of butterflies and honey. Flocks of birds arrived overhead, stopping off on their way back to spring in Europe, and John was shouting out their names. I felt I was in a psychedelic dream, the light had become so intense.

The year before I had been reading Paul Bowles, an outstanding American writer who lives in Tangier. My eyes had become rivetted to this sentence: 'The area around the Tafraoute Oasis is like the badlands of southern Dakota only writ large, with fingers of granite, and high peaks all around'. I looked this place up on the map and found it, on the south side of the Anti Atlas range, an old French Foreign Legion Post on the edge of the sub-Sahara. Christmas 1987 seemed a good time to check it out and I eventually arrived there after an epic journey from Yorkshire by bus. I was astounded to see so much granite in one place. For miles and miles around the Oasis were boulders and crags, some hundreds of feet high, set on a plateau with a backdrop of mountains rising to almost 9,000 feet, above the Ameln valley to its north.

On my first day I walked out into the desert. It was not like the movies, with large dunes, but flat, sandy and stony, and known as *hammada*. I went first to a rock above the village of Agard Oudad, a large pinnacle hundreds of feet high with real climbing potential, known as the Chapeau Napoleon, then, with the help of a Berber tribesman I had met, I found the painted boulders. A Belgian artist had recently spent months out in the desert painting the rock faces in bold colours, a work on an immense scale. Imagine going up to Stanage one day and finding out that someone had painted a large section of the edge blue, or turning up at Napes Needle to see it painted purple! Some of these surfaces are 100 feet high and many of the detached boulders, overhanging on all sides and without an easy route to the top, are coloured all over. I decided that this painter must be no mean climber and totally mad! It is a startling concept and the boulders have now become really quite celebrated – I hope the artist received a grant from the Moroccan Tourist Board! I asked my Berber guide what he thought about it all. He simply smiled, shrugged his shoulders and murmured, '*Labass*! It's OK.'

I had returned to Britain uncertain what to say about Tafraoute. It was already much visited by tourists as a classic oasis site of palm trees, rock and desert, but it seemed that no one had climbed there before. Climbing solo, wearing only trainers, it was hard for me to assess the worth of the area as a future venue. Although the granite is basically firm, much of its surface is exfoliated because of the great variations in temperature. However, some of the rock faces and boulders are covered with desert 'varnish', and are sound. In all honesty, the major attraction of climbing is the beauty of the place – the brightness of the light, the breathtaking views and the sunsets which, on my first visit, made every other I had ever seen seem tame by comparison.

Mr Big – Ron Fawcett. (Photo: Dennis Gray)

I had some fun out in the desert, bouldering on my own. On one occasion I had set the self-timer on the camera, leapt on to the face of a 20-foot wind-eroded boulder, and started to climb up it. Just below its summit I became stuck – it was as round as a baby's bottom. I tried to climb down but could not and after a few moments I began to get anxious. Below me large rocks were waiting for me to jump, yet try as I might I could not get sufficient purchase with my hands to make the pull over the top. The sweat was pouring into my eyes and I had visions of falling, breaking a leg and having to crawl back across the sands, when as if by magic a hand appeared over the top of the boulder! I grabbed it and risking all swung up and over the top to meet a grinning youth, a young Berber out herding goats who had apparently been watching me all the way up. He had scaled the opposite side of the boulder – easier, but still a taxing climb – wearing green plastic sandals! Some of the Berbers are definitely born climbers.

Tafraoute seemed to me then a paradise, especially since I could live there so cheaply, and I was tempted not to tell anyone in the climbing world about it. The locals were still very friendly (although they thought I was crazy going out into the desert each day running and bouldering!) and I feared what popularity of the area outside the Oasis might do to its unspoiled nature. Eventually I decided that good things have to be shared with friends and one night I showed John Beatty some photographs and talked about Tafraoute; the next thing I knew, Ali Baba (because of his black beard) had organised Ron Fawcett and me to go there with him as a trio. In March 1968, we flew to Agadir as supernumeraries on a charter flight made up exclusively of package tour holiday victims – a cheap but ghastly experience.

We reached Tafraoute in a day and a half, first taking a grand taxi to Tiznit, then a bus up to the Oasis. I was delighted at my friends' reactions to the place as I showed them around with a propriety air. The boulders immediately captured Ron's imagination. There are many square miles of them, all unclimbed, and although a large number are composed of bad rock, we found sufficient sound material to keep us enthralled for a week. Climbing behind Ron was unnerving, for his reach was much longer than mine. On one boulder I stuck below the top and shouted to Ron, 'What's the finish like?'

'Ee, it's not too bad,' he shouted back. I jumped for it, only to find that the top was smooth and not at all incut! I only just managed to pull over to safety; I was 15 feet off the ground with a terrible landing, and my words to Ron are unprintable – something like, 'You are a bloody big banana!'

Our explorations revealed that the whole plateau is climbing territory. John Beatty and I enjoyed a memorable day out when we made a traverse of the rock faces high up at the head of a valley, above a village to the south of Tafraoute. We found incredible wind-eroded formations – one rock was shaped exactly like an elephant, trunk and all. Some of the scrambling was exciting and afterwards, comparing notes – we had become separated in the immensity of this desert because John tends to wander off to photograph anything which captures his imagination – we found we had almost dogged each other's footsteps. There was nobody about in this wild desert country except the nomadic tribesmen.

These journeys around Tafraoute more than anything changed my feeling towards the desert. I had seen it as a hostile environment, all right for men on camels but not a place to go walking and climbing, and uninteresting in its apparent sameness. Now I feel drawn irresistibly back again and again to desert country. In the Sahara I almost cried tears of joy as I walked across my first real sand dunes, south of Tamegroute, and looked from their summits into the emptiness of an immense desolate wilderness. In 1989, I led a trek in the Sahhro mountains to the north in the sub-Sahara, firstly through country with wonderful rock scenery, then through wild granite mountains like Bou Gaffer, an impressive rock peak to which you have to *climb* before you can gain its summit by any route. From there you can look southwards and see the Sahara reaching out its fingers towards you.

The appeal of Tafraoute is still as strong – its unspoilt nature, its rocks, its people, its Oasis attract me as much as ever. Word is now out about the area, and many climbers are starting to go there, but I hope that, as it becomes popular, we can make sure that precisely those things that draw us can be preserved.

Morocco's problem is that it cannot move away from being a Third World country and become modernised without losing part of its unique culture, built up over centuries of isolation as the land of the Maghreb, the 'country furthest west'. Its tradition is so important. In January 1990 I ran in the Marrakesh Marathon. At its start there were Gnaoua drummers, snake charmers and chanters, while out on the course literally thousands of people lined the route, many in their traditional

John Beatty bouldering at
Tafraoute. (Photo: Dennis Gray)

costumes, shouting enthusiastic encouragement. Once outside Marrakesh we were running through date palmeries. The sun shone out of an azure sky, and the kid who finished in front of me was a Berber from the Atlas, 17 years old and wearing the universal plastic green sandals! The brightness and the gaiety could not have been anywhere but in Morocco, and that evening in Marrakesh I sat alone on a roof-top looking at the stars, and was glad to see that the night there never really grows dark!

Issues and Conclusions

Yesterday was yesterday and today is today!
Moroccan saying

Then's then, and now's now!
Yorkshire saying

Writing this book has forced me to compare mountaineering 'then', when I began to climb in 1947, and mountaineering 'now'. When I was a young boy it was almost a secret society; whilst hitch-hiking I was often stopped by a policeman who would point at the rope sticking out of the top of my rucksack and demand, 'Where are you going? Off to commit a crime?' Few people had heard of climbing, and those who had thought it akin to Russian roulette – a perverse and irresponsible activity. These days it is a major sport with an infrastructure of professionals dealing with a demand for designer clothes and specialist equipment, technical instruction, information, and even public relations! The difficulty now is whether mountaineering and rock climbing can preserve their creed and sub-culture if they simply become over-organised activities.

Previous generations took the preservation of the traditions of the sport seriously, perhaps too seriously, so that to re-read a tome like Frank Smythe's *The Spirit of the Hills*, or Wilf Noyce's *The Springs of Adventure*, is a feat in itself. They come from another age, but perhaps they have a point in emphasising the importance of the *spirit* of mountaineering. For me it is about fun and adventure. The fun lies in simply enjoying it, and not giving anything, including achievements, more significance than it deserves. The need for adventure is different. In older people I wonder whether it is an immaturity, a refusal to grow old, to button down to the daily round of earning a living, to become a 'respectable' citizen and never kick over the traces.

We have to acknowledge this spirit of adventure, and be honest about it. There are those who do the sport a great disservice because of the way they report it and represent it. Mountaineers do not have some special high place in the hall of character development – many I have known have been anti-social and some have been criminal – although most of them love life and are risk-takers. The popular press demands its heroes and needs to talk about courage and self-sacrifice. In everyday life these are admirable traits, and are the basis of civilisation's onward progress, but they are totally inappropriate when attributed to climbers. If we are honest, the majority of us are in the sport for anarchistic, idiosyncratic and selfish reasons.

It is hard for the non-climber to understand the climber's motivation, just as those in 'authority' (the Sports Council, for example) find it hard to see why we do not want to proselytise and build up the numbers of converts to the sport by promotional activities. In Britain we have a finite wilderness arena that is already threatened on conservation grounds, and to bring in newcomers who have not made the important first step of self-commitment would be a mistake. There is also the moral question of the high-risk nature of the sport. It is bad enough when someone who is a climber is injured or killed, but it is totally wrong for someone who is not a committed participant to be exposed to a risk of injury or death that they have never really understood.

I am not trying to be sensationalist when I say that over 50 of my friends have died climbing. Some people think that only the unwary or incompetent get injured or killed, but this is not the case. I have known some of the leading mountaineers of any generation be terribly unlucky or miscalculate the risks, and pay the ultimate price. The great majority would never have guessed that this would be their fate. Each time it happens you are made to question your commitment, and to examine your life as a climber. My four decades in the sport have been the basis for such a rich existence that I cannot bring myself to declare that I would have been better off dedicated to science or art and literature.

Mountaineering's hold over its participants must seem a mystery at times to those who have either to live and work with them or who love them. I know that my own family has suffered because of my need to climb and travel; I neglected my wife, and she ended up bemused by this imperative. As I have grown older this need has not diminished, but has become stronger and stronger – at times I would sell my soul to the devil if it meant I could get out on to the hills or rocks, or even on to an artificial climbing wall sometimes! I have always climbed in order to know life more fully. Climbing has given me clear objectives – the conquest of a route, a face, a peak – and in this there has been no inner conflict about whether it was right or wrong! There has been the added bonus of the aesthetic appeal of wilderness areas and mountain and crag scenery and, most of all, friendships. In retrospect the people I have met and the friends I have made have been an important reason for maintaining such a long love affair with the sport. I am sad that so many of my companions have died, but I am proud to have known them; a few of them were like family to me and I pay homage to their memory.

Another positive benefit of the sport is that a love of mountaineering will lead you to travel and come into contact with people from different cultures, hear about their lives and study their religion, and make friends from such a basis. I have found by trial and error that travel from the point of view of learning is best done alone, away from the constraints and cushioning of a group from your own culture. This is the best arrangement for adventures to develop, and it can be as demanding walking in the sub-Sahara as it ever is on a rope with companions on an ice slope in the Himalaya.

Climbing, like life in general, will continue to change, develop and make progress but, from a perspective of so many years as a climber, I can report that Benjamin Franklin was right when he said, 'The golden age was never the present age!' From time to time I have been convinced that mountaineering had lost its way, but somehow, through the good sense or sheer bloody-mindedness of its participants, it has continued to evolve positively. It is now faced with threats to its future well-being – environmental problems, over-organisation by some well-meaning individuals and outside bodies and commercialisation and the increasing involvement of sponsors. Fortunately, all such difficulties still resume a smaller perspective when you are faced with a Cairngorm blizzard, or a difficult move thirty feet above a point of protection, or a wonderful sunset at the end of a day's cragging.

Legislators may legislate, and fame-seekers or money people may contract and manipulate, but these things remain as the essential nature of the sport, representing what matters most to the majority of the participants.

I am optimistic and more convinced than ever that the mass of active climbers will always go out and do their own thing. In 1970 I wrote in *Rope Boy* that to enjoy climbing we need a little organisation and a lot of freedom, and twenty years on this is still the case. I suspect that if the Sports Council were to connive with a National Park to surround a crag with barbed wire and guard dogs, that crag would be climbed just as often as before. Appeals to protect a particular site from over-use or environmental damage do not fall on deaf ears – climbers usually want to preserve what they see as 'belonging' to them – but I feel that the majority, like the earlier generations of mountaineers, will have little time for heavy-handed bureaucratic methods.

Many older climbers were upset when organised competitions developed in rock climbing, but they had to happen as a logical concomitant of the rise in standards, which now demand total dedication and intense training regimes from the top performers. The talented, naturally gifted person who can rock climb to the highest levels without training is becoming rarer, and in another decade it will probably be unheard of for any outstanding climber not to train scientifically. This will require a total dedication, leaving no time for working to earn a living, and climbing competitions can provide the answer of a yardstick of performance for sponsors. Perhaps now promising athletes will cease to be expected to give up all their time without the prospect either of some recognition or material gain.

Preserving an informal, friendly approach in climbing will be difficult but not impossible – many other sports have adopted systematic training regimes and still maintained 'good fellowship'. As long as competitions are confined to specially constructed artificial walls and continue to pose no threat to the natural crag environment, they will not affect the mainstream activity of our sport adversely. Some people argue that, because these events are held in relatively safe conditions, climbing every where will have to be made safe with bolts placed in all climbs, but this implies that young climbers cannot appreciate the difference between pure 'sports climbing' and 'adventure climbing' out on a crag. I think they can. If you fall off a crag it is natural that you might hurt yourself. Those who participate in competitions are attracted by a challenge; it may be a different kind of challenge from the one which first led them to climbing, but it is none the less still a challenge. None of us want to change the way demands are made in our sport, otherwise we would never have been out on the rocks in the first place.

Climbing is now facing the greatest crisis in its history in terms of protecting its traditional mores and ethics. Growing numbers are responsible for this more than competitions; we are now a mass market, and the sport is up for grabs to be exploited! The media and potential sponsors, including industrialists, are all interested, and we climbers need to be aware of the possibility of damage being done to the sport. We must make sure that a large proportion of any future income is ploughed back in conservation work, to combat the erosion caused by so many of us on the mountains and crags, and in access work. It must be used for the benefit of many, and not just to line the pockets of a few. The BMC needs more and more support, and its elected officials need to be alive to the potential of such sources of income.

When I started to write this book I was aware of being at one of life's crossroads. I never, ever thought I would get old, and I can remember that when I was 15 years of age and climbing with Arthur Dolphin, then in his late twenties, I thought, 'Gosh, he climbs well for an old person!' A spirit of adventurousness seems, however, to have nothing to do with age; some people never have it, whilst some old people are brimming over with it (and you can experience as much in the way of adventure spiritually alone on Ilkley Moor in a storm as you can on a high peak in the Himalaya). I once met a 70-year-old woman who had hitch-hiked just two years earlier from Cairo to Cape Town. She drank us under the table on red wine and regaled us all evening with stories of her adventures. She did not lack maturity, on the contrary, she was not over-ripe and knew how to enjoy life. This is a gift so precious that sooner or later you have to look into your own experiences to see whether you have used it wisely, and think of how best to use it in future.

I am not too self-critical, and I am not unhappy with how I have spent my time so far. I have done many things – most of them badly – and I have been lucky to travel widely and know some of life in depth, with all its joys and sadnesses. I have never found a religion to believe in, despite having studied a few, but I hope I respect other people's beliefs. (One of my friends was a Quaker, and I admired what he believed; his example has affected me all my life). I want to continue to travel and to climb in my quest for enlightenment, adventure and experience. There are still many challenges open for me. I must continue to strive to be a wise parent and be a support when and if my children need me. I want to visit the many countries I have never been to, and explore further those I have only been to in transit. To those who have yet to travel my advice is pack your rucksack and *go*, before it is too late, and before what you seek is irreversibly changed.

I will continue in my search for some wisdom and truth, but one thing I already know is that the most satisfaction in life is to be had in making other people happy and being of service to them. In this way I can put something back of what I have been privileged to gain in my existence so far. Finally, I will always climb. However badly I do it, however much crabbed age forces me to slow down, and walk up little hills or climb up easy rock faces, I cannot stop. It is a need in me that must be met, for it is my contact with nature, and this I have loved above all else. We have only one world and this, our environment, is really a wonderful place.

Index

Italic numerals denote page numbers of illustrations.